QUI

MW01100801

QUICK ESCAPES®
TORONTO

Second Edition

26 WEEKEND TRIPS
IN ONTARIO

BY

DAVID E. SCOTT

REVISED AND UPDATED BY
HELGA LOVERSEED

The Globe Pequot Press

GUILFORD, CONNECTICUT

ABOUT THE AUTHOR

David E. Scott has been a writer, photographer, publisher, and editor for almost four decades. He has lived in many countries and toured, at last count, ninety-seven. His travel books, articles, and photographs have earned national and international awards.

Mr. Scott's previous books include *On the Road* (published by the London Free Press); *The Ontario Getaway Guidebook, A Taste of Ontario Country Inns, Ontario for Free,* and *Ontario Place Names* (all published by Whitecap Books); and *Great Canadian Fishing Stories That Didn't Get Away* (published by General Store Publishing). He has also contributed chapters to Canadian guidebooks for Penguin, Berlitz, Fodor's, and World of Travel. Mr. Scott makes his home in Ailsa Craig, a small town about 150 miles west of Toronto.

Copyright © 1997, 2000 by David E. Scott

Photo credits: Pp. 10, 26, 38, 58, 130, 151, 190, 199, 205, 220, 230, 239, 257, 273, 289: Ontario Ministry of Economic Development, Trade and Tourism; p. 121: Stephen Leacock Museum. All other photos by the author.

Cover photo: © Robert K. Grubbs, New England Stock Photography
Cover design by Laura Augustine
Interior design by Nancy Freeborn
Maps by M.A. Dubé

Quick Escapes is a registered trademark of The Globe Pequot Press.

Library of Congress Cataloging-in-Publication Data
Scott, David, 1939–
    Quick escapes Toronto : 26 weekend trips in Ontario / by David E. Scott. — 2nd ed.
        p. cm. — (Quick escapes series)
    Includes index.
    ISBN 0-7627-0469-1
    1. Toronto Region (Ont.) — Guidebooks. I. Title. II. Series.
    F1059.5.T683S36 1999
    917.13'541044—DC21   99-14878
                                                    CIP

Manufactured in the United States of America
Second Edition/First Printing

CONTENTS

INTRODUCTION

Each of the twenty-six chapters in this book describes a destination within reasonable driving distance of Toronto that contains sufficient attractions and recreational facilities to keep you entertained and fully occupied for at least a weekend. For many of these destinations, spending two to three days is just scratching the surface; feel free to stay longer, if you have the time, and delve a little deeper.

Three chapters push the "quick escape" concept to the limit: Moosonee at the foot of James Bay requires a twelve-hour drive; Manitoulin Island is an eight-hour journey, including the ferry trip; and the Agawa Canyon Train Excursion out of Sault Ste. Marie is eleven hours from Toronto. But these are major Ontario adventure trips, and no guide to getaways in and around Toronto would be complete without them. I have stripped them to the bone in order to fit them into three- or four-night escapes. You can do them in that time frame, but if you can spare it, take a week for each and dawdle through these very special areas of mid-North Ontario.

As you travel around Ontario, you'll find that Ontarians are the province's greatest attraction. Hundreds of them have cheerfully dropped what they were doing and provided me with excellent suggestions, told me about little-known or unadvertised points of interest, or simply taken the time to chat about their hometowns or areas. There are many pleasant, friendly, and helpful Ontarians out there and I thank each and every one of them. (All were unaware, by the way, that I was gathering material for a travel guidebook because I always pay my own way, do not accept "freebies," and only tell tourist boards what I'm doing *after* I've done it.)

It is not the purpose of this book to persuade you to go to places I have written about. That would be a waste of everybody's time because tastes differ widely. What I've tried to do in these pages is tell you honestly and accurately what's out there and what it's like. That information will help you decide whether a destination and its attractions are where you want to spend time and money. If I've done my job properly I may have saved you time and money by dissuading you from going somewhere you always thought you wanted to go. Or, better yet, inspired you to visit some place you hadn't known existed.

And if I've helped you, perhaps you'd be kind enough to help me: If on the way to or from these destinations you discover something wonderful or fascinating that I missed—a great restaurant, specialty shop, tearoom, or scenic attraction—please take a moment to share your find with me and future readers of revised editions of *Quick Escapes® Toronto*. You may write to me care of The Globe Pequot Press, P.O. Box 480, Guilford, CT 06437.

Thanks for that, and happy travels in the province whose license plate bears the slogan YOURS TO DISCOVER.

> The information listed in this guidebook was confirmed at press time. We recommend, however, that you call establishments before traveling to obtain current information.

TRAVEL TIPS FOR VISITORS TO ONTARIO

Customs and Immigration

U.S. citizens crossing Canada's border either way may be required to prove their citizenship with a passport, birth certificate, or baptismal certificate. Naturalized U.S. citizens should carry their naturalization certificate. Permanent U.S. residents who are not citizens should carry their Alien Registration Receipt Card.

Citizens of all other countries except Greenland and residents of St. Pierre et Miquelon must have a valid passport and may also need to show a visitor's visa. Travelers under the age of eighteen and unaccompanied by an adult must have a letter of permission from a parent or guardian in order to travel in Canada.

Currency

All prices indicated in this book are given in Canadian dollars. Canadian currency is in the same denominations as U.S. currency, and Canada uses coins instead of paper for $1.00 and $2.00. The $1.00 coin is known as the "loonie" because of the loon pictured on its obverse side; there's no official nickname for the $2.00 coin, although "twoonie" is gaining popular acceptance.

The rate of exchange between U.S. and Canadian dollars varies almost daily, and not all retail operators are scrupulously fair about offering correct exchange rates. U.S. visitors to Canada are advised to exchange their U.S. dollars for Canadian dollars at Ontario Government Currency Exchange offices at border points, Toronto or Ottawa International Airports, chartered banks, or trust companies. Banks are generally open 10:00 A.M. to 4:00 P.M. Monday–Thursday and 10:00 A.M. to 6:00 P.M. Friday. Most trust companies are open 9:00 A.M. to 6:00 P.M. weekdays and 9:00 A.M. to noon Saturday.

Ontario Government Currency Exchange offices are also located at the following Ontario Travel Information Centres: Cornwall, Fort Erie, Fort Frances, Niagara Falls, St. Catharines, Sarnia, Sault Ste. Marie, Windsor, and Hill Island (Highway 137 at Thousand Islands Bridge near Ivy Lea).

Credit Cards

Most major credit cards, including MasterCard, Visa, American Express, Carte Blanche, En Route, and Diners Club, are widely accepted in Ontario.

Gifts

Visitors to Ontario may send gifts to friends or relatives in Canada or bring gifts with them without paying duties provided each gift is valued at less than $60 Canadian and does not consist of tobacco, alcohol, or advertising material. Gift packages sent by mail should be clearly marked Gift and the value should be indicated. Gifts valued at more than $60 Canadian are subject to duties on the value above $60.

Duty-Free Shops

Motorists crossing the U.S.–Ontario border at one of ten major points may shop in duty-free stores on either side of the border for goods to be taken directly to the other country. (This is a case of caveat emptor; some duty-free "deals" are no deal at all. Check out in the private sector the cost of what you're planning to buy before you go for a "deal" at a duty-free shop.)

Duty-free shops are located at the following border points: Fort Erie, Fort Frances, Lansdowne, Niagara Falls, Queenston, Prescott, Rainy River, Sarnia, Sault Ste. Marie, and Windsor.

U.S. Duty-Free Exemption

U.S. residents returning to the States after forty-eight hours or longer in Canada may take back up to $400 U.S. of merchandise duty-free, once every six months. This may include 1 liter (35 ounces) of alcohol, 200 cigarettes, or 100 cigars (that are not of Cuban origin). After a visit of seventy-two hours or longer, if the $400 exemption has already been claimed in the previous six months, an exemption of only $100 is allowed. After less than forty-eight hours in Canada, a returning U.S. resident is duty-exempt on $25 worth of merchandise.

Firearms and Ammunition

You may bring a hunting rifle or shotgun into Ontario for hunting or competition purposes if you are eighteen years of age or older. You are also allowed to bring, duty- and tax-free, 200 rounds of ammunition for hunting or 1,500 rounds for use at a recognized meet, up to a total of 5,000 rounds.

Firearms manufactured as fully automatic are prohibited entry regardless of any conversion. Also, no firearms less than 26 inches in length or with a barrel shorter than 18.5 inches are allowed, except to be used in an approved shoot, in which case a temporary permit is required in advance from a local police agency. In other words, handguns are not welcome in Canada.

Fishing and Hunting

Licenses are required for fishing and hunting in Ontario and may be purchased from most sporting goods stores, tourist outfitters, hunting and fishing lodges, and Ministry of Natural Resources district offices. For information on seasons, regulations, and license fees contact Ministry of Natural Resources, Natural Resources Information Centre, Macdonald Block, Room M1-73, 900 Bay Street, Toronto ON M7A 2C1; (416) 314–2000.

Hospital and Medical Services

Check before leaving home to find out whether your health insurance plan extends outside your home country. Visitors are not eligible for coverage under the Ontario Hospital Insurance Plan (OHIP).

If you are taking medicine prescribed by your doctor, bring an adequate supply and a copy of the prescription in case you need a refill or a customs inspector suspects those pills may be something other than a prescription drug.

Beer, Wine, and Liquor

Anyone over the age of nineteen may buy beer, wine, or liquor from government stores. You can get beer from Brewers' Retail stores and liquor, wine, and sometimes beer from Liquor Control Board of Ontario (LCBO) stores. Licensed establishments sell alcoholic beverages from 11:00 A.M. to 1:00 A.M. and may require proof of age.

In Ontario it is illegal to consume alcohol anywhere except in a private residence or licensed establishment. Your hotel or motel room qualifies as a private residence. Police patrol public beaches and waterways looking for violators.

Driving a motorized vehicle while impaired by alcohol is illegal in Ontario and may result in a heavy fine, suspension of your license, imprisonment, or all of the above. Impairment is determined by a Breathalyzer test; anyone with a reading higher than 80 mg (0.08 percent of alcohol per 100 ml of blood) is considered impaired. You may be convicted for refusing to take a Breathalyzer test. Motorized vehicles include boats with motors, snowmobiles, all-terrain vehicles, motorbikes, and even riding lawn mowers.

Pets

Dogs and cats over three months of age entering Canada from the U.S. require certification, signed by a licensed veterinarian, that they have been vaccinated against rabies. The certificate should provide a complete and legible description of the pet, as well as the date of vaccination. Animals are required to have been vaccinated within the preceding thirty-six-month period and at least thirty days prior to reentry to the U.S.

Taxes

Welcome to Tax Country! Just about everything you buy is subject to a 7 percent federal Goods and Services Tax (GST) and an 8 percent provincial tax. Keep receipts for every purchase you make because visitors to Canada may claim a refund on that 7 percent GST on accumulated purchases worth a minimum of $100, provided the goods are taken out of Canada within sixty days. Tax charged on hotel and motel accommodation is also eligible for refund.

Rules of the Road

Radar warning devices are not permitted in Ontario *even if they are turned off and are only being transported between states or provinces where they are permitted.* Police are empowered to seize such devices on the spot, and heavy fines may also be imposed.

Seat belts must be worn by adults and children over 18 kg (40 pounds) if the car is designed with them; taxis, buses, and school buses are excepted. Infants from birth to 9 kg (20 pounds) must travel in a rear-facing child restraint system. Children weighing 9–18 kg (20–40 pounds) must travel in a child restraint seat.

Studded tires are not permitted on Ontario roads.

Windshield coatings that do not allow a clear view of the interior of the vehicle are not permitted in Ontario.

Right turns on red lights are permitted unless otherwise marked. You must first come to a complete stop and may make the right turn when the way is clear.

Speed limits are posted in kilometers and enforced by everything from "ghost" cars to aircraft. The highest speed permitted in Ontario is 100 km/h (62 mph) on freeways. Trans-Canada Highway routes in Ontario have a limit of 90 km/h (56 mph). The speed limits on rural highways and county roads vary from 80 to 90 km/h (50 to 56 mph) and are posted. In urban or heavily populated areas, speed limits range between 40 and 60 km/h (25 and 37 mph) and are posted.

Road Signage: In 1998 the provincial government introduced easy-to-follow road signage throughout the province. The new blue and white signs guide motorists from major highways to accommodations, conservation areas, cultural centers, farmers' markets, historical sites, museums, and other tourist attractions. The signs include the name of the attraction, a symbol indicating what it is—a bed with a roof over symbolizes a hotel, for example—the distance, and the direction that motorists have to follow.

Automobile documents: A valid driver's license from any country is good in Ontario for up to three months.

An important note on car insurance: Ontario is a "no-fault" province. This means if someone wrecks your car, you are responsible for paying to repair or replace it. Check with your insurance agent before crossing the border to make sure you are protected!

Weather

Ontario's weather is similar to that of the U.S. states it abuts—New York, Michigan, and Minnesota. Our summer is June through August and it can get steamy hot. The farther north you go, the cooler it gets, particularly at night. In spring and fall be ready for cold snaps, and in winter . . . well, we're not nicknamed "The Great White North" for nothing! Temperatures are measured in degrees Celsius.

FREE INFORMATION ABOUT ONTARIO

A wealth of well-researched and professionally produced travel and tourism information is available from the Ontario Ministry of Economic Development, Trade and Tourism, and it's all free!

To order material, just dial (800) ONTARIO between the hours of 8:00 A.M. and 6:00 P.M. Eastern Standard Time. The office is open daily mid-May to Labor Day (first Monday in September) and Monday to Friday the rest of the year. When requesting information, specify your areas of interest: antiques hunting, boating, camping, fishing, dining, hiking, and so on. In every recognized category of travel and recreation, the Ministry has excellent, up-to-date resource materials to help you do your thing in Ontario.

The Ministry also produces the best available road map of Ontario. Be sure to ask for one. There's also a list available of hotels, motels, lodges, inns, resorts, and rental cabins in the province, and a four-color magazine-format book entitled *The Ontario Travel Planner,* describing the attractions in each of Ontario's twelve tourism regions.

Another useful publication is the **events calendar** (published in summer and winter), which describes a multitude of special activities around the province—such as fall fairs, winter carnivals, home shows, dog and cat shows, aboriginal powwows, sporting events, theater productions, and even bird migrations.

The map and booklets are available at Travel Information Centres at border points and across the province, but it's to your advantage to get them well ahead of your visit so you can better budget your time for precisely what you want to see and do.

Help Us Keep This Guide Up to Date

Every effort has been made by the authors and editors to make this guide as accurate and useful as possible. However, many things can change after a guide is published—establishments close, phone numbers change, facilities come under new management, etc.

We would love to hear from you concerning your experiences with this guide and how you feel it could be improved and be kept up to date. Though we may not be able to respond to all comments and suggestions, we'll take them to heart, and we'll also make certain to share them with the author. Please send your comments and suggestions to the following address:

The Globe Pequot Press
Reader Response/Editorial Department
P.O. Box 480
Guilford, CT 06437

Or you may e-mail us at:
editorial@globe-pequot.com

Thanks for your input, and happy travels!

SOUTHWESTERN
ONTARIO
ESCAPES

Windsor and Amherstburg

FOLLOWING THE MIGHTY RIVER

2 NIGHTS

Casino • River picnic • Wine tasting • Boat watching • History

Windsor has cleaned up its act in the past few decades. Those who haven't visited for a number of years will recall Windsor as a dirty industrial center continuously economically unbalanced by auto industry layoffs or strikes. The city then was a grungy slum squatted on the south bank of the Detroit River enjoying the vista of its neighbor's shiny high-rises and offering only a junky, weed-infested waterfront in return.

These days the skyline of Detroit is even more dramatic, and Windsor's petticoats have become manicured riverside parklands. They abound in colorful flower beds, dotted with benches, fountains, and statuary. They are restful oases, and Windsorites and visitors have taken to them with a vengeance. Youngsters toss Frisbees, teens cultivate their tans, and young and old stroll along the banks while keeping watch for traffic on the always-busy river. The railroad tracks and sidings that once littered the riverbank are gone, and parkland extends all the way upriver to Walkerville.

DAY 1

Morning

LUNCH: There's no way around the 370 km (231 miles) of Highway 401 to Windsor, but you can break it up with a great lunch at one of Ontario's most elegant hostelries, Ingersoll's **Elm Hurst Inn.** You can also unwind by meandering along their nature trail or using the putting green. Shoppers and

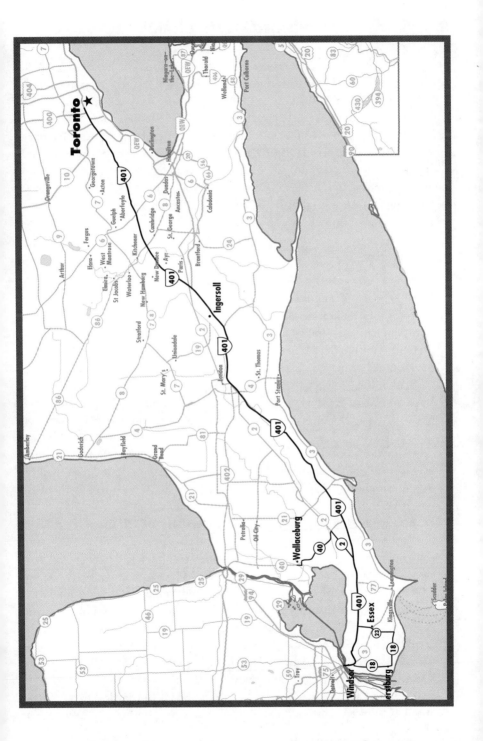

browsers will enjoy the **Carriage House Gift Shop.** The inn is at exit 218, 148 km (92 miles) west of Toronto. Lunch is served in the Victorian country dining room from 11:30 A.M. to 2:00 P.M., and the daily special is an $11.95 buffet with salad and dessert bars. Reservations: (519) 485–5321.

If you're not pressed for time, drop in at the **Ingersoll Cheese Factory Museum and Sports Hall of Fame.** Turn right as you exit Elm Hurst and it's just up the road on your left. Early cheese-making equipment is in a replica 1860 Oxford County cheese factory. Two barns house early farm machinery, tools, and a blacksmith shop. The Sports Hall of Fame recalls area sports highlights. No admission charge; donations accepted.

Afternoon

Back on Highway 401 to Windsor, which is Canada's twelfth-largest city, with 200,000 people. Windsor's biggest drawing card used to be Detroit and all that a city of four million people can offer, but it now has lots to see in its own right. The cities are linked by the **Ambassador Bridge** and the **Windsor-Detroit Tunnel.** The bridge, 2.8 km (2 miles) long, is the world's longest international suspension bridge.

Start at the Convention and Visitors Bureau at Suite 103, City Centre, 333 Riverside Drive West, where you can get free brochures and advice. (Be sure to pay your parking meter because Windsor police are among the fastest ticket writers in Canada.)

From the Convention and Visitors Bureau walk to **Ouellette Avenue.** The half-mile stretch between Riverside Drive and Wyandotte Street used to be just another grungy downtown street. Now it's resplendent with trees, flower beds, benches, and cafes with outdoor patios.

Also within walking distance is the **Art Gallery of Windsor.** It's at 3100 Howard Avenue, in the Devonshire Mall, and has fifteen exhibition areas with constantly changing displays of contemporary and historic Canadian and foreign art. Open Tuesday–Friday 10:00 A.M. to 7:00 P.M., Saturday 10:00 A.M. to 5:00 P.M., and Sunday noon to 5:00 P.M.; closed Monday. No admission fee.

Windsor's **Community Museum** is in the 1812 **François Baby House** at 254 Pitt Street West, and exhibits include a hands-on history room for children. The Battle of Windsor, the final incident in the Upper Canada Rebellion, was fought in the Baby orchard in 1838. Open Tuesday–Saturday 10:00 A.M. to 5:00 P.M., Sunday 2:00 to 5:00 P.M. No admission fee.

Windsor has many riverside parks, including **Jackson Park–Queen Elizabeth II Sunken Gardens.** This sixty-five-acre park at Ouellette Avenue and

Tecumseh Road has a four-acre rose garden with 12,000 bushes in 450 varieties.

Coventry Gardens and Peace Fountain is 3 km (2 miles) east of downtown on Riverside Drive. The fountain shoots 15,000 gallons of water per minute 70 feet in the air. It operates May through October, 11:00 A.M. to 11:30 P.M. daily, and is illuminated with colored lights at night.

DINNER AND LODGING: The family-owned **Ivy Rose Motel** at 2885 Howard Avenue is one of Ontario's most unusual and best-value motels. Walter Skally runs the place as though his guests are friends of the family—which many have become. It's a home away from home for many business travelers, and many return for social events such as Skally's summer barbecues or Christmas parties. The Christmas parties are so popular "we often have to ask people if they'd mind doubling up," Skally explains. "They usually don't mind because they already know each other." Another unusual thing about the Ivy Rose is the furniture. Skally doesn't like commercial furniture and doesn't see why his guests should have to live with it. The result is ninety-one personalized units, each furnished like a bedroom/sitting room. On the premises are an outdoor pool, a barbecue patio, and picnic areas.

The **Ivy Rose Restaurant** gets heavy traffic from motel guests and locals. It offers home-style cooking and a vast menu for breakfast through dinner, with large servings of excellent food and a smorgasbord that usually has rare roast beef. The restaurant is adjacent to **Skally-wags,** a sports bar and lounge.

To reach the Ivy Rose Motel, follow the U.S. tunnel turnoff from Highway 401 westbound. Exit onto Howard Avenue and follow it until it ends at a stop sign, then turn right. You'll pass through a residential area for 1.5 km (1 mile). The motel is 95 meters (100 yards) past the Devonshire Mall, on your left. Room rates: $52–$130. Reservations recommended year-round: (800) 265–7366.

Evening

If hitting Casino Windsor tonight, you might want to warm up your luck on the *Northern Belle* **Casino,** a Mississippi-style paddle wheeler with 800 slots, thirty-eight table games, and a food court at its mooring at 350 Riverside Drive East.

Casino Windsor, at 445 Riverside Drive West, is one of Canada's premier commercial tourist attractions, and the lines at the slots are often half a dozen deep. There are three floors of everything from roulette to Pai Gow Poker, as well as 1,700 slots, a restaurant, and lounges. The Casino Windsor and the *Northern Belle* never close.

DAY 2

Morning

BREAKFAST: Save time and enjoy good quality and friendly service at Ivy Rose Restaurant. Save room for the picnic you're going to have in Amherstburg.

The Devonshire Mall is across Howard Avenue from the Ivy Rose and has 165 shops and restaurants, including specialty food shops loaded with goodies in the **Picnic Garden.** If you can't complete your picnic shopping list there, try the stalls of the more than seventy vendors at **Market Square,** open Tuesday–Thursday 7:00 A.M. to 4:00 P.M., Friday 7:00 A.M. to 6:00 P.M., and Saturday 5:00 A.M. to 4:00 P.M. Windsor's market deserves to be called a farmers' market more than most because there are so many farmers on the two cluttered floors where you can buy produce, rare cheeses, meats, and pastries.

Take Highway 18 south toward Amherstburg. You'll be following the east bank of the **Detroit River** and will see all kinds of "lakers" and "salties" steaming up and down Canada's busiest waterway. There are small parks where you could picnic, but the shaded grounds of **Fort Malden National Historic Park** just north of Amherstburg, or **Navy Yard Park** in downtown Amherstburg, are special.

Amherstburg has had a busy and illustrious history, but now many of the 8,500 residents are retired folk and their quiet town 25 km (16 miles) south of Windsor doesn't often make the national news. Its small parks are great for picnics from spring through autumn and for watching the procession of commercial and pleasure boats on the river. Navy Yard Park, with flower beds guarded by old anchor chains, has benches overlooking Bois Blanc Island and the narrow main channel. It's pleasant to loaf here on a warm day and soak up both sunshine and a sense of history from the strategic position commanded by Fort Malden just upstream.

Fort Malden National Historic Park, first known as Fort Amherstburg, was the British base when Detroit was captured in the War of 1812, though its history goes back to 1727, when the Bois Blanc Mission occupied the area. The first permanent white settlers came in 1784, when former Indian Department officers were allowed to settle here. In 1796 Detroit was evacuated by the British and a new military post was established at Fort Amherstburg.

In 1838 Fort Malden was in the news again when its garrison and the local militia repelled four attempts by the "Patriot" Filibusters (supporters of the Rebellion of 1837–38) to invade Canada. The fort was garrisoned by British regiments until 1851 and then occupied by military pensioners until 1859 when it was abandoned.

Today the eleven-acre park includes remains of the original earthworks, a restored barracks, a military pensioner's cottage, two exhibit buildings, and picnic facilities. Start at the interpretation center, where a slide show details the fort's history. Then stroll through parkland to the museum, which comes in two parts: Ground-floor displays detail the life of military officers in the 1812 era and show their personal and professional effects. Upstairs, artifacts and paintings depict naval engagements of the War of 1812. The 1819 brick barracks facing the museum are fully restored and furnished. The fort is operated by Parks Canada and is open daily 10:00 A.M. to 6:00 P.M. June through Labor Day, 10:00 A.M. to 5:00 P.M. during the rest of the year. No admission fee. (519) 736–5416.

The **North American Black Historical Museum** on King Street tells of daring escapes by U.S. slaves and of the underground railway system they used in their flight to Canada. Between 1800 and 1860 approximately 30,000–50,000 made the trip to Canada, their Promised Land.

In warmer weather many swam across the Detroit River to Amherstburg, and in winter many crossed on the ice—though not always without breaking through and being swept to their deaths. An 1848 church and a 1798 log cabin contain exhibits, artifacts, and biographies pertaining to that era. Photographs, crafts, and art displays trace the journey of black people from Africa through slavery to freedom. Open Wednesday–Friday 10:00 A.M. to 5:00 P.M., Saturday–Sunday 1:00 to 5:00 P.M.; closed November through mid-February. Admission $3.00, $1.00 for seniors and students. (519) 736–5434.

The **Park House Museum** was originally built in 1796 on the U.S. side of the Detroit River. The owner, a Loyalist who didn't want to leave his new home on the American side after the Revolutionary War, dismantled it, floated the materials across the river, and reassembled it here in 1799. (This may have been the world's first "prefabricated house.") The log home with clapboard siding and cedar shake roof has been restored to the pre-1850 era. There are pioneer artifacts and demonstrations of tinsmithing, candle-dipping, spinning, and weaving. Open Tuesday–Friday, 10:00 A.M. to 5:00 P.M. June through August, 11:00 A.M. to 5:00 P.M. September through May. Admission $2.00.

DINNER: For gracious dining with continental service amid coveys of duck decoys and breads baked in-house, try **Ducks On The Roof Restaurant.** Yes, there are—ducks on the roof, that is. Six at last count . . . and 117 decoys scattered through the restaurant, which is on Highway 18, 3 km (2 miles) south of Amherstburg. The first batch of ducks was put there in the 1950s when the place was a hunting and fishing camp. "Ducks On The Roof" overtook its proper name, and when Brian Lucop and John Tersigni bought the place in 1987 they kept the name . . . and the ducks. The European-style service is formal, but there is no formal dress code.

Main dishes are accompanied by fresh-baked bread, pear-shaped potato croquettes, and vegetables served in individual steamers. Soup is served from pewter pots at the table, and salads are made right before your eyes. One of the specialties—surprise!—is half a roasted duck with a choice of apricot or honey garlic sauce, flamed at the table. Other entrees include steak, lamb, fish, quail, rabbit, chicken, lobster, and shellfish. Prices $12–$31 per person per meal. Reservations advised.

LODGING: Duffy's Tavern and Motor Inn proudly proclaims itself to be "The best host on the Canadian coast." There have been a lot of changes since the original building was a private residence in 1800. The thirty-five roomy, well-appointed units are in two- and three-story layers with all rooms overlooking an outdoor pool, the Detroit River, and Boblo Island. **Duffy's Tavern,** adjacent to the motel, has a million-dollar view and family-style dining with an emphasis on seafood. Rates are $80–$126. Reservations recommended year-round. (519) 736–2101.

DAY 3

Morning

BREAKFAST: Watch the river traffic from Duffy's Tavern. The breakfasts are large, the service fast and friendly.

Zigzag across county roads to Essex, via Routes 18, 12, 23, and 8—a lot of numbers to travel 30 km (20 miles). **Southwestern Ontario Heritage Village,** 8 km (5 miles) south of Essex on Essex County Road 23, is a turn-of-the-century village on fifty-four wooded acres displaying fourteen historic buildings from neighboring communities. There are a train station with railroad artifacts, a United church originally built for Methodists, a school, a general store, a barber/cobbler shop, and an assortment of furnished pioneer homes. In summer, volunteers show visitors how pioneers baked, operated weaving looms, and dipped candles.

Also on the grounds is the **Transportation Museum of the Historic Vehicle Society of Ontario, Windsor Branch,** which houses a fine collection of modes of travel, from snowshoes to buggies to vintage cars. A 1918 Dodge, built for the wife of Dodge's founder, has detachable running boards designed to provide traction on muddy surfaces—in other words get the car "running" out of the mud. The museum's prize possession is the world's only 1893 Shamrock. This adorable two-seater was the second prototype built by the Mira Brothers. When it didn't run either, the brothers abandoned their career as auto manufacturers. Open 10:00 A.M. to 5:00 P.M. daily July through August; during April through June and September to mid-November, open Wednesday–Sunday only. Admission $3.50 adults, $2.50 seniors and students. (519) 776–6909.

Head for Highway 401 and home, or continue on to **Uncle Tom's Cabin** near Dresden for more background on the history of slavery in America. For Dresden, take exit 63 east of Tilbury and Highway 2 into Chatham, then Highway 40 north to Wallaceburg.

LUNCH: Try **Oak's Inn** at the south edge of Wallaceburg. The family-owned motel has a licensed patio, lounge, and restaurant. Lunches are good and reasonably priced.

Afternoon

Continue north on Highway 40 into Wallaceburg and turn east on Highway 78, which takes you to Dresden. Uncle Tom's Cabin is 1.6 km (1 mile) west of Highway 21 on Park Street West, well marked from Dresden.

Uncle Tom's real name was Reverand Josiah Henson. Ordained a Methodist minister in 1828, he was overseer of his master's plantation in Kentucky. In 1830, threatened with separation from his family, he escaped with his wife and four children to Canada. He was one of the founders of the Dawn Institute near Dresden, a cooperative settlement of 100 families of ex-slaves, and he also served as pastor of the Methodist Episcopal Church. In 1849 he met writer Harriet Beecher Stowe, who used him as her model for Uncle Tom in her 1852 book *Uncle Tom's Cabin*.

At Henson's 1842 cabin, visitors can see the bubbly, irregular window glass and the square-headed handmade nails holding tulipwood siding to hand-hewn beams. Also on the grounds are an 1850 church, a former slave house

Uncle Tom's Cabin near Dresden.

where new escapees first savored their freedom, and a museum of rare books and documents on the abolitionist era. Scattered through the museum are handcuffs, clubs, ball-and-chains, whips, and head irons—graphic testimony of the inhumane treatment of African slaves in the U.S. less than a century and a half ago.

The museum is open daily mid-May through mid-October, Monday–Saturday 10:00 A.M. to 4:00 P.M., Sunday noon to 4:00 P.M. Admission $5.00. (519) 683–2978.

To return to Highway 401, follow Highway 21 through Thamesville and take exit 109 onto Highway 401.

THERE'S MORE

Willistead Manor is a mansion in Windsor that was the home of Edward Chandler Walker, second son of Hiram who founded Walker's Distillery in 1858. No expense was spared on the thirty-six-room spread, built in 1904 in the Tudor-Jacobean style of a sixteenth-century English manor house. Walker died nine years after moving into the manor, and in 1921 his widow deeded the property to the town of Walkerville. Tours are available daily September through November; on the first and third Sundays January through June; every Sunday afternoon and Wednesday evening 7:00 to 9:00 P.M. in December; and Sunday–Wednesday afternoons in July and August.

If you want see how one of the world's best-known whiskeys (Canadian Club) is made, there are daily two-hour tours of **Hiram Walker–Allied Vintners Distillery,** at Riverside Drive and Walker Road in Windsor, during summer at 10:00 A.M. and 2:00 P.M. Visitors must be at least nineteen years old. The tour involves considerable walking and stairs. No charge but reservations are required: (519) 254–5171.

SPECIAL EVENTS

Second and third weekends of June. Carrousel, Windsor. More than twenty nationalities and cultures are represented in pavilions where visitors can sample food and drink and enjoy dances and performances.

Early July. International Freedom Festival, Windsor and Detroit. Since 1959 these cities have combined their national birthday parties (Canada Day, July 1, and Independence Day, July 4) into a massive bash. During the two-week period leading up to July 4, there is a nonstop entertainment smorgasbord of more than 100 special events on both sides of the Detroit River. The party wraps up with a massive fireworks display over the river on July 4. More than a million people watch what is billed as North America's largest fireworks display.

OTHER RECOMMENDED RESTAURANTS AND LODGINGS

Windsor

Alabazam, 1515 Ottawa Street. (519) 252–8264. Windsor's only Creole eatery. This trendy, two-story bistro-style restaurant has an outdoor patio, a sit-down/stand-up bar, and open kitchen. Try their bread pudding and Chantilly cream for dessert.

Chatham Street Grill, 149 Chatham Street West. (519) 256–2555. Casual and refined with a touch of west-coast flair. Tempting menu includes pasta, gourmet pizzas, eggs Benedict, certified Angus beef, and more.

Windsor Hilton, 277 Riverside Drive West. (519) 973–5555 or (800) 445–8667. Just a stroll away from Windsor Casino, and every room commands a view of the Detroit River and skyline.

FOR MORE INFORMATION

Convention and Visitors Bureau of Windsor, Essex County, and Pelee Island, Suite 103, City Centre, 333 Riverside Drive West, Windsor ON N9A 5K4. (519) 255–6530 or (800) 265–3633.

Brantford and Paris

A BUDGET VISIT TO THE TELEPHONE CITY

1 OR 2 NIGHTS

*Where the dial tone began • Mohawk Church
Birthplace of the Women's Institute • Village-hopping*

Brantford has suffered many major industrial conflicts, setbacks, and closures over the years, and perhaps it's those uncertainties that have inspired its residents to make the most of their unique historical and cultural assets. Whatever the case, there's lots to see and do in and around this city of 85,000. And if the historic sites aren't enough to put Brantford on the tourist map . . . the city is the hometown of hockey superstar Wayne Gretzky and boasts a sports complex that bears his name.

DAY 1

Morning

Take Highway 401 west to exit 282 and Highway 24 south to Brantford, only 100 km (65 miles). As you enter the city, Brantford Mall is on your left. The next major intersection is Toll Gate Road. Turn right, cross over Highway 403, and at Paris Road turn left. The Brantford Welcome Centre is on your right. Here you can get free brochures, maps, and advice. In two days you won't have time to see and do everything Brantford and the area have to offer, so pick whatever appeals to you from the touristic smorgasbord that follows.

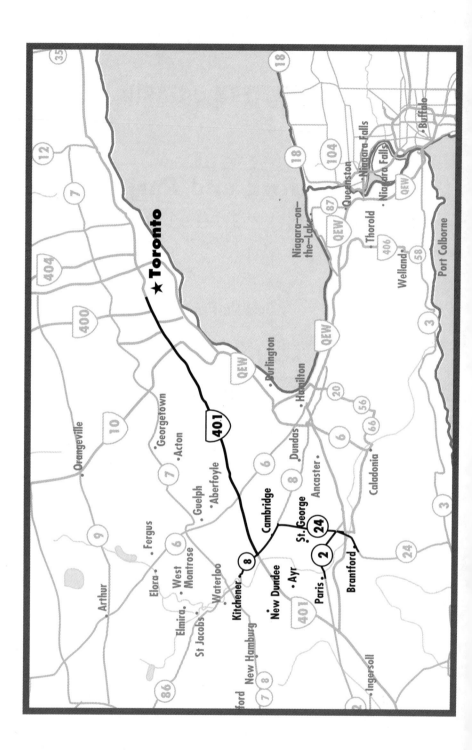

Brantford's nickname is The Telephone City because it was here that Alexander Graham Bell invented the telephone and made the first long-distance telephone call. Bell was the son of a professor of vocal physiology, and his interest in voice mechanics intensified when his mother became deaf. The family moved to Brantford in 1870, and the following year Alexander accepted a speech-teaching post in Boston, Massachusetts. At night he experimented to find a way to send several telegraph messages simultaneously over one wire.

He spent all his vacation time at Brantford and in the summer of 1876 received the first successful telephone call between two communities—Brantford and nearby Mount Pleasant. The first long-distance telephone call was made a few days later between Brantford and Paris, a distance of 13 km (8 miles).

The **Bell Homestead** is a national historic site open year-round daily except Monday. About 90 percent of the furnishings are original from the 1870–81 period, when the Bells lived there. Next door is the **house of Reverand Thomas Henderson,** moved from its original location in downtown Brantford.

Henderson was a Baptist minister who left the church when he recognized the profit potential in telephones. His home became the first telephone office and now is a museum of telephone artifacts that demonstrate how the telephone works. One display shows a switchboard operator of the 1880s at her board wearing a six-pound headset supported by shoulder straps.

The earliest telephone on display is a replica of Bell's 1875 contraption; the original is in Washington's Smithsonian Institution. Many of Bell's telephone experiments were made in Boston, supporting the claim that the telephone was invented there. Bell, however, declared Brantford the place where the telephone was invented and said so publicly many times. A memorial at West and King Streets, unveiled in 1917 with Bell present, clearly heralds the fact that the telephone idea was conceived in Brantford and that the first telephone message originated there.

There is no admission charge to the Bell or Henderson homes, which are at 94 Tutela Heights Road (follow the signs from downtown). (519) 756–6220.

Joseph Brant was principal chief of the Six Nations Indians, who knew him as Thayendanegea. He was born in 1742 at Wellington Square (now Burlington) and educated at a Protestant school in Lebanon, Connecticut. In

Site of the first telephone call.

the American Revolutionary War he fought for the British, and in 1784 he led his followers to Brantford, where they settled on his tract of Crown land.

The year after Brant moved to the area, a grateful King George III built a chapel in the village, and it stands to this day. The simple, white-painted frame building is known as the **Mohawk Church,** though in 1904 by Royal assent it was given the name His Majesty's Chapel of the Mohawks (now changed to Her Majesty's). It is the oldest Protestant church in Ontario and the only Indian Royal chapel in existence. Eight stained-glass windows depict the history of the Six Nations people, and the interior woodwork, particularly on the ceiling, is a study in precision carpentry. Open daily 10:00 A.M. to 6:00 P.M. July through August. For the balance of the year open by appointment only Wednesday–Saturday 10:00 A.M. to 6:00 P.M., Sunday 1:00 to 5:00 P.M. At 291 Mohawk Street, near the Bell Homestead. Call (519) 758–5444 beforehand.

LUNCH: St. George is a village 14 km (9 miles) north of Brantford whose main street is lined with tea shops, arts and crafts outlets, boutiques, specialty shops, and antiques stores. For a memorable lunch, try **The Potter's Cafe** in the neighboring village of Troy. The light, delicious fare includes chicken and broccoli encased in phyllo pastry and served with cheese sauce, or grilled Cajun shrimp with guacamole, wrapped in a tortilla. Prices: $6.00–$10.00. The pottery is open to the public, and you can watch the skilled craftspeople turn out mugs, casseroles, and wine decanters in a variety of stunning colors and shapes.

Afternoon

Three km (2 miles) west of St. George on Blue Lake Road is the home of Adelaide Hunter. Her 1857 birthplace and home until her marriage is a fully furnished turn-of-the-century house now known as the **Adelaide Hunter-Hoodless Homestead Museum.** In 1897, in nearby Stoney Creek, she organized the first Women's Institute, an organization through which rural women can discuss their problems and work together to improve their lives. Hunter-Hoodless also led the crusade to bring domestic science courses to Ontario schools and raised funds to build MacDonald Institute at Guelph. Open February 20 to December 20, Monday–Friday 10:00 A.M. to 4:00 P.M.; from mid-May to mid-October also open Saturday noon to 5:00 P.M. Admission $2.00. (519) 448–1130.

The **Woodland Cultural Centre,** at 184 Mohawk Street near the Mohawk Chapel, is a museum that preserves and promotes the culture and heritage of the First Nations. In 1831 the building was a boarding school for Native children, but it has been modernized and now contains displays and exhibits demonstrating Woodland Indian culture. Special events are held here, such as the snowsnake tournament in late January. A gift shop offers jewelry, baskets, leather items, posters, and souvenirs. Open Monday–Friday 9:00 A.M. to 4:00 P.M., Saturday and Sunday 10:00 A.M. to 5:00 P.M. Admission $4.00 for adults. (519) 759–2650.

The handsome former home of Ontario's fourth premier, Arthur Sturgis Hardy, houses the **Brant County Museum,** which has displays covering the early days of Brantford and the Six Nations Indians. There is an excellent collection of Brantford pottery. Open year-round, Wednesday–Friday 10:00 A.M. to 4:00 P.M., Saturday 1:00 to 4:00 P.M.; from May 1 to August 31 also open Sunday 1:00 to 4:00 P.M. At 57 Charlotte Street, corner of Wellington Street. Admission $2.00. (519) 752–2483.

Brantford's art gallery, the **Glenhyrst Art Gallery of Brant,** contains a permanent collection of paintings, graphics, sculpture, and photography as well as rotating exhibits. It's located in the main house of Glenhyrst estate at 20 Ava Road, a beautifully landscaped site with a nature trail, overlooking the Grand River. Open Tuesday–Friday 10:00 A.M. to 5:00 P.M., Saturday and Sunday 1:00 to 5:00 P.M. No admission charge. (519) 756–5932.

A store 5 km (3 miles) north of Brantford on Highway 99 merits inclusion. The name, **Belholme Trading Company,** doesn't reflect what is probably the largest retail inventory of wicker and rattan pieces in Canada. Room after room is filled with furniture, bowls, baskets, birdcages, trunks, lamps—anything that can be fashioned from wicker or rattan. Open 9:00 A.M. to 9:00 P.M. weekdays, 9:00 A.M. to 6:00 P.M. Saturday, and noon to 5:00 P.M. Sunday. (519) 752–2022.

There's another attraction in Brantford that you won't find listed in any tourist literature. The city has 35 km (22 miles) of perfectly level cycling, walking, or jogging trail at the top of a dike built around the city to protect it from floodwaters of the Grand River. The dike, 12 feet wide at the top, cuts through parkland around the city and passes near all the major attractions. Access to the dike is possible at the Bell Homestead or at Lions Park, Mt. Pleasant Street at Gilkison Road.

DINNER: Brantford's best dining is found north and south of the city. The **Olde School Restaurant** is on Highway 2 West at Powerline Road, a few kilometers north. Gus Iliopoulos spent more than $1 million converting the 1870s Moyle School House into a 225-seat restaurant serving continental cuisine and specializing in steaks and seafood. Rural school artifacts are worked into the decor of the lovely building, with entertainment offered every day in the Piano Lounge. Lunches and dinners are served daily, and there's a Sunday brunch from 11:00 A.M. to 2:00 P.M. For dessert, try a chocolate mouse—that's right, mouse! Entrees range from $16 to $20. Reservations: (519) 753–3131.

LODGING: Brantford does not yet have a major downtown hotel or any accommodation of significant historical or architectural interest. The "budget" reference in this chapter heading applies to the **Four Star Inn,** one of the best values in Ontario. The motel is at 568 Colborne Street East and the property backs on Dalhousie Street. (Those streets are Brantford's main one-way traffic arteries, and guests can enter or exit on either.) The rooms aren't fancy but they've got everything provided at places that charge twice as much, and the Moniz family are gracious hosts. Doubles cost $55 per night. (519) 753–8424.

Evening

The **Sanderson Centre for the Performing Arts** opened in 1990 in the 1919 **Temple Theatre,** designed by New York architect Thomas Lamb and restored to its turn-of-the-century opulence. The centre presents an ambitious schedule of performers like Anne Murray, Mexico's Ballet Folklorico, Moe Koffman, and the Massenkoff Russian Folk Festival. **Tourism Brantford** at 1 Sherwood Drive or the theatre's Visitor Centre can provide information on what's available at the time of your visit.

DAY 2

Morning

BREAKFAST: Stop in for your morning meal at Brant Park Inn, at 19 Holiday Drive.

Take Highway 24 north and follow the signs to **Paris.** It's only 10 km (6 miles). Paris calls itself The Prettiest Town in Ontario. That claim could be successfully challenged by a number of communities, but it holds up in Southwestern Ontario, where the town of 8,600 at the confluence of the Nith and Grand Rivers is a lovely respite from flat farm country. There's no glamorous connection with the other Paris: this one was named for its extensive plaster-of-Paris beds.

The best viewpoint overlooking Paris is near the top of the hill on Highway 2 just west of town. At the point where they join, the Nith and Grand Rivers have carved steep valleys through the Niagara Escarpment. There are small waterfalls and a gracefully curved dam.

There are fine examples of century-old homes in Paris—many of which would be more attractive with a fresh coat of paint. No tourism entrepreneurs have yet capitalized on the very real beauty of this little town, which has been bypassed by major highways. There's a pleasant small-town mood, and free angled parking is available on both sides of the main business section.

Take time to wander along both sides of River Street, which is the main street, and then explore the quiet, tree-shaded side streets. The more prestigious homes line River Street as it climbs a steep hill to the north. **Penmarvian,** a gorgeous mansion on your right as you head north out of town, was built by the town's founder, Hiram "King" Capron. It was later the home of John Penman, founder of Penman's Clothing, who left it to the Presbyterian Church as a home for retired ministers.

Lions Park, a block west of River Street beside the Nith River, is a pretty spot; en route you'll notice some **cobblestone homes.** The houses are made of rows of smooth stones the size of hockey pucks embedded in mortar. Several kilometers north and east of town is the 1845 cobblestone **Paris Plains Church.**

John M. Hall's House of Quality Linen on River Street is worth a visit. It is a living museum in a turn-of-the-century retail dry-goods establishment, and the stock of quality linen and textile goods draws shoppers from miles around. Open 9:00 A.M. to 6:00 P.M. Monday–Wednesday, 9:00 A.M. to 9:00 P.M. Thursday and Friday, 9:00 A.M. to 6:00 P.M. Saturday, and 1:00 to 5:00 P.M. Sunday.

Several doors up the street there's a plaque on the front of a building in which Alexander Graham Bell received the **world's first long-distance telephone call** from Brantford on August 10, 1876.

Paris has a number of factory outlet stores in its compact downtown area, including **Mary Maxim** for sweaters, afghans, and knitting yarns.

LUNCH: Try the **Spruce Goose,** which has excellent home-style cooking. It's on the second floor of a blue-painted building at 12 Broadway Street West in Paris.

Afternoon

If you've "done" Brantford and are spending a second night there, Paris is a good jumping-off spot for some small communities you may have never heard about but will find delightful to visit—if you enjoy sleepy villages. The two-lane secondary roads linking them are usually lightly traveled, and village-hopping is a fun way to spend a few hours. Most contain antiques or curiosity shops and a tearoom serving home-baked goods.

To the south, **Burford** has antiques, gift, and novelty stores, as do the picturesque villages of **Ayr** and **New Dundee** to the north. You're also near the many attractions of **Kitchener, Cambridge,** and **St. Jacobs** (see Southwestern Ontario Escape Six).

DINNER: Al Dente in Brantford is highly recommended, especially if you're watching your diet. This eatery, at 250 King George Road, specializes in pasta—from penne to lasagna—with every conceivable sauce and filling. Entrees run the gamut from vegetable cannelloni flavored with low-fat mozzarella cheese (a mere 600 calories), to a traditional fettucini Alfredo flavored with garlic and a rich cream sauce—not as slimming as some dishes, but worth the extra calories.

Dinners cost $12–$20. (519) 753–4303.

LODGING: The Four Star Inn

DAY 3

Morning

BREAKFAST: The Greenwich Family Restaurant at 200 Greenwich Street is popular for its generous servings of home-style cooking.

After breakfast, return home.

THERE'S MORE

Myrtleville House Museum at 34 Myrtleville Drive in Brantford is a pioneer museum in an 1837 Georgian farmhouse built by Irish immigrant Allen Good and furnished with family heirlooms from Ireland and with locally made pieces. One of the outbuildings is a working blacksmith forge containing turn-of-the-century agricultural tools. Open April through September, Tuesday–Sunday 10:00 A.M. to 4:30 P.M. Admission $2.75. (519) 752–3216.

The **Canadian Military Heritage Museum** and the **Canadian Vintage Motorcycle Museum,** at 347 Greenwich Street in Brantford, house war artifacts showcasing Canada's military history from the 1700s to the present. The motorcycle museum portrays the development of the motorcycle for military and civilian use. Open April through September, Tuesday–Sunday 10:30 A.M. to 4:30 P.M.; October through March, Saturday and Sunday 1:00 to 5:00 P.M. Admission $3.00. (519) 759–3553.

A collection of memorabilia from famous local athletes is in the **Brantford and Area Sports Hall of Recognition** housed in the **Wayne Gretzky Sports Centre** in Brantford. Among those represented are Gretzky, Tom Longboat, Todd Brooker, and Jay Silverheels (better known as Tonto in the TV series *The Lone Ranger*).

SPECIAL EVENTS

Late May. Riverfest Craft Show, Brantford. Handmade items from forty local crafters—wooden objects, candles, children's toys.

Late May. Brantford Riverfest. Family weekend with entertainment, children's events, fireworks, crafts, canoe race.

End of May–early June. Springtime in Paris Art Show. Local artisans display creations of fine art, crafts, jewelry.

First week of June. Art show and sale, Paris. Watercolors, oil paintings, hand-painted glass.

Second week of July. International Villages Festival. Multicultural festival held at various ethnic and community halls featuring ethnic food, dances, entertainment, cultural displays.

End of August–early September. Paris Fall Fair, one of the biggest country fairs in the province.

Late September. Miniature Show and Country Fair, Paris. Miniature dolls, dollhouses, furniture, craft boutiques, country fair. At Paris Agricultural Fair Grounds on Silver Street.

OTHER RECOMMENDED RESTAURANTS AND LODGINGS

Brantford

Huckleberry's Family Restaurant, 603 Colborne Street East, about a 2-block walk from the Four Star Inn. Extensive menu and reasonable prices.

Sherwood Restaurant, 799 Colborne Street East. Family-style cooking and a good value for breakfast, lunch, or dinner.

Brant Park Inn and Conference Centre, 19 Holiday Drive. (519) 753–8651. For a hotel experience with all the trimmings, pay $156 for a room with Jacuzzi and fireplace. The hotel has indoor and outdoor pools and a full-service dining room. Regular rooms cost $69 per double.

Paris

Davidson Motel, Highways 5 and 54. (519) 442–4417. Seventeen units, a budget property with comfortable rooms.

FOR MORE INFORMATION

Tourism Brantford, 1 Sherwood Drive, Brantford, Ontario, N3T 1N3. (519) 751–9900.

SOUTHWESTERN ONTARIO

Elora and Fergus

BACK TO THE BASICS

1 OR 2 NIGHTS

Elegant digs • Superb dining • Fun browsing
Elora Gorge • Mennonite countryside

The 3,000 folks of Elora are used to having the lenses of movie, television, and tourist cameras pointed at them. Their picturesque town on the Grand River swarms with visitors, and the arrival of a film crew is not an unusual occurrence. The historic limestone architecture of the town lends itself to period films and TV commercials that are supposed to evoke Europe or life in pioneer days. One of Canada's few remaining five-story gristmills is the anchor of this living movie set and is restored as one of the nation's most elegant inns.

Elora has attracted entrepreneurs who operate gift shops, gourmet restaurants, and boutiques in the ancient stone buildings along a quiet street that dead-ends at the mill. The restaurants have patios on that street, and some have rear decks over the Grand River. In summer Elora could easily be mistaken for a riverside village in the United Kingdom or Europe.

It was a Scotsman who started it all in 1832. William Gilkison bought land surrounding falls on the Grand River at its confluence with Irvine Creek. He named the community that developed after his brother's ship, which had been named after the cave temples of Elora in India.

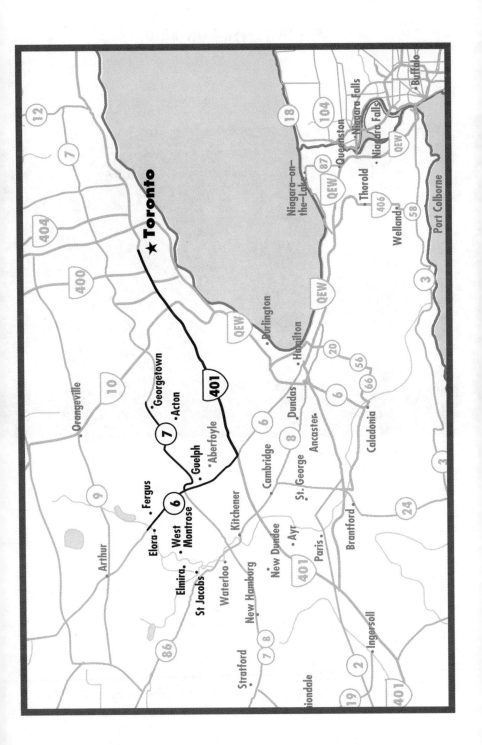

Beautiful Elora Gorge.

DAY 1

Morning

Unless traffic is extraordinarily heavy, it shouldn't take you more than ninety minutes to reach Elora or Fergus from Toronto. The fastest route is Highway 401 west to exit 295, then Highway 6 into Fergus and County Road 18 west to Elora. To better set the mood for the Elora-Fergus experience, take Highway 7 west through **Norval, Georgetown, Acton,** and **Rockwood,** and at Guelph pick up Highway 6 north. (In Norval, Georgetown, and Acton you'll find boutiques and shops worth browsing.)

In Elora, check into the five-star **Elora Mill Inn.** The lounge has a wood-beamed ceiling like an English pub and the dining room has one of those menus food-lovers fantasize about. The lounge, dining areas, and most of the sixteen rooms in the original mill overlook the cliff-lined gorge of the Grand River, which is floodlit at night. The guest rooms are all different, but the decor of each one starts with a hand-painted Mexican ceramic bathroom sink, and the pastel colors continue through the room.

The beds are covered with Mennonite quilts, and all rooms contain antiques, from prints of Elora as it looked a century ago to antique mirrors and washstands. In the public rooms there are photographs of the mill before and during its mammoth restoration project.

What was a jumble of broken machinery and chunks of the collapsed roof is now the spacious lounge. The dining rooms seat 200 in pine chairs around huge fireplaces and beneath enormous hand-hewn beams. At night guests can open their windows and be lulled to sleep by the roaring waters of the Grand as it charges through the narrow gorge. Sixteen more rooms and suites are in four adjacent stone buildings. Five of the annex rooms are suites with sitting areas and wood-burning fireplaces.

Room rates at Elora Mill are $150–$220, the highest rate for a suite with fireplace or Jacuzzi. Dinner entrees are $20–$30. A number of packages are available. The midweek package is $230 per couple per night, which includes accommodation, a three-course dinner, and a full breakfast. The Elora Mill is located at 77 Mill Street West, Box 218, Elora ON N0B 1S0. (519) 846–5356.

LUNCH: Consider a light one at a cafe or restaurant on the street leading to the Old Mill. Most establishments post menus outside so you can make a choice before choosing a table overlooking the river. (A light lunch is suggested because if you enjoy good food, you'll want to have a full-size appetite tonight at the Old Mill!)

Afternoon

If the weather is good, put on your walking shoes or hiking boots and wander through **Elora Gorge.** Pathways with sturdy guardrails follow the cedar-lined banks, which in places are sheer drops of more than 100 feet. There are caves, rapids, and waterfalls along the very pretty gorge, in which Indians believed their spirits lived. Sections of the trail are rough with loose gravel and sharp stones, and often wet from weeping springs. The trip should not be attempted in high-heeled or leather-soled shoes.

On a Saturday or Sunday, visit the **Fergus Farmers' Market.** Another Scotsman, Adam Fergusson, founded Fergus on the Grand River in 1834. This pretty town with a population of 6,000 is 4 km (2.5 miles) northeast of Elora and has more than 200 nineteenth-century buildings still in use. One is an 1887 stone building by the river that used to be a foundry but is now a large and popular farmers' market open on Saturday and Sunday year-round.

When you've "done" the market, take the **Fergus Walking Tour.** Residents treasure both their Scottish heritage and the town's historic limestone buildings. Many of the buildings bear plaques that tell when and for whom the buildings were constructed and, in the case of houses, the occupation of the original owner. One prized building is the community's oldest surviving log cabin, originally home to James Edwards, a local character known as The Major, who was the grave digger.

The **Abraham Groves Grist Mill and Electric Light Company** is so named to honor the doctor who performed the first successful appendectomy. He was the first to sterilize medical instruments by boiling them and the first to remove bladder stones through the abdomen.

The **Templin Gardens** are restored English gardens on the Grand River Gorge in downtown Fergus and are a pleasant place to stroll.

DINNER: Chef Randy Landry of Elora Mill Inn has created menus that make salivating reading for lovers of fine food. The cuisine is a mix of Canadian and European. There are the staples of steak, roast beef, lamb, fowl, and fish, and such imaginative entrees as Tweed of Salmon Elora, a fresh Atlantic salmon fillet wrapped in spinach and encased with melted Brie in a light puff pastry.

LODGING: Elora Mill Inn.

Evening

When you're able to push yourself away from the table, consider a stroll around town before making it an early night to be lulled asleep by the rushing waters just outside your window.

DAY 2

Morning

BREAKFAST: If the weather is fine, try one of the cafes just down the street. Some offer exotic varieties of coffees and teas and have fresh baked croissants and other goodies.

If you're spending a second night, consider visiting **Kitchener Farmers' Market** to pick up supplies for a picnic at **West Montrose,** site of the only remaining covered bridge in Ontario.

You'll be traveling through Mennonite country and will see members of this sect dressed in black and driving horse-drawn buggies. Mennonites are peaceful people—peaceful to the point of being conscientious objectors who refuse to participate in wars. They have strict moral conduct, in most cases do not indulge in tobacco or alcohol, and resist modern inventions. To watch them go about their business is to experience a lifestyle from another era— that of our forefathers when life involved more grueling physical work but was not as complicated, fast-paced, or downright hectic. Spend a day roaming Mennonite country and you'll find you're not driving as fast as usual. You'll also find that you have time for that second cup of coffee after lunch or dinner and that you're not in quite as much of a hurry as usual.

Take Highways 6 and 7 to downtown Kitchener, where **Market Square** is the city's showpiece. The complex, complete with clock tower, is enclosed in green-tinted glass. In addition to the 100 vendors offering fresh meat, poultry, fish, farm produce, and crafts, there are seventy shops and boutiques.

From Market Square take Highway 86 north to **St. Jacobs,** where you won't be able to resist the allure of shops and boutiques offering everything from handcrafts to maple sugar candy. Continue north on Highway 86, and a few kilometers from St. Jacobs turn onto County Road 21. Follow the signs to **Elmira,** where there's more boutique browsing.

LUNCH: When you're shopped out, take County Road 86 east for a few kilometers to the sign for West Montrose. As you enter the hamlet of West Montrose you'll see the bridge. The land surrounding the covered bridge is privately owned, but the owners, who live directly across the street from the riverbank area where you'll want to picnic, usually are gracious about granting permission. Be sure to leave the picnic site as clean as you found it.

While you're having your picnic, you're likely to see some of those black buggies drive through the bridge. If the clip-clop of the horses' hooves stops for a few beats, chances are the bridge is earning its nickname of the **Kissing Bridge.**

THERE'S MORE

Be the only person on your block—or in your city—to have seen the **World's Largest Culvert.** On Highway 6, go 19 km (12 miles) north to Arthur and turn west (left) on Highway 9. After approximately 12 km (9 miles) turn left on County Road 10. The culvert is 2 km (1.25 miles) west of the village of Rothsay. The world's largest soil and steel bridge spans the Mallett River on Wellington County Road 10. If you want to be reassured that you have seen and/or photographed the world's largest culvert, call the County of Wellington Engineering and Road Department at (519) 837–2600.

SPECIAL EVENTS

Victoria Day (May 24) weekend. Great Teddy Bear Caper, Fergus. All teddy bears and their handlers are welcome to join in all manner of fun and compete for a long list of prizes.

Summer weekends. The Fringe Festival, Elora. Free concerts throughout the village.

Three weeks in July. Elora Festival. Considered the finest music/choral festival in Ontario, set around a quarry lake.

Second Saturday of August. Fergus Highland Games. One of the largest Highland Games and Scottish festivals in North America.

OTHER RECOMMENDED RESTAURANTS AND LODGINGS

Fergus

Highlander Inn, Bridge Street. (519) 843–3115. Great comfort food and traditional Scottish fare, including the best roast beef for miles around.

The River's Edge, Queen Street (in the Fergus Market). (519) 787–9303. Pastas are this eatery's specialty. Daily buffet lunch.

Breadalbane Inn, St. Andrews Street West. (519) 843–4770. Luxurious accommodation and fine dining.

FOR MORE INFORMATION

Fergus and District Chamber of Commerce, 2nd Floor, Fergus Market Building, corner of Queen and St. David Street West, Fergus ON N1M 2W7. (519) 843–5140.

Elora and District Chamber of Commerce, 1 MacDonald Square, Elora ON N0B 1S0. (519) 846–9841.

Goderich and Bayfield

THE NAME-DROPPERS' TOUR

2 NIGHTS

An octagonal town • School on wheels • Dutch windmill
Double sunset • Delightful inns

Goderich has the largest harbor on the Canadian side of Lake Huron, and in shipping season the visitor can count on seeing "lakers" loading grain or salt from the elevators at the dock. The salt is mined beneath Lake Huron from the mine head adjacent to the dock.

Going to and from Goderich you can pass through Waterloo, Stratford, New Dundee, Dublin, Zurich, Paris, Lucan, and London. If you're a travel snob, you can impress the folks at your next social gathering by dropping such lines as "had a great cheese in Zurich last month," or "the weather was super in Paris this spring . . ."

With an uncharacteristic lack of tact, Queen Elizabeth II once referred to Goderich as "the prettiest town in Canada." Other municipalities have challenged Her Majesty's comment, but the town of 7,500 does command a fine site atop a bluff overlooking Lake Huron, the valley of the Maitland River, and the harbor formed by the river.

Dr. William "Tiger" Dunlop planned the town site in 1828. He named it after Viscount Goderich, chancellor of the exchequer when the British government sold land in the Huron Tract to the Canada Company (where Dunlop was a bureaucrat). Streets radiate from an octagonal civic park, in the center of which is Huron County Court House.

Goderich has blocks of stately old brick homes on tree-shaded, manicured lots. Many of the houses have towers and turrets and deep verandas. It's the kind of community that invites a summer evening stroll.

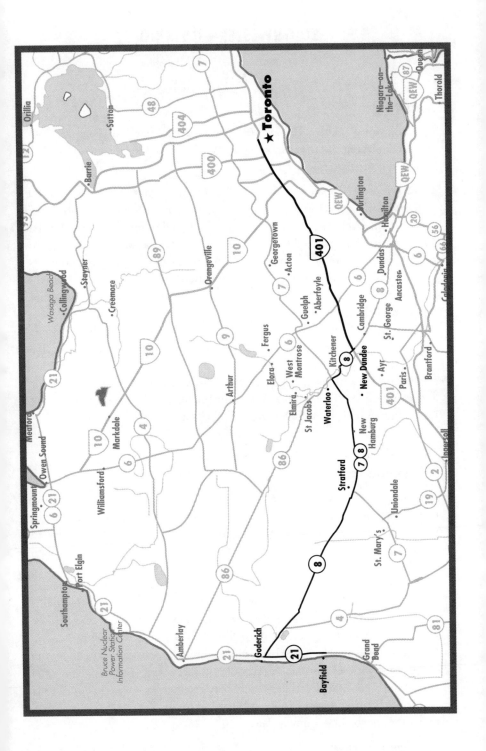

SOUTHWESTERN ONTARIO

DAY 1

Morning

On Highway 401 drive 105 km (66 miles) west to exit 278 (Highway 7/8). (If you're playing the travel snob game, **Waterloo** is 3 km [2 miles] north of where you turn west on Highway 7/8.)

LUNCH: From Highway 7/8 about 11 km (7 miles) west of the exit, take the well-marked **New Dundee** cutoff south (Regional Road 12). In 8 km (5 miles) you'll reach the quaint village of New Dundee and the **Great British Emporium.** The licensed tea/lunchroom is at the rear of an 1887 Victorian country store at 169 Front Street, where the original wooden floors, counters, and shelves are heaped with quality items ideal for browsing—knickknacks, gadgets, toys. It's the sort of place where you could check off a lot of names on your Christmas list.

For lunch choose among budget-priced traditional English dishes like savory pie and ploughman's lunch or quiche with seasonal garnishes. A traditional Scottish cream tea is accompanied by warm scones with butter, preserves, and Devon cream. Or there are toasted crumpets, warm shortbreads, and raspberry and rhubarb pie. Going for broke? Try the Boozy Cheesecake. Open year-round, Tuesday–Saturday 10:00 A.M. to 5:00 P.M., Sunday 11:00 A.M. to 5:00 P.M.

Afternoon

Continue on Highway 7/8 westbound to Stratford, where you may want to make a detour to **Festival Theatre** overlooking the Avon River (see Southwestern Ontario Escape Ten). Often the river's banks are covered with strollers and picnickers, and its surface is dotted with white swans and paddleboats. Festival Theatre is well marked; stay in the right lane as you enter Stratford.

Take Highway 8 out of Stratford through Mitchell, Dublin, and Seaforth to Clinton. At Clinton turn south on Highway 4 and follow signs to the **School on Wheels.** Canadian National Railway Car 15089 was one of seven "schools on wheels" covering 7,200 km (4,500 miles) of railway lines in Northern Ontario. The schools on wheels brought education to children in settlements without permanent schools of their own. Each week a train moved the school cars to sidings where they remained for a week. Pupils were given sufficient homework to keep them busy until the classroom returned, sometimes as much as a month later.

The Clinton connection was Fred and Celia Sloman, who lived in, and taught from, Car 15089 from 1914 to 1964. During that time the school graduated more than 1,000 children including the Slomans' five children, who were raised in the car. The only remaining train classroom has been restored to the way it looked when the Slomans lived on board. Open May 24 to Labor Day, Thursday and Friday 2:00 to 5:00 P.M.; Saturday, Sunday, and holidays 1:00 to 5:00 P.M. Closed in inclement weather. (519) 482–9583.

When you reach Goderich you may wish to spend some time in **Goderich Jail**—or *Gaol*. On a hot day it's deliciously cool inside the 2-foot-thick stone walls. The building is a three-story octagonal structure surrounded on seven sides by 20-foot-high stone walls separating exercise yards. The eighth side contains the jail governor's residence.

Civil libertarians were likely piqued when the jail was designed in 1839 because containment of criminals was given priority over their comfort. But Canada's concern for care of criminals saw no exception here: the daily rations were half a pound of meat and one pound of bread per prisoner. Two executions were held here; the first, in 1856, was Canada's last public hanging. The jail closed in 1972.

The jail occupies one of the finest sites in town, at 181 Victoria Street North, high on the south bank of the Maitland River, commanding a view across the valley mouth to Goderich harbor. But the only people to benefit from that billion-dollar view were guards keeping an eye on the exercise yards from a raised walkway. The exercise yard walls are smooth and capped with loose stones designed to fall with a clatter if a prisoner reached that height. The governor's home, which faces the town, is furnished in the mid-1800s period.

Open daily Victoria Day to Labor Day, 10:00 A.M. to 4:30 P.M.; Labor Day to November 30, open weekdays 10:00 A.M. to 4:00 P.M. and Sunday 1:00 to 4:30 P.M.; closed Saturday. Admission for adults is $4.00. (519) 524–2686.

Huron County Pioneer Museum in Goderich is an astonishing collection of 15,000 pieces of Canadiana in the town's former Central School and seven additions. It's part monument to founder and first curator J. Herb Neill, and its mandate is to explain how area settlers lived. There are theme rooms—a fully-equipped dentist's office, doctor's office, blacksmith's shop, and other rooms set up as they would have appeared in the 1800s—and areas for Indian and Eskimo crafts, agricultural implements, and displays of mammals, birds, butterflies, and fish.

Neill devoted most of his life to the museum and built many of the exhibits that demonstrate how pioneer inventions worked—stump pullers, wood splitters, and other machines created by ingenious settlers to make their work faster or easier. At 110 North Street, which runs north off the square. Open May 1 to Labor Day, Monday–Saturday 10:00 A.M. to 4:30 P.M., Sunday 1:00 to 4:00 P.M. During the rest of the year open Monday–Friday 10:00 A.M. to 4:30 P.M., Sunday 1:00 to 4:30 P.M.; closed Saturday. (519) 524–2686.

DINNER: Robindale's has superb food at a good value. There are four dining rooms in the 1870-vintage home at 80 Hamilton Street (which also leads off the square). Owners Rob McGregor and Dale Dolson say they have tried to make their culinary offerings "like the sort of meal you'd get at Grandma's house" . . . and would that Grandma could cook so well! Servings are generous; some appetizers could serve as a complete meal for a light eater. There are stained-glass windows and hand-carved cherry fireplaces where burning wood crackles on cold nights. Dinner Monday–Sunday. Prices in the $13.50–$19.95 range. Reservations recommended: (519) 524–4171.

LODGING: Hotel Bedford, on the southwest corner of the octagonal town "square," has a popular eatery—**Duke Phase 2.** The newly renovated dining room offers daily specials and full-course meals with all the extras for $4.95–$15.95. Room rates are $59–$89 including continental breakfast. The 1896 hotel is fully refurbished with new pine frame beds, pine wainscoting, and bathroom fixtures. Each room also contains at least two pieces of refinished original furniture—washstands, dressers, or chairs. In **Bruno's Ristorante** pub food is available, and there's a dance floor where a DJ spins music on Thursday nights. (519) 524–7337.

Evening

Go down West Street toward the harbor. Before starting down the steep hill, turn left onto Lighthouse Street, which takes you to the lighthouse. If you want to see two sunsets, climb down the stairs to the boardwalk and watch the first sunset at water level. If you climb back up those stairs fast enough, you'll be able to watch the second sunset—and possibly even see the **Green Flash,** an optical illusion sometimes visible at the split second the sun disappears over the horizon.

DAY 2

Morning

BREAKFAST: You've paid for it, so enjoy the continental breakfast in the bright and attractive dining room at the Hotel Bedford.

Directly across the square from the hotel at 10 The Square is **Vandelys,** a deli with a deservedly excellent reputation. Ask the folks there to set up your picnic lunch. They've got it all—soups, salads, sandwiches, quiche—and it's all made right there. Prices are moderate. On your stroll back to the hotel and your car, walk half a block down West Street and see if you can browse in **Culbert's Bakery** without buying something delightful for dessert.

Take Highway 21 south for 31 km (19 miles) to **Bayfield.** British Admiralty surveyor Henry Wolsey Bayfield envisioned the place named after him as an important trade center with goods moving in and out by rail and ships using the Lake Huron harbor into which the Bayfield River empties.

A number of others evidently shared Bayfield's dream because when the railroad did come north—and miss the town by 45 km (28 miles)—there were twelve hotels built and waiting for the boom. All the hotels closed and the village slumbered until the 1970s when city folk began retiring to the country and were drawn to Bayfield by its beauty.

The town sits high on a bluff over Lake Huron and the Bayfield River, which forms a natural harbor between sandy beaches. When the miniboom started, handsome brick homes and century-old frame stores along the main street were renovated by enthusiastic entrepreneurs whose promotion and advertising have raised the village's population to over 1,000. Fortunately at least two of the original hotels have survived, and tonight you'll drink in one and dine and sleep in the other.

Chrome and neon don't suit the mood of Bayfield, and neither one is allowed to mar its nineteenth-century ambience. There's a modern marina in the river mouth, where millions of dollars worth of powerboats and yachts are berthed, but apart from automobiles and TV antennas, there isn't much modern in evidence in the village. The main street is shaded by huge old willow trees, relics of the past bristle in antiques shop windows, and the drinking and dining spots are redolent with historical flavor.

LUNCH: As you enter Bayfield from Highway 21, a square park will be on your left. That's **Clan Gregor Square,** and all summer long families gather for

A 95-foot-high Dutch windmill just north of Bayfield.

picnics and reunions in the shade of the ancient trees. You can have your picnic here or down at the beach.

Afternoon

Three km (1.9 miles) north of Bayfield, turn right off Highway 21 on the gravel road at the golf course and drive 4 km (2.5 miles) to a full-size Dutch windmill 95 feet from the ground to the tip of the sail. It was a seventeen-year labor of love for Frank de Jong, who charges $3.50 admission for tours from mid-May through mid-October. The **Folmar Windmill** is the only wind-driven saw- and gristmill in North America, and the ingenious harnessing and conversion of wind energy is fascinating to see.

Climbing around the mill, you'll have worked up an appetite, so return to Bayfield and look for **Admiral Bayfield's Bakery and Deli.** It's on your left as you enter the village's Main Street, down a driveway just past the **Albion Hotel.** French fries and soft drinks are the only items sold from the food stand. Owner Terrence Bullen, who also operates the adjacent tearoom, serves the best french fries in Ontario.

You'll probably want to spend some time strolling up and down Main Street and window-shopping among the boutiques and shops. Several vendors offer excellent ice-cream cones. Before dinner you might want to indulge in an apéritif at the Albion Hotel, a popular watering hole.

DINNER AND LODGING: At the **Little Inn** on Main Street—and it's wise to make a dinner reservation because its cuisine enjoys a wide reputation. Entrees cost $11–$29; the top price is for their trademark rack of lamb. Don't gamble on a room at the Little Inn at any time of year. This special getaway draws its fans from hundreds of miles away. There are thirty rooms, some in the original inn and others in an addition. Some rooms have saunas and fireplaces. The inn has a small spa with sauna and whirlpool. Room rates $115–$225. For information write: Little Inn of Bayfield, P.O. Box 100, Main Street, Bayfield ON N0M 1G0. (519) 565–2611.

DAY 3

Morning

BREAKFAST: The Little Inn bakes its own goodies to serve with morning coffee, and some of the eateries on Main Street have outdoor patios.

When you're ready to head home, follow Highway 4 for 16 km (10 miles) to St. Joseph and Highway 84 for 16 km (10 miles) to **Zurich.** Note the Swiss-inspired town hall. The **Tasty Nu Bakery** is closed on Sunday, but any other day it's open. It's in the middle of the town's business block and has superb breads and rolls.

Continue on Highway 84 to Hensall and turn south on Highway 4, which passes through Lucan to London. From London take Highway 401 home.

THERE'S MORE

Huron County Marine Museum is down by the Goderich dock and open daily 1:00 to 4:30 P.M. May 24 to Labor Day. Artifacts and photographs relating to Goderich's role in the Great Lakes shipping trade are displayed in the forward cabins and bridge of an old freighter. (519) 524–2686.

SPECIAL EVENTS

Early May. Lucan Spring Craft Show and Sale. In Lucan Community Centre.

Early July. Festival of Arts and Crafts, Goderich. Live entertainment, demonstrations in Courthouse Park.

Second weekend of August. Celtic Roots Festival, Goderich. Celebration of Irish, Scottish, and Celtic traditions with music, dance, song, and arts and crafts in Lions Harbour Park.

Second weekend of August. Bayfield Antiques Fair. In Bayfield Arena.

Late August. Zurich Bean Festival. Pancake and sausage breakfast, entertainment, antique car show, street market, horseshoes, frog jumping, bean dinner, dance.

Third weekend of September. Miniature Show and Country Fair, Paris. Miniatures (dolls, dollhouses, furniture), craft boutiques, country fair at Paris Agricultural Fair Grounds.

OTHER RECOMMENDED RESTAURANTS AND LODGINGS

Benmiller

Benmiller Inn, 7 km (4 miles) inland from Goderich on County Road 31. (519) 524–2191 and (800) 265–1711. Luxurious five-star country inn complex with forty-eight super-deluxe rooms and suites in four beautifully restored historic buildings, three of which used to be working mills. Situated on seventy-five acres of hilly, forested land adjacent to a 150-acre conservation area. Indoor swimming pool, games rooms, saunas, and indoor jogging track.

FOR MORE INFORMATION

Goderich Tourist Office, 57 West Street, Goderich ON N7A 2K5. (519) 524–6600.

SOUTHWESTERN ONTARIO

Grand Bend, Petrolia, and Wallaceburg

SUN AND SAND

2 NIGHTS

Beach scene • Canada's first oil boomtown
Pioneer history • Exotic animals

The highway signs that announce you're entering the village of Grand Bend also tell you the resort town has a population of 1,000. This must puzzle summer visitors who find it takes them up to an hour to inch their car up and back down the main street, a distance of 8 blocks round-trip.

On sunny summer weekends up to twenty-five or thirty times the number of permanent residents cram into this speck on the map that straddles the mouth of the Ausable River. Grand Bend is a beach—a fine, deep beach of golden sand on the shores of Lake Huron. Its habitués call it simply "The Bend." When the sun is hot, bronzing bodies stretch as far as you can see, the lake is dotted with all types of watercraft although the marina still appears full, and the sky is full of parasailers and hang gliders.

Grand Bend is also full of people with money to spend, and the main street takes on a carnival atmosphere of people watching people and people queuing for ice-cream cones, french-fried potatoes, and cold drinks. Those are nonalcoholic drinks, of course, because with the May 24th weekend comes a battalion of extra Ontario Provincial Police officers who dedicate their summer to making sure nobody takes a bottle of beer to the beach. There's also a police patrol boat to ensure that boat operators are quenching their thirst with nonalcoholic drinks.

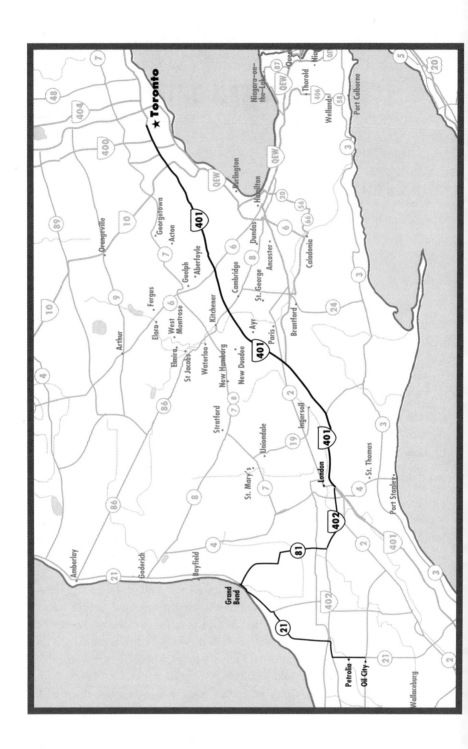

Grand Bend's long, deep beach.

There are few places in Ontario with more to do when the weather is pleasant. During the day, relaxing at the beach and strolling along the sidewalks are the main activities. When the sun goes down, people congregate in the bars, restaurants, discos, coffee shops, and snack bars. Then there are amusement arcades, miniature golf, and the Huron Country Playhouse Theatre—and the main street is still thick with strollers far into the night.

DAY 1

Morning

Take Highway 401 west 185 km (116 miles) to London, and just past London take Highway 402 toward Sarnia. About 40 km (25 miles) west of London, take exit 65 and Highway 81 north to Parkhill. Follow Highway 81 into Grand Bend.

LUNCH: There are good restaurants at Ingersoll (exit 218 from Highway 401; see Elm Hurst Inn in the Southwestern Ontario Escape One) and family-style restaurants in Strathroy and Parkhill.

In Grand Bend you can have a full or light lunch at Oakwood Inn Resort Golf and Country Club or Pine Dale Motor Inn, your lodging options for the night, or wander Grand Bend's main drag and sample the burgers, sandwiches, fries, and other fast food offered every few storefronts. This town hasn't earned its popularity from fine dining (although you'll have good food at either inn); it's food-on-the-hoof for most and this works for most.

Afternoon

Folks usually come to Grand Bend to people-watch, but there are some attractions of merit.

If you head 8 km (5 miles) south of town on Highway 21, the main gate to **Pinery Provincial Park** is on your right. The park has 1,000 campsites and is often fully booked on summer weekends. It contains a series of parallel sand dunes ranging from water level on the 10-km-long (6-mile-long) beach to 100 feet high farther inland. The park protects one of the largest oak and pine forests in Southwestern Ontario. A slow-moving river, a branch of the Ausable, roughly divides the park from north to south and is popular with canoeists and bird-watchers. More than 200 species of birds have been identified here. The Pinery has nine well-marked hiking trails that double as cross-country ski trails in winter and 80 km (50 miles) of roadways. A convenience store in the area rents bicycles and canoes.

Just north of the park entrance on the other side of Highway 21 is **Lambton Heritage Museum.** This is no assortment of oddities from the community's attics; it's a large collection with a full-time curator and staff. The main exhibit center is housed in a modern structure and holds more than 15,000 artifacts, including one of the most extensive collections of pressed glass in Canada.

Behind the museum building a pioneer village has been assembled from historically significant buildings. Two large barns house agricultural devices and a collection of sleighs, cutters, and wagons. A showpiece of the museum is one of the last horse-drawn ambulances ever made. There are several furnished pioneer log homes and a reconstruction of the 1874 frame Mary-Ellen Memorial Chapel, in which summer weddings are sometimes held.

One particularly interesting exhibit is a small wooden building known as the Springvale Beef Ring Slaughterhouse. In the pre-electric-freezer era, a group of thirty to forty families agreed to coordinate their weekly beef and pork supply. They built a small slaughterhouse on skids that was hauled to a farm, where one member of the group acted as butcher. The families took turns contributing a beast of specified weight and quality to the slaughter-house, and cuts of meat were allotted on a prearranged schedule. The butcher's fee was paid by all of the families, and when he died or retired the slaughter-house was dragged off to the farm of the next butcher.

Adults are charged $3.75 admission to the museum, which is open Monday–Friday 10:00 A.M. to 5:00 P.M., weekends and holidays 11:00 A.M. to 5:00 P.M.; closed on weekends November through February. The museum is on the east side of Highway 21, 8 km (5 miles) south of the traffic light in Grand Bend. (519) 243–2600.

Between Lambton Heritage Museum and Grand Bend (on your right as you return to Grand Bend) is the small, family-owned **Grand Bend Zoo.** It's on a side road just off Highway 21; follow the signs. The zoo boasts Ontario's largest variety of monkeys and a fine collection of everything from llamas to yaks, baboons to coatimundis, and leopards to peccaries. What makes this zoo special is its setting. Display areas are separated by shaded pathways through the forty-acre site. The animals are like pets to owner Ted Relouw and his family, and you don't get that feeling of concrete and steel bars evident in most municipal zoos. There's a small admission fee. Open daily 10:00 A.M. to 7:00 P.M. mid-May to mid-September and only on weekends until mid-October. (519) 238–2769.

DINNER AND LODGING: At the junction of Highways 81 and 21 turn right. In less than a mile you'll see the entrance to **Oakwood Inn Resort Golf and Country Club** on your left. In the last decade the Oakwood Inn Resort has become one of the finest little resort complexes in Ontario. There are ninety rooms, four cabins, and a honeymoon cottage. Some rooms have whirlpools and fireplaces. In the main lodge you'll find one of Ontario's best-designed indoor swimming pools. The pool is surrounded by wide aprons under skylights and decorated with greenery and expensive lounge furniture. The pool area overlooks a deck that in turn affords a view between old cedars to the first and tenth fairways of the golf course. A Jacuzzi and saunas are in the pool area, which also has a massive granite fireplace. Wall decorations throughout the resort are framed blowups of turn-of-the-century black-and-white photographs of local scenes. The pool area is attached to the clubhouse, which contains the bar, lounge, and dining area, built of red pine logs in 1930. Oakwood is not on the beach, but just a short stroll away it has a section of beach for the use of guests. Open year-round with a variety of getaway packages. Rates range from $79 to $223. For more information, write: Oakwood Inn Resort Golf and Country Club, Box 400, Grand Bend ON N0M 1T0. (519) 238–2324.

Evening

From the end of June to Labor Day, Huron Country Playhouse offers straw-hat theater in a barn just east of town. For information or tickets call (519) 238–8451.

DAY 2

Morning

BREAKFAST: At the Oakwood Inn Resort.

Take Highway 21 south through Forest, west for 9 km (6 miles) on Highway 402, and south again to Petrolia, a total distance of 70 km (43 miles). Follow signs to **Petrolia Discovery.** This working museum presents the history of Canada's petroleum industry, which started 25 km (16 miles) southeast at Petrolia and 10 km (6 miles) south at Oil City.

Petrolia was Canada's first oil boomtown after the liquid gold was discovered at Oil Springs in 1855. Within two decades there were fifteen wells pumping, 100 drilling rigs, and fifteen refineries. From here, pioneer oil men traveled the globe, discovering most of the major oil fields in eighty-seven countries.

Oil is still pumped in a sixty-acre field in this town of 4,800, and guides take you on a tour. Open daily 9:00 A.M. to 5:00 P.M. from the first Saturday in May to Labor Day. Open Monday–Friday from Labor Day through October. Arrangements may be made to tour the site after the regular season by writing: The Petrolia Discovery, Box 1480, Petrolia ON N0N 1R0. (519) 882–0897.

LUNCH: The **Oil Rig Restaurant** at 415 Albany Street in Petrolia will keep you in this afternoon's theme. (They have a model of an oil derrick in the middle of their dining room!) Photos of early oil days line the walls. The menu runs from soup and salads to family-style full-course meals. Their onion soup is memorable. (519) 882–1232.

Afternoon

On your way to the Oil Rig Restaurant from Petrolia Discovery, you passed the impressive **Victoria Hall** at 411 Greenfield Street. The building houses the town offices and council chambers and **Victoria Playhouse,** a 425-seat theater that offers a wide variety of dramatic entertainment year-round. The hall was built in 1889 and gutted by an arsonist in 1989. The outside walls survived and the interior was rebuilt by 1992. Tours can be arranged, or you can get information on what's playing during your visit, by calling (519) 882–2350.

The **Oil Museum of Canada** is 10 km (6 miles) south at Oil City. The museum is on the site of North America's first oil well and has working wells. Artifacts trace the history of the industry and the evolution of machines that run on oil or its by-products. Open daily 10:00 A.M. to 5:00 P.M., May 1 to October 31, and open year-round for tours or by arrangement. Admission $3.75. For information write: Oil Museum of Canada, Kelly Road, R.R. 2, Oil Springs ON N0N 1P0. (519) 834–2840.

The **Wallaceburg and District Museum** charges a $2.00 admission to its collection of community artifacts at 505 King Street. Inside there's a children's toy display, the world's largest faucet, a film room, an old-time hardware store, a barbershop, a fine collection of photographs of the early days of Wallaceburg, and a schoolroom. From June through September, open 10:00 A.M. to 4:00 P.M. Tuesday–Saturday and 1:00 to 4:00 P.M. on Sunday. October through May hours are Monday–Friday 10:00 A.M. to 4:00 P.M.

DINNER AND LODGING: Check in at the family-owned **Oak's Inn,** which has an indoor pool and sauna, patio, lounge, and restaurant. The Oak's Inn dining room is known for its prime roast of beef and roast chicken. Entrees are $7.00–$12.00. The inn is at 80 McNaughton Avenue on the south side of town just off Murray Street, or Highway 40. Room rates $50–$80. (519) 627–1433.

Evening

They've been racing horses at **Dresden Raceway,** 1244 North Street, since 1875, and today's race-goers can watch from a three-tiered grandstand with

2,300 seats. Bets are taken (and wins, if any, paid out) in Canadian or U.S. dollars. There are four races a week, usually Wednesday, Friday, and Saturday evenings at 7:45 and Sunday at 1:30 P.M. (519) 683–4466.

DAY 3

Morning

BREAKFAST: At Oak's Inn.
Take Highway 40 through Chatham, 27 km (17 miles) to Highway 401, and head for home.

THERE'S MORE

The **Libbey-Canada Factory Outlet** on Garnet Street has become a major tourist draw for Wallaceburg. There are factory prices on hundreds of glassware items from ashtrays to drinking glasses, terrariums to tumblers, decanters to flower vases. Most of the inventory is heavy glasswork, the sort of stuff used in restaurants and sold in bargain outlets, but there's a wide choice in several large rooms. Open Tuesday–Saturday 9:30 A.M. to 5:30 P.M. (519) 627–9715.

In Chatham, the **Chatham-Kent Museum,** the **Thames Art Gallery,** and the **Chatham Railroad Museum** are all free. The Chatham-Kent Museum at 75 William Street North in the Chatham Cultural Centre has five galleries that highlight the history of the city. The Thames Art Gallery, also in the Chatham Cultural Centre, features exhibitions of local, national, and international art. Both the museum and the gallery are open year-round, Tuesday–Sunday 1:00 to 5:00 P.M. (519) 354–8338. The Chatham Railroad Museum is in a restored 1955 Canadian National Railroad baggage car at the intersection of Queen, McLean, and William Streets. Displays include artifacts from the Chatham, Wallaceburg, and Lake Erie railways. Open May through September, Monday–Friday 9:00 A.M. to 5:00 P.M., Saturday and Sunday, noon to 5:00 P.M. (519) 352–3097.

SPECIAL EVENTS

Early May. Annual Antique Show and Sale, Chatham.

Early May. Kite Fly, Oil Springs. Kite flying for all ages on grounds of Oil Museum of Canada, with prizes and play yard for children.

Second week of June. Oil Patch Quilt Show and Sale, Oil Springs. Quilts, awards, books, museum, play yard at the Oil Museum of Canada.

Late July to early August. Summer Bazaar and Festival, Forest. Two weekends feature entertainment and activities, including pageant, music, outdoor displays, farmers' market, demonstrations, vendors, and children's events.

Second week of August. Antique Motor and Boat Outing, Wallaceburg. Competition between antique cars, boats, fire engines, and motorcycles.

Labor Day weekend. Festival of International Buskers, Grand Bend. Organized by the Township of Stephen, Village of Grand Bend, and Town of Bosanquet. Entertainers, musicians.

Mid-September. Quilt Show and Sale, Grand Bend. At Lambton Heritage Museum.

Mid-October. Christmas Craft Sale, Grand Bend. Folk art, stained glass, pottery, Christmas decorations. At Lambton Heritage Museum.

Mid-October. Pumpkinfest, Petrolia. Pumpkin carving, games, demonstrations at Petrolia Discovery site.

OTHER RECOMMENDED RESTAURANTS AND LODGINGS

Grand Bend

Coral Reef Inn, on Highway 21 just south of the traffic lights on Highway 21. (519) 238–2081. It has a popular bar/lounge with dartboards, and its small dining room serves excellent seafood, steaks, and North American cuisine year-round at reasonable prices.

Pine Dale Motor Inn, 107 Ontario Street South. (519) 238–2231. Fully booked most weekends. Forty-one units so comfortable that people enjoy their weekend even if the weather doesn't cooperate. Some of the guest rooms have extra-long beds and the carpeting is extra-deep pile. A whirlpool and sauna are adjacent to the indoor pool, as is a games room. Guests can eat next door at Aunt Gussie's, a family-style eatery.

FOR MORE INFORMATION

Sarnia Lambton Tourism, P.O. Box 248, Grand Bend ON N0M 1T0. (519) 238–2001

Town of Petrolia, P.O. Box 1270, Petrolia ON N0N 1R0. (519) 882–2350

SOUTHWESTERN ONTARIO

Guelph, Kitchener-Waterloo, and St. Jacobs

THE HEART OF MENNONITE COUNTRY

2 NIGHTS

A poet's residence • Mennonite and Hutterite country
The world's longest bar • Antique vehicles • Liquor museum

In Guelph, when you pass the same point for the second or third time and want somebody to curse at, let fly at John Galt. He founded Guelph in 1827 and laid out what *Encyclopedia Canadiana* charitably calls "the interesting radial street pattern." That pattern might have been just swell in horse and buggy days, but it's mighty confusing for today's visitor. Fortunately the locals are used to—and generally good at—providing directions, and the places you'll want to visit are well signed.

Guelph is also a very pretty city. As you go around and around trying to find your way, you'll notice the many lovely homes and buildings of locally quarried limestone. To be fair to Galt, he had to contend with a hilly terrain and the confluence of the Speed and Eramosa Rivers. The Roman Catholic Church has helped strangers by building the Church of Our Lady, which dominates the city from a central hilltop. It's nicknamed "The Cologne Cathedral of Canada" for the cathedral after which it was modeled, and it's a great point of reference for those who are perplexed that they're lost in a city of only 96,000.

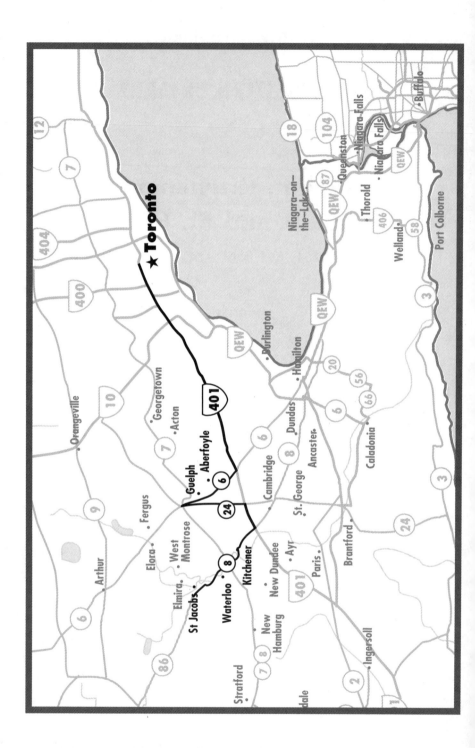

SOUTHWESTERN ONTARIO

DAY 1

Morning

Take Highway 401 west to exit 299 and turn north on County Road 46. If you luck out with traffic, you should reach that intersection thirty to forty minutes after leaving Toronto. As you drive north on County Road 46, you'll see the **Aberfoyle Mill,** the venue recommended for tonight's dining, on your right after about 3 km (2 miles). Continue on to Guelph.

LUNCH: Experience the "biggest living room in town." That's how the "in" restaurant **Van Gogh's Ear** describes itself. It's at 10 Wyndham Street North and is easier to locate with the new sign instead of just the enormous bronze ear that used to be your only guide. There's regular table seating, but many prefer to settle into a couch and eat from coffee tables. There's a full traditional menu for lunch and dinner, as well as bar food. Daily specials cost $4.00–$6.00 for lunch and $5.00–$8.00 for dinner. (519) 821–9864.

Afternoon

Guelph is easily appreciated year-round, but a visit in early November makes a poignant lesson for the generations that missed the World Wars. Lieutenant Colonel John McCrae was born here; he was a physician who died in France in World War I while serving in the medical corps. He was also a poet and wrote the immortal lines of "In Flanders Fields." His poem inspired the use of the poppy as a universal symbol of remembrance.

The modest stone home at 108 Water Street West (off Old Highway 6, or Gordon Street) from which McCrae left to go to war is now a museum, **McCrae House.** McCrae's bedroom and the kitchen are furnished with original effects. The rest of the house is filled with memorabilia relating to his successful career as a physician and author of medical texts and to his involvement in the Boer War and World War I. The staff can answer questions about this man whose promising career ended at age forty-five.

Admission is $3.00 for adults, and for another $2.00 you can get a ticket to **Guelph Civic Museum** at 6 Dublin Street, which is open year-round. McCrae House and Guelph Civic Museum are open daily 1:00 to 5:00 P.M. (519) 836–1221.

Take Highway 7 east from Guelph toward Acton and turn right onto Wellington County Road 44. The **Halton County Radial Railway** is well marked. A museum contains historic streetcars, radial cars, and work cars, and you can ride antique vehicles on a 2-km (1.3-mile) track. Note: The railway is only open May through October, 10:00 A.M. to 5:00 P.M. daily. (519) 856–9802.

DINNER: Reservations are recommended at the popular **Aberfoyle Mill.** It's 8 km (5 miles) south of Guelph on Brock Road. Scottish immigrant George MacLean built the mill in 1859 and in 1867 won a gold medal at the Paris World's Fair for his oatmeal. Owners John and Terri Manolis don't list oatmeal on their menu, but they do offer rack of lamb and stuffed chicken served amid a clutter of Canadiana claimed to be Canada's largest private collection.

The mill equipment has been returned to working order, and water still rushes out the tailrace at one end of the dining room. Lunch and dinner are served daily, except that on Saturday no lunch is served and on Sunday there's brunch. Dinners cost $13–$24. (519) 763–1070.

LODGING: The **College Inn,** on the south side of Guelph at 716 Gordon Street, has an outdoor pool, workout room, dining room, and bar/lounge that serves finger foods. Rates $84–$114. (519) 836–1240 or (800) 563–9240.

DAY 2

Morning

BREAKFAST: At the College Inn.

Take Highway 24 south 14 km (9 miles) to Highway 401 west and take the second exit (275) for Homer Watson Boulevard. Follow signs a short distance to **Homer Watson House and Gallery.** Watson, Canada's first landscape artist of note, produced more than 1,200 canvases between 1855 and 1936. Most were inspired by the rolling countryside of the region where he spent all his life. His early Victorian, high-gabled house near the banks of the Grand River is now an art gallery and museum that displays his paintings. Open early April through mid-December, Tuesday–Sunday noon to 4:30 P.M., Thursday until 8:00 P.M., and holiday Mondays. (519) 748–4377.

Doon Heritage Crossroads is a bit farther north off Homer Watson Boulevard. Just minutes from the swish and roar of Highway 401, this sixty-acre site tranquilly brings alive the lifestyle of people who lived near the main highway of the early 1800s, the Huron Road. Visitors wander tree-shaded roadways where neither automobiles nor the noises of the urban complex to the north intrude. Staff at the village wear period costume, and some work at old-time activities—spinning yarn, tabby-weaving rag mats, or in the case of

Chief Palemoon at Iroquois Village, spinning the tales and legends of his people. A day at the village with a picnic lunch is a painless way to show children what life was like in the nineteenth century.

Demonstrations and crafts are featured in the replica Waterloo Township Hall. A museum building has a Conestoga wagon used by early settlers, displays of early shops, and stuffed birds. On the grounds are the Petersburg Railroad Station with its Canadian Pacific locomotive out front and the Shantz and Shuh barns containing farm implements, Victorian hearses, baby carriages, churns, and butcher equipment. Each building has costumed interpreters. Across a covered bridge is Doon Village, where there's an 1836 village store. Old-time candies, pottery, sketches, postcards, and rag rugs made at the village are for sale. The village also has a fully equipped saddlery and harness shop, an 1835 printing shop, and the 1851 post office from Wellesley.

Open daily 10:00 A.M. to 4:30 P.M. May 1 to Labor Day, 10:00 A.M. to 4:30 P.M. Labor Day to December 31. Closed January 1 to April 30. Admission $5.50 adults, $3.50 seniors and students. (519) 748–1914.

Continue north on Homer Watson Boulevard to Ottawa Street, turn right, and then go left on King Street, which takes you into the heart of Kitchener. The city of Kitchener is the seat of Waterloo County, and Waterloo is a city that abuts Kitchener so closely the two are called Kitchener-Waterloo and known colloquially as "K-W." Waterloo, according to historical records, has been called that since it was settled around 1800 by Swiss-German Mennonites from Pennsylvania.

Kitchener, on the other hand, has gone through many names. When settled, around 1800, it was called Sand Hill. That changed to Ebytown to honor Bishop Benjamin Eby, who settled what is now downtown Kitchener in 1807. In 1841, German immigrants honored their homeland by naming the place Berlin. In 1916, however, when anti-German sentiment was running high, the name was changed to Kitchener, after Lord Kitchener, who drowned at sea that year. K-W now has a combined population of 250,000 and a wide ethnic mix, though German names predominate. Nor is there any chance of mistaking that major ethnic ingredient: There's a huge **glockenspiel** on Benton Street beside Speakers' Corner, and every October since 1967 the city has hosted its popular Oktoberfest.

There are farmers' markets all over Ontario, but **Kitchener Farmers' Market** at the corner of Frederick and Duke Streets is particularly well known. It isn't the oldest or biggest but it's been around since 1869 and is now housed in magnificent quarters at **Market Square.** The block-size complex is enclosed in green-tinted glass and has seventy shops, boutiques, and snack bars and a large Eaton's Department Store. One hundred market vendors offer meats, poultry, fish, sausages, baked goods, pickles, vegetables, plants, sauerkraut, flowers, jams, and handcrafts. Open Saturday 5:00 A.M. to 2:00 P.M. From mid-May through mid-October there's a Wednesday market from 7:00 A.M. to 2:00 P.M.

Continue north on King Street to **Waterloo.** The only way you'll know you're there is by the sign that welcomes you. Waterloo is one of the stops on the recently created **Ale Trail,** a self-guided route that takes you to six of the microbreweries for which the area has become renowned. The breweries make a wide range of traditional European-style lagers and ales, based on the methods used by the early settlers who came here at the beginning of the 1800s. The flavorful brews are served in many of the region's pubs, restaurants, and inns. Maps are available from Ale Trail, P.O. Box 21026, Campus Postal Outlet, 35 Harvard Road, Guelph ON N1G 4T3.

LUNCH: In nearby Waterloo, at the corner of William and Caroline Streets, is **Yukiko's Cafe.** Labeled by its owners as a patisserie, Yukiko's offers a variety of sandwiches—try smoked salmon on fresh baked bread and, for dessert, hazelnut-pumpkin cheesecake or the chocolate and orange variety. The fare is unusual and amazingly delicious.

Afternoon

Take King Street south to Victoria Street, turn left, and follow signs to **Woodside National Historic Park.** William Lyon Mackenzie King, prime minister of Canada for twenty-two of the years from 1921 to 1948, spent his teenage years in a rented ten-room house called Woodside, built in 1853 and now a national historic park. There's no particular imprint of the lifelong bachelor prime minister, whose diaries reveal his belief in mysticism, portents, and communications with the dead, but the house has been furnished to reflect the period of the King family occupancy.

That period was the sunset of the Victorian era, when the appearance of comfort, opulence, and hospitality was created by cramming excessively ornamental furniture and bric-a-brac into every room. It was de rigueur in that era to throw into one room as many different patterns as possible—three or four different wallpapers and wild prints, chintzes, and floral patterns on draperies, chairs, carpets, and rugs. In the reception room, potted tropical plants vie for attention with plaster busts, beadwork, hanging plates, and petit-point mottos.

In summer, guides wear period costume on weekends, operate a children's program, and present slide shows and projects like bread-baking. Open May to December daily 10:00 A.M. to 5:00 P.M., closed Remembrance Day. Admission $2.50. (519) 571–5684.

West across King Street and a block south of Victoria Street is **Joseph Schneider Haus** at 466 Queen Street South. This home of one of the region's earliest pioneers has been restored and furnished to the 1820s era, when Joseph Schneider built it for his family. Costumed staff do quilting, bake apple schnitzels, shear sheep, and tend the garden. A modern museum wing has changing exhibits of folk and decorative art. From Labor Day to Victoria Day, open Wednesday–Saturday 10:00 A.M. to 5:00 P.M., Sunday 1:00 to 5:00 P.M. The rest of the year, open daily 10:00 A.M. to 5:00 P.M. Closed Christmas, Boxing Day, and New Year's Day. Admission $2.25. (519) 742–7752.

Take King Street North and branch off on Weber Street to the left. Just as you leave Waterloo, two farmers' markets face each other across Weber Street North. One is **Waterloo Farmers' Market** and the other is **K-W Stockyards and Farmers' Market.** Both offer the usual market produce but also have flea markets and arts and crafts. Open Saturday 7:00 A.M. to 2:00 P.M. and Thursday 7:00 A.M. to 5:00 P.M. from June until early October.

Stay on Weber Street North and follow signs to **St. Jacobs.** It's a little village of 1,500, but there are enough things to see and do in and around it to keep you busy for several memorable days and nights. Here in the **heart of Mennonite and Hutterite country,** you'll see members of these two sects at any hour of the day or night driving their distinctive, black, horse-drawn carriages or cutters.

If you're a serious dieter, consider a getaway in a different place. This area is one of the last bastions of real food in the province. Restaurants serve mostly German fare: no-nonsense home-style good food and plenty of it. The region is also a shopper's paradise, especially the towns of St. Jacobs and Elmira, about 8 km (5 miles) north.

The entire village of St. Jacobs is an attraction in its own right. Most of the buildings along the main street (King Street) were built in the 1850s, and care has been taken to ensure they appear now as they did then. There are antiques shops, gift boutiques, candy shops, and places like the **Village Bakery** offering fresh-baked bread. In two buildings facing each other across King Street at the Conestoga River, there are more than forty shops and boutiques. The **Riverworks Retail Centre** is on the east side and **St. Jacobs Country Mill** is on the west side. Tucked into the latter building are the **Village Silos,**

Mennonites in their horse-drawn black carriage.

former grain storage silos from the flour mill ingeniously converted to retail outlets.

At the **Meeting Place,** 33 King Street, displays and videos explain the history, culture, lifestyle, and beliefs of the Mennonites. The explanation starts with a twenty-eight-minute documentary film. There are photos, slide presentations, a replica of a Swiss cave, and a Mennonite meeting house of the type still used by Old Order Mennonites. Open in summer Monday–Friday 11:00 A.M. to 5:00 P.M., Saturday 10:00 A.M. to 5:00 P.M., and Sunday 1:30 to 5:00 P.M. Open November to April, Saturday 11:00 A.M. to 4:30 P.M. and Sunday 2:00 to 4:30 P.M., or other times by appointment. Admission is by donation, suggested at $3.00 adults, $2.00 students. (519) 664–3518.

The **Maple Syrup Museum of Ontario** chronicles the history and techniques of the manufacture of maple products. A small sugar shack is built into the display, and products are for sale. Located at 8 Spring Street (just west of King), the museum is open daily year-round except January and February, when it's open every day except Monday. Free admission. (519) 669–2423.

DINNER: The **Stone Crock** has restaurants in St. Jacobs and Elmira. They're folksy places with home-style cooking, salad bars, and dessert tables that have caused more than one Weight-Watchers member to burn a membership card. The St. Jacobs Stone Crock is on King Street 1 block south of Benjamin's Inn, and the Elmira restaurant, which includes a bakery, delicatessen, and gift shop, is at 59 Church Street. Open Monday–Friday 7:00 A.M. to 8:30 P.M. and Sunday 11:00 A.M. to 8:30 P.M. Reservations recommended: St. Jacobs, (519) 664–2286; Elmira, (519) 669–1521.

LODGING: Benjamin's Inn is a lovely re-creation of the 1852 Farmer's Inn. The original hand-hewn wooden beams remain, and even the horse-watering trough by the outside pump has been restored. Nine rooms on the second floor are furnished with antiques, and the beds are covered with Mennonite quilts. Continental breakfast is served on an enclosed veranda and included in the rate of $95 per couple. There's a restaurant with open-hearth fireplaces, pine ceiling beams, lots of greenery, and French-Mediterranean cuisine.

In summer there's a secluded outdoor patio surrounded by riots of flowers where the chef grills dishes. At 17 King Street. (519) 664–3731.

Evening

Kitchener's cultural mecca is the **Centre in the Square,** a modern, red-brick building offering entertainment year-round. The **Kitchener-Waterloo Symphony Orchestra** performs here, as well as big-name singers, comedians, native folk groups, barbershop groups, the **Waterloo Regional Police Male Chorus,** dancers, opera singers, and other performers for all age groups. To find out what entertainment will be offered during your visit, or for reservations, call (519) 578–1570 or (800) 265–8977 from anywhere in Canada.

Or, you might like to visit **Lulu's**. This unique nightspot, just south of Kitchener on the west side of Highway 8 (King Street South), can seat 2,000 customers at 450 tables and on bar stools, and there's room for another 1,000 standing along the longest and second-longest bars in the world. (The world's longest bar is 333 feet; the second-longest is 310 feet.) Lulu's also claims to be Canada's *largest* bar. Everything is big: The parking lot holds 1,500 cars. Since Lulu's opened in 1984 it's been packing 'em in to watch performances by big-name rock entertainers. Open Thursday–Saturday nights 4:30 P.M. to 1:00 A.M. and sometimes Wednesday nights for special concerts. There's a cover charge, and jeans are not permitted. (519) 650–0000.

DAY 3

Morning

BREAKFAST: At Benjamin's Inn.

Drive home on Highway 401 if you're in a hurry, or wander along Highway 7 through Guelph, Acton, Georgetown, Norval, and Brampton.

THERE'S MORE

Nature trails and wildlife gardens are featured at the vast **University of Guelph Arboretum** on Arboretum Road on the east side of the University of Guelph campus. The arboretum contains a wide array of plant collections, and there are 2,900 varieties of trees and shrubs on the property. Open year-round. No admission charge.

At **Kortright Waterfowl Park** in Guelph, there's a captive collection of more than ninety species of waterfowl. They're in a natural setting that is ideal for observation or photography. Open March through October on Saturday, Sunday, and statutory holidays, 10:00 A.M. to 5:00 P.M. On Niska Road off Kortright Road. Adults $2.15, students $1.50. (519) 824–6729.

There are two major water theme parks in Kitchener. **Bingeman Park** (pronounced Bing-a-man) is at 1380 Victoria Street North off Highway 7. It has a wave pool and waterslides, minigolf, go-carts, and a golf driving range. Open daily May through September. Free parking and admission to the grounds. Adult pass to all attractions is $18.95; child's pass is $15.95. The waterpark pass costs $10.50 for adults and $8.50 for children under twelve. (519) 744–1555.

Sportsworld is a thirty-acre park at 100 Sportsworld Drive off Highway 8, just north of Highway 401. It has a wave pool, waterslide, tube ride, children's play pool, amusement rides, minigolf, and an indoor driving range. The driving range is open year-round and all facilities open the first Saturday in June; hours are 10:00 A.M. to dusk daily. A passport to all attractions costs $19.95 for adults, $15.95 for children five to eleven; a midway pass for unlimited amusement rides is $10.00. (519) 653–4442.

SPECIAL EVENTS

Mid-May. Antique Roadshow and Fair, Kitchener. Have your heirlooms, treasures, and antiques identified and appraised by experts from Ritchie's Auctioneers, Woodside National Historic Site.

Early June. Donkey Day, Guelph. Donkey and pony rides, donkey demonstrations, nature walks, barn visits, hay rides, food and gift booths. At the Donkey Sanctuary of Canada, Puslinch Road.

Mid-June. Antique Automobiles and Parts. Have a look behind the scenes as Doon Heritage Crossroads highlights their collection of antique automobiles and parts.

End of June to early July. Settlers' Days Immigration Celebration, Kitchener. In honor of the area's first pioneers, the Joseph Schneiders, this event focuses on their pioneering skills and the contributions of more recent immigrants to the area. Joseph Schneider House.

Third week of August. Handwerk, Kitchener. An outdoor festival featuring artisans who practice traditional nineteenth-century crafts, such as tinsmiths, quilters, cabinetmakers, and blacksmiths, demonstrating their crafts and offering unique items for sale.

First week of October. Great Canadian Maturity Show, Kitchener. Exhibits focus on products, services, and opportunities for the fifty-plus age group, entertainment, videos, demonstrations. At Kitchener Memorial Auditorium Complex.

First week of October. Country Craft Festival, Kitchener. Crafts made by artisans from Southwestern Ontario. At the Knights of Columbus Community Hall.

Mid-October. Oktoberfest, various locations. Canada's largest Bavarian festival featuring festhalls, food and drink, music and entertainment, family and cultural events.

OTHER RECOMMENDED RESTAURANTS AND LODGINGS

Elmira

The Stone Crock Restaurant, 59 Church Street. (519) 669–1521. Has an a la carte menu, country buffet, and salad bar. On the premises are a bakery and delicatessen, as well as a gift shop featuring Mennonite quilts and country calicos, coal oil lamps, scented candles, and soaps.

Heidelberg

Olde Heidelberg Brewery, County Road 15, 8 km (5 miles) west of Highway 86, just north of the Waterloo markets. (519) 699–4413. Bavarian lager brewed in five big copper vats in the front window. Honky-tonk piano, shuffleboard, pool tables, and music for sing-alongs. Daily dinner specials, $8.00–$10.00 per person.

Olde Heidelberg Motel, same address as brewery. (519) 699–4413. Clean, large, fully-equipped motel rooms with two double beds.

St. Jacobs

Jakobstettel Guest House, 16 Isabella Street. (519) 664–2208. Twelve large rooms in an 1898 red-brick mansion. Five-acre grounds with gardens and huge shade trees bordering the millrace. Outdoor pool and clay tennis courts. Breakfast served, snacks available.

FOR MORE INFORMATION

Guelph Visitor and Convention Services, 55 Wyndham Street North, Guelph ON N1H 4E4. (519) 837–1335.

Cambridge Visitor and Convention Bureau, 531 King Street East, Cambridge ON N3H 3N4. (519) 653–1424.

Kitchener-Waterloo Area Visitor and Convention Bureau, 2848 King Street East, Kitchener ON N2A 1A5. (800) 265–6959.

For St. Jacobs: Township of Woolwich, c/o Elmira and Woolwich Chamber of Commerce, 5 First Street East, Elmira ON N3B 2E3. (519) 669–2605.

London and Port Stanley

TOWN AND COUNTRY WEEKEND

2 OR 3 NIGHTS

A ride on a double-decker bus • Museums • Indian village
Jumbo monument • Rail excursion

Most Canadians know London because it's home to the University of Western Ontario and the headquarters of London Life Insurance Company and Labatt's Breweries, or because of General Motors' major operation there. The city is nicknamed "The Forest City" and there are more than 50,000 trees on city property. Canada's eleventh-largest city is full of parks—1,500 acres of them, including 1,000 acres along the Thames River.

London has been described as "a microcosm of Canadian life" and is considered so typically Canadian it is often used as a test market for new products. If something will sell in London, it will sell anywhere in Canada. In its own low-key way, London has a lot to interest the casual visitor. To see all the sights in and around London takes a week. The best are listed here; select enough to fill the afternoon of Day 1 and the morning of Day 2. Then you're off to relax in a super country inn in a picturesque Lake Erie fishing village.

DAY 1

Morning

Take Highway 401 west 185 km (116 miles) to exit 186 and follow Wellington Road north through the city to York Street. Turn left on York and after 2 short blocks go right on Richmond. Pall Mall Street is 6 blocks north on

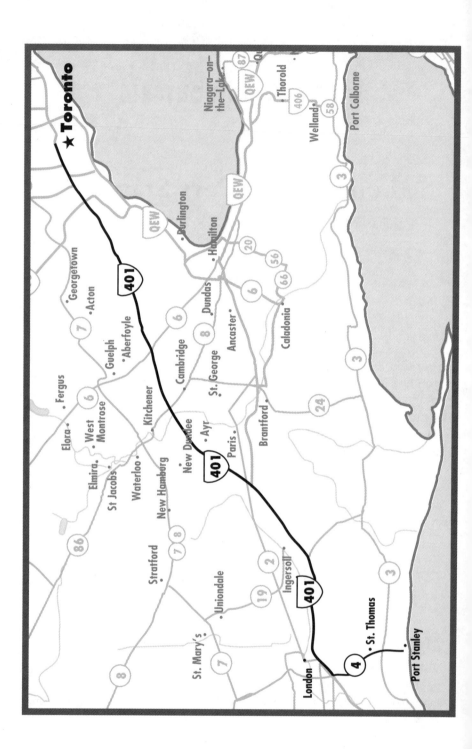

Richmond. Turn right on Pall Mall. **Station Park Inn,** where you'll be staying, will be on your left at 242 Pall Mall.

LUNCH: Two blocks south of the hotel on Richmond at Central Avenue, **Joe Kool's** offers salads, sandwiches, rotisserie chicken, burgers, Tex-Mex dishes, and pizza in the $5.00–$6.00 range.

Afternoon

The best way to get an overview of London is on a **Double-Decker London Bus Tour.** From Kool's you can cut diagonally across Victoria Park (the equivalent of 2 blocks) to City Hall, where tours leave daily at 10:00 A.M. and 2:00 P.M. in a red London double-decker bus. The morning tour stops for twenty minutes at **Storybook Gardens** and the afternoon tour stops at **London Art Gallery.** Tours operate late June to Labor Day and cost $7.50 per person, including taxes. They take you past fifty of London's major attractions, give you a sense of direction in this easy-to-find-your-way city, and help you decide which places you'll return to for a longer visit. (Although carved by the Thames River and several tributaries, London has a good network of major streets in grid format to get you easily to the city perimeter.)

Here are London's best attractions:

Storybook Gardens is probably the major attraction. It's operated by the city's Public Utility Commission, which charges one of the lowest rates to any theme park in the country: $5.25 for adults and $3.25 for children. The park is on the Thames River in 281-acre Springbank Park. You enter over a drawbridge and through the enchanted castle, past many characters from children's stories. Children can slide down the hill that was the undoing of Jack and Jill, crawl through the throat of Willie the Whale, or climb the ropes of Little Miss Muffet's web. There's also a zoo. Open early May to Labor Day. On Springbank Drive West. (519) 661–5770.

London Princess Cruise operates June through October from Storybook Gardens on the Thames River. The boat offers two-hour lunch and dinner cruises daily and a brunch tour on Sunday. From June through August there are forty-five-minute afternoon cruises every hour. Adults $6.95, children $4.95. Reservations recommended, and required for all meal cruises. Dinner tours cost $23.95; brunch tours are $18.95. At 696 Headley Drive. (519) 473–0363.

Unlike many Canadian military museums, the **Royal Canadian Regiment (RCR) Museum** is well lit, well planned, and squeaky clean. It's at

Canadian Forces Base London, at the corner of Oxford and Elizabeth Streets in Wolseley Hall, itself a national historic site. The RCR is Canada's senior regular force infantry regiment. There's a nominal admission fee but no charge for servicemen and -women or members of their families. Open daily year-round except Monday and holidays. (519) 660–5102.

Covent Garden Market has been a London fixture for well over a century and is one of the few farmers' markets open six days a week, year-round, 8:30 A.M. to 6:00 P.M. It's at 130 King Street (one-way east) and has indoor parking above it. You can buy local produce, flowers, fresh baked goods, and even a goldfish or kitten. Some vendors import foreign-grown spices, fruits, vegetables, and specialty and gourmet foods. Although the market was closed for renovation when this edition went to press, it is scheduled to reopen in fall 1999.

London Regional Children's Museum is a mini Ontario Science Centre on three floors of the former Riverview School at 21 Wharncliffe Road South. The museum was designed just for children, but a lot can be learned and enjoyed by adults, too. Children can be archaeologists digging up bones, crawl through caves to discover stalactites and stalagmites, or enter a manhole to learn what's beneath the street. Materials and tools are provided for such activities as filing soapstone or making your very own ajagaak. (When you've made yours, see how skillful you can be with it!) Open daily, small admission fee.

London's oldest surviving residence, **Eldon House,** was built in 1834. The Harris family occupied it for its first 126 years, and the fixtures, fittings, and furnishings are authentic and complete. The sheathed frame house, built in Georgian and Regency styles, is at 481 Ridout Street North. The Harrises were inveterate travelers, and the house and its walls are heavy with china and crystal from England, brassware and rosewood furniture from India, swords from Japan, and numerous hunting trophies from Africa. On Wednesday through Sunday, June through August, tea is served on the lawn from 2:00 to 4:00 P.M. Open daily year-round except Monday. (519) 661–5169.

London Regional Art Gallery is as interesting to look at from the outside as its exhibits are on the inside. It's contained in six joined glass-covered structures whose ends are the shape of croquet hoops. At 421 Ridout Street North, on a site called Forks of the Thames because it overlooks the north and south branches of the Thames River. No admission fee. Open daily year-round noon to 5:00 P.M. except Monday. (519) 672–4580.

At 1600 Attawandaron Road in northwest London, **London Museum of Archaeology and Iroquois Indian Village** houses more than 40,000 Indian artifacts along with a gallery of artists' conceptions of the Attawandaron Indians' life on the museum site more than 500 years ago. Nearby is a reconstructed multifamily longhouse on its original site on Wonderland Road, south of Highway 22. Archaeologists still comb the site for flints, arrowheads, and shards of pottery. Open daily 10:00 A.M. to 5:00 P.M. May to September; from September to December open Tuesday–Sunday 10:00 A.M. to 5:00 P.M. Admission $3.50. (519) 473–1360.

If you're over forty, the name Guy Lombardo and his Royal Canadians should bring back memories. New Year's Eve? The big countdown to midnight in New York's Times Square? Guy Lombardo was born in London, and the city has honored him by naming a bridge after him and operating the **Guy Lombardo Museum** at 205 Wonderland Road South, in Springbank Park. Many who enjoyed his music don't know that Lombardo fit two careers into his seventy-five-year life. There was Lombardo the musician and Lombardo the speed freak on water. The museum covers both facets of his colorful career. Lombardo built a series of boats and drove them like a madman to win every major speedboat trophy in the United States. The museum is short on artifacts but long on old phonographs, plaques, and letters. Open daily 11:00 A.M. to 5:00 P.M. mid-May to Labor Day. Admission $2.00. (519) 473–9003.

London's oldest building, the **Old Courthouse and Gaol,** is also one of its most impressive. The wrecker's ball came awfully close to the Old Courthouse and it got some of the wall of the former Middlesex County Gaol. But a citizens' group successfully fought city hall. In 1981, after a $2.5 million facelift, the Old Courthouse, which was modeled after Malahide Castle in Ireland, reopened as the home of Middlesex County Council. On weekday afternoons a guide shows visitors the fine oak paneling, the marble first floor and stairs, the warden's office in one of the 48-foot-high corner turrets, and the grand quarters of the council meeting room. Behind the courthouse is a restored solitary confinement cell, which was in use until 1977. No admission charge. (519) 434–7321.

Upstairs in the Old Courthouse is the **First Hussars Museum,** a one-room collection of artifacts of the First Hussars Regiment in London, which was formed in 1856 as the First London Volunteer Troop of Cavalry. No admission charge. (519) 434–7321.

There are twenty-five historic buildings in **Fanshawe Pioneer Village** just northeast of the city limits. From May through August the village is open daily, and costumed villagers chat with visitors about life in early Canada and demonstrate trades of the period. From Highway 401 take Highway 100 north to Oxford Street West and go west to Clarke Road. Take Clarke Road north 3 km (2 miles) to the entrance. Admission $5.00. (519) 451–2800.

Longwoods Road Conservation Area is 25 km (16 miles) southwest of London, 6.5 km (4 miles) west of the village of Delaware on Highway 2, and about 5 km (3.1 miles) west of Highway 402. There's a resource center with Native history displays and **Ska-Nah-Doht Indian Village.** (Doht is pronounced like "dough" and the name means "a village stands again.") This is a re-created 1,000-year-old Oneida Indian settlement surrounded by a palisade of small tree trunks and entered through a maze. Inside are two longhouses and the framing for a third. A longhouse was the home of an extended family, up to forty or fifty people, all related through the clan mother. Inside and outside the palisade are various elements of Indian life: a deer run, a burial area, food storage areas, animal skin stretching racks, a fish trap, a sweat bath, maple sap works, drying racks, a mortar and pestle, and an agricultural area. The grounds are open year-round daily 9:00 A.M. to sunset. The Indian village and resource center are open year-round Monday–Friday 9:00 A.M. to 4:30 P.M., and also on weekends (same hours) May 24 to Labor Day. Admission $2.75. (519) 264–2420.

DINNER: The **Marienbad Restaurant** and **Chaucer's** next door are within walking distance of your hotel. They are at 122 Carling Street, which runs west off Richmond Street. Both restaurants' fare is Central European and so is their uncontrived ambience of paneled walls and pillars that appear to have supported the roof for centuries—in fact, since 1854. They serve hearty fare—goulash, schnitzels, rouladen, chicken Kiev, and sauerbraten at very reasonable prices. (519) 679–9940.

LODGING: The Station Park Inn, at 242 Pall Mall, has 126 roomy, elegantly furnished suites priced at $125. (800) 561–4574.

Evening

The **Grand Theatre**, only several blocks from the Marienbad Restaurant, is a first-rate professional repertory theater that has been entertaining Londoners since 1901. Their season runs October through March. Evening curtain is usually 8:00 P.M. Tickets ($26–$47) may be ordered toll free in Ontario, (800) 265–1593, and paid for by credit card.

DAY 2

Morning

BREAKFAST: Oscar Taylor's Restaurant adjacent to your hotel is fine for breakfast, or cross the street to the **Five 'n' Diner**, part of **Paradise Bakery**. Breakfast rolls, breads, and croissants don't come any fresher!

During the morning complete your list of things to see and do in London.

LUNCH: Downtown, there is no better deal for a full lunch than the **Ridout Tavern** at Ridout and York Streets. There are choices of hot entrees and vegetables and a salad bar, and you'll get a lot of change from a $10 bill. It's your basic Ontario tavern where regulars eat with their baseball hats on and scoop food into their mouths with their knives, but servings are fast and generous, the food is consistently excellent, and it's the sort of place that has to be experienced. There's a large, free parking lot.

Afternoon

After lunch take Wellington Street South, which is also Highway 4 and later becomes Wellington Road. Follow signs for **St. Thomas** and on its outskirts you can see the **statue to Jumbo the circus elephant,** killed there in a railway accident. There is no charge to see the statue—10 percent larger than life-size—of the largest elephant ever in captivity. He traveled North America with the Barnum and Bailey Circus and died on his second visit to St. Thomas.

During his tours, Jumbo became friendly with the tiny clown elephant Tom Thumb. One evening in 1885 the two elephants were being led along the railroad tracks to their sleeping quarters after that night's performance. An unscheduled train suddenly appeared out of the fog, and Jumbo and Tom Thumb were trapped between the parked circus train and a steep bank Jumbo refused to descend. As the elephants raced for safety, they were overtaken by the train. Tom Thumb suffered a broken leg but Jumbo was hurled into the parked cars and a tusk was driven into his brain.

Adjacent to the Jumbo monument is a railway caboose containing the summer office of the St. Thomas Chamber of Commerce and a gift shop with Jumbo kitsch, open daily 9:00 A.M. to 9:00 P.M.

Less than a block from the statue, at 32 Talbot Street, is the **Elgin County Pioneer Museum** in the 1848 house of Dr. Elijah Duncombe. One interesting exhibit is what was perhaps the world's smallest horse. The 12-inch-high horse became the pet of an English woman, and when it died she had it stuffed and brought it with her when she immigrated to Canada in 1895. An annex contains pioneer agricultural tools and railroad artifacts from the days when St. Thomas was known as the Railway City. Open year-round, Tuesday–Friday 10:00 A.M. to noon and 1:00 to 5:00 P.M.; Saturday and Sunday 2:00 to 5:00 P.M. Next door at 30 Talbot Street, the **Elgin Military Museum** is an ambitious collection tracing the involvement of the people of Elgin County in wars from the War of 1812 to Vietnam. Open Tuesday–Friday 1:00 to 5:00 P.M., Saturday 10:00 A.M. to noon and 2:00 to 5:00 P.M., and Sunday 2:00 to 5:00 P.M.

Get back on Highway 4 and drive to its end in **Port Stanley** on Lake Erie. The village is slowly struggling back to the heyday it enjoyed earlier this century when big bands were the rage and Port Stanley had Canada's largest ballroom. When entertainment tastes changed, the ballroom stood empty for a decade and then burned.

After you've checked into your inn, have a look around the little resort town. There are some great shops for browsing: three for antiques, four for art, eight for gifts, and ten for clothing. Down at the beach there's **Mackie's**. Some "Porters" swear Mackie's hot dogs and orange soft drinks, served there since 1911, are the best snack food in the world.

It isn't hauled by a steam locomotive, but the **London and Port Stanley Railroad (L & PS)** still packs in trippers year-round. The L & PS was built in 1856 between London and Port Stanley and was intended as a main trade artery between Canada and the U.S. International trade didn't materialize but the railroad survived on excursion traffic until 1957.

Railroad enthusiasts have restored some passenger cars and 14 km (10 miles) of rail line. The train runs Sunday afternoons year-round; Saturdays during May, June, and September through November; and daily July and August. Passenger cars are hauled by a diesel engine and, when scheduled, run rain or shine from the old Port Stanley Railway Station near the drawbridge.

DINNER AND LODGING: In 1985 a schoolteacher and a lawyer who wanted to be innkeepers acquired the historic ten-room **Kettle Creek Inn** on Main Street, built in 1849 as the summer home of Squire Samuel Price. Jean and

The 1849-vintage Kettle Creek Inn, a cozy hostelry in Port Stanley.

Gary Vedova renovated the property and have established a fine reputation for their cuisine. Specials change daily, but there's usually fresh Lake Erie perch, Atlantic salmon, or a local venison dish. Entrees run $16–$19.

There are two suites and five rooms in the original inn and five rooms and three suites in an annex. All of the rooms and suites overlook a courtyard, and each, instead of being numbered, is named after a local artist whose works hang in the rooms and are for sale. The suites have gas fireplaces and double whirlpool tubs. Room rates are $90–$185 for a double. A two-night package is $315 for a room and $500 for a suite. (If midweek, deduct $20 per night.) (519) 782–3388.

DAY 3

Morning

BREAKFAST: Have breakfast at the inn and, unless you opted for the two-night package, head for home. Take Highway 4 north to County Road 7, turn right, and drive to the village of Sparta where there are several good antiques shops and artists' studios. From Sparta take County Road 36 north to Highway 3, then jog right on Highway 3 to Highway 74, which will take you north to Highway 401.

THERE'S MORE

Wally World Waterpark at the southwest edge of London, Southday and Wonderland Roads, is a water theme park with a wave pool, eight giant water slides, and a 1,000-foot-long river ride. There are also batting cages, minigolf courses, and a go-cart track. The park is open late May through Labor Day, Monday–Friday 11:00 A.M. to 7:00 P.M., Saturday and Sunday 10:00 A.M. to 8:00 P.M., weather permitting. An all-day pass for water activities costs $14.00 for adults, $10.00 for children four to twelve. Go-cart rides cost $2.25 per lap or $7.50 for five laps. (519) 473–1737.

Western Fair Raceway is the major standardbred racing venue in Southwestern Ontario. The track is at Western Fairgrounds, Queen's Park, at King and Ontario Streets. (From Highway 401, take exit 189, drive north on Highbury Avenue, and turn left on Dundas Street.) From October through June, post time is 7:30 P.M. on Thursday, Friday, and Saturday. Free admission. For admission to the clubhouse there's a charge of $2.00 for adults; children are free. Top of the Fair Clubhouse serves dinner 8:00 to 9:00 P.M. on race nights and has a deservedly excellent reputation for its prime rib. Entrees cost $13.95–$17.50. Reservations strongly recommended. (519) 433–3247.

SPECIAL EVENTS

Mid-May. Rubber Ducky River Race, London. Fundraiser for Heart & Stroke Foundation. Fifteen thousand rubber ducks race down the Thames River to Harris Park where there are concession stands, pony rides, entertainment, and a play center for kids.

Mid-May. Forest City Show Jumping Tournament, London. The Canadian Olympic Equestrian Team and other famous horse-and-rider teams compete for the $50,000 Cuddy International Grand Prix and other prizes in Labatt Park. The RCMP Musical Ride also performs.

Last weekend of May. First showing of Art in the Park, London. Original works by local artists, shown every Sunday 11:00 A.M. to 4:00 P.M. through Labor Day in Springbank Park.

Early June. International Air Show, London. Annual event featuring flying demonstrations of some of the world's most advanced aircraft.

Early June. The London International Children's Festival. Children's performers and games for small fry.

End of June. The London Street Performers Festival, London. Musicians, jugglers, and street artists give a European flair to downtown London.

End of June. Royal Canadian Big Band Music Festival, London. Live music and dance demonstrations in Victoria Park, concerts at Wonderland Gardens, and special display at Galleria London.

First three weeks of July. The Great Walleye Hunt & Rainbow Roundup, Port Stanley. Event raising money to stock rainbow trout.

Third weekend of July. Home County Folk Festival, London. Big-name Canadian folk acts perform in Victoria Park.

July and August. Port Stanley Festival Theatre. Light entertainment, comedies, plays, and musicals.

Early August. London Balloon Festival. At Harris Park.

Early September. Annual Western Fair, London. Parade, midway, livestock shows, grandstand performances.

OTHER RECOMMENDED RESTAURANTS AND LODGINGS

London

Under the Volcano, 300 Colborne Street. (519) 679–2296. Mexican fare including beef, chicken, or seafood chimichangas and deep-fried ice cream. (Note: For more dining options get a free *Restaurant Guide* from your hotel or one of the three welcome centers listed below.)

Delta London Armouries Hotel, 325 Dundas Street. (519) 679–6111. A twenty-story silver-mirrored tower that rises from the center of the 1905 London Armoury. The lobby is a greenhouse of vines, trees, plants, and fountains wrapped in marble and accented with rich woods and old yellow brick. Indoor swimming pool.

Michael's On The Thames, 1 York Street. (519) 672–0111. Overlooking the Thames River. Maitre d' Jack DiCarlo has become something of a local celebrity with his impromptu song-and-dance acts.

FOR MORE INFORMATION

Free London tourist literature is available at three locations: the Welcome Centre (on your right as you enter London northbound on Wellington Road from Highway 401); City Hall at 300 Dufferin Avenue; or in summer, a trailer at Highways 4 and 22 (Richmond Street and Fanshawe Park Road in Masonville Mall). Or contact: Tourism London, 300 Dufferin Avenue, London ON N6B 1Z2. (519) 661–5000.

Pelee Island, Point Pelee, Kingsville, and Leamington
LIFE AT A TURTLE'S PACE

2 NIGHTS

Birds • Butterflies • Ferry ride • Turtles • Wine tasting

You can see Pelee Island a few minutes after the ferry steams away from the dock at Kingsville or Leamington. It is just a gray-green smudge on the horizon—low and flat out there in the middle of Lake Erie, 26 km (16 miles) south of the Canadian shore and 37 km (23 miles) north of Ohio. The trip takes an hour and a half, and from mid-March to mid-December the island is served by the MV *Pelee Islander* and MV *Jiimaan,* which link it to the two Canadian ports and Sandusky, Ohio ($7.50 one-way per person over twelve, $16.50 one-way per automobile; for information and reservations call 519–724–2115 or 800–661–2220). In winter there are regularly scheduled and charter flights from Windsor.

This is a quiet, laid-back place except during one of its three "people" seasons, when it's likely one of the noisiest places in North America. In summer up to 1,200 visitors, 60 percent from Ohio, cram into 200 privately owned and rental cottages. The rest of the year the 300 permanent residents quietly go about their business of planting and harvesting crops, tending vineyards, and maintaining rental boats and cabins.

The noisiest season is during three weekends in October when 700 hunters per weekend come to shoot 20,000 pheasants. The municipality has raised pheasants for hunts since 1932, and the proceeds considerably reduce taxes. Township clerk Brett Kelly reckons the hunts inject more than $750,000

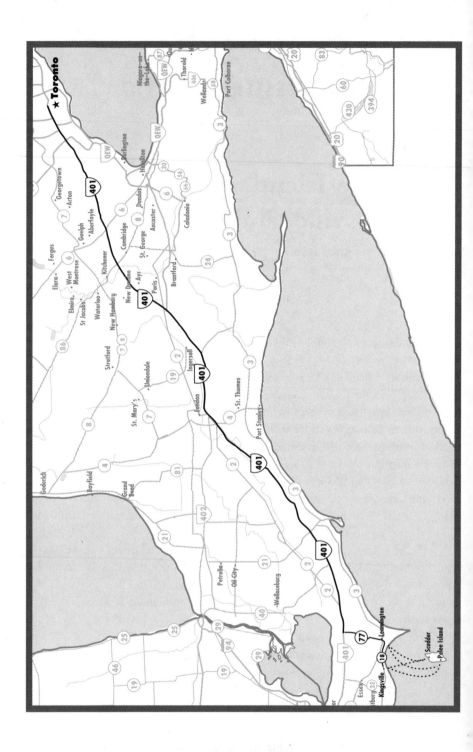

a year into the island's economy from licenses, accommodations, meals, and employment of beaters. The limited hotel accommodations sell out early so hunters rent room and board from islanders.

You can ferry your car to the island or rent a bicycle and enjoy cycling on the pancake-flat terrain. (If you bring your car, fill up the tank before you get here; there is a gas station, but it isn't open every day.) Whichever you choose, be prepared to respond to friendly waves from islanders. It's that kind of place. "You're a friend who has come to visit," an islander once explained. "If you were a tourist, you'd be sticking that camera in my face wanting to take my picture and I don't even have a good face."

Note: This escape is based on the premise you have reserved one of the few rooms on the island and made ferry reservations for your vehicle. If it's a spur-of-the-moment trip, you can always get passenger space on the ferry, but you may have to limit your island sightseeing and spend both nights in Leamington or Kingsville.

DAY 1

Morning

There's no practical way to avoid the 300-km (188-mile) drive west on Highway 401 to exit 48 just west of Tilbury, where you take Highway 77 south 24 km (15 miles) to Leamington, or from Leamington continue on Highway 18 another 15 km (9 miles) to Kingsville. On arrival at Leamington or Kingsville, go directly to the ferry office on the dock to reconfirm your reservations and sailing time.

LUNCH: If you're taking the Leamington ferry, eat at the **Leamington Dock Restaurant,** which has windows overlooking Lake Erie and the hustle and bustle of arriving and departing boats. Fresh fish dishes, steaks, chops, poultry and roast beef. The yellow perch plate is $8.00; daily special is $7.00. Reservations (needed only for lunch or dinner on weekends): (519) 326–2697.

For those departing from Kingsville, **King's Landing** overlooks the dock and, in addition to being a top-notch dining spot in an 1863 building, is allegedly the home of George, a cordial ghost. The **Upper Deck Lounge** is a popular pub, and in fine weather there's drink and finger-food service on its deck overlooking the harbor and full dining service downstairs. Daily specials start at $6.00; the yellow perch or pickerel dinner costs $10.00. Reservations: (519) 733–2231.

Afternoon

As the ferry closes on the 14.5-by-5.5-km (9-by-3-mile) island, the only distinguishing landmarks are a few brightly painted cottages along the tree-lined shore. The ferries dock at either **West Dock** or **Scudder Dock.**

If you land at West Dock—the biggest mark on the little brochure and map you'll be given with your ferry ticket—there isn't much to see. The largest building, resembling a tiny, gray citadel, is the town hall. It also contains the **Pelee Island Heritage Centre,** a collection of island artifacts worth a browse. Open daily 11:00 A.M. to 5:00 P.M. May through mid-November. Admission $2.00 adults, $1.00 students.

There are two landmarks as you approach Scudder Dock. (Dr. John Scudder initiated an elaborate drainage system in 1885 so crops could be grown.) On your left are the remains of a lighthouse, and dead ahead is a ramshackle, weatherbeaten grain elevator looking strangely out of place, surrounded in summer by colorful watercraft.

Check into your hotel and then you're ready for a quick look around.

From West Dock you can see to the south the 352-foot-high **Perry's Victory and International Peace Monument** commemorating one of the decisive battles of the War of 1812. The marker honors American commander Captain Oliver Hazard Perry, who engaged the English at Put-in-Bay Island, Ohio, in 1813. Perry won control of Lake Erie by sailing straight into the British fleet firing broadsides. He became a national hero and is remembered for succinctly reporting: "We have met the enemy and they are ours."

Pelee Island is not the most southerly place in Canada, a claim belonging to neighboring Little Middle Island, one of the Bass Island group. But a line drawn east and west through Pelee Island would pass through northern California, northern Spain, and southern Italy.

In 1865 three Kentuckians discovered the island and its moderate climate, found it conducive to growing grapes, and founded **Vin Villa Vineyards.** They cut two 40-by-60-foot vaults in the solid rock for storing wine and above them built Vin Villa, a pretentious limestone manor house. Prohibition killed the winery, Vin Villa burned, and the islanders resumed producing wheat, corn, and tobacco. The agricultural cycle came full circle in 1979 when a consortium started a vineyard whose grapes now are shipped to Kingsville and processed into Pelee Island wine.

The brochure with map given to you with your ferry ticket lists numerous "points of interest," but you can cut the list to half a dozen because places like the gas station, the liquor store and four churches are included. By slowly wandering along the main road ringing the island you can see all but six of the "sights." The exceptions are just off that ring road:

Vin Villa. There's a replica of Vin Villa next to the liquor store at West Dock or you can go to the site, where several limestone walls remain. If you're agile you can scramble down into the wine storage vaults to admire the high, curved limestone ceilings. None of the snakes you're certain to encounter are poisonous.

Indian grinding stone. A pumice-like rock outcrop with circular indentations made by Indians sharpening their axes, arrows, and spearheads.

Huldah's Rock. A large rock near Vin Villa from which a lovesick Indian maiden supposedly jumped to her death. (Huldah must have been a very determined suicide because the top of the rock is only a few feet above lake level and the water no more than waist deep.)

Pheasant Farm. Daily 9:00 A.M. to noon there's usually someone around to answer your questions and explain why the pheasants wear what look like sunglasses on their beaks. (It's so they can't peck each other's eyes out.) There are also cages with a dozen or more species of exotic pheasant. Free tours can be arranged anytime by calling (519) 724–2064.

Old Lighthouse ruins and **Lighthouse Nature Reserve.** As you leave the parking lot for the short hike through the nature reserve to the lighthouse ruins, pick up one of the sticks you'll find lying about. Use it to rustle tall grasses ahead of you, warning basking snakes of your approach. Move quietly and you may see some of the 5-foot-long ones swimming in the brackish pools beside the pathway.

Pelee Island Wine Pavilion. Here you take a short guided tour and sample their wines. A barbecue lunch that you cook for yourself is available. The tour, including the vineyards, a small historical museum, a video, and wine tasting, takes sixty to ninety minutes. Tours and lunches available daily 11:00 A.M. to 6:00 P.M. May through September. The cook-your-own barbecue lunches cost $5.00–$9.00. (519) 724–2469 or (800) 597–3533.

DINNER: In warm weather, try a fresh fish dinner on the licensed patio of **Pelee Passage** a few steps from your hotel. They also have steaks and hamburgers. The patio is a lively social center at which you can catch the sunset. (519) 724–2266. Or, catch the view and sunset from your full-menu hotel dining room. Both of these dining spots are reasonable.

Point Pelee National Park, a birdwatcher's paradise.

LODGING: The **Pelee Island Hotel** has a one-night package for two for $80 including passes to the **Winery Tour and Tasting** and Pelee Island Heritage Centre, plus a full breakfast. The rooms are small with four-piece bathroom en suite and will not recall the Ritz, but they're comfortable, and owners Darith and Bruce Smith are very hospitable. There's a large bar/lounge called **Bootleggers** that's popular with locals, and the dining room overlooks the dock and lake. (519) 724–2912.

DAY 2

Morning

BREAKFAST: You've already paid for it, so have it at the hotel. Enjoy good coffee, toast, eggs, and bacon with a gorgeous view.

You'll have time before sailing on the midmorning ferry to browse the Heritage Centre and the **Trading Post,** a gift shop near the dock. First, check at the ferry office on the dock to reconfirm your departure time and the dock from which your ferry will sail.

Kingsville is Canada's most southerly town, but most Canadians know it as the former home of conservationist Jack Miner and the current home of **Jack Miner Bird Sanctuary.** The sanctuary is 5 km (3 miles) north of town. Take Division Road and look for Essex County Road 29. There's no admission charge.

Jack Miner was thirteen years old in 1878 when his family moved here from Ohio. He was an avid sportsman and hunter but came to the conclusion that no species could survive both its natural enemies and man. In 1904 he dug ponds on the family farm, planted trees, and introduced four Canada geese with clipped wings. That number grew to the 50,000 that now winter on that and an adjoining property. From 1910 to 1940 Miner lectured on conservation, convincing kings and presidents of the need for it and earning the Order of the British Empire (OBE) "for the greatest achievement in conservation in the British Empire." The Jack Miner Migratory Bird Foundation is open daily year-round except Sundays.

There's a two-story museum in the former stables containing a wealth of Miner memorabilia and a pond where feed is provided for the far-from-shy geese and ducks. Although the Miner family compound and museum are closed on Sundays, the fields across the road swarm with migrating geese. At 3:00 and 4:00 P.M. daily, including Sunday, the birds are flushed for **"air shows."** Best times to view migrations are late March and late October to November.

Another place to see birds—though nothing so plebeian as geese and ducks—is **Colasanti's Tropical Gardens and Petting Farm.** It's between Kingsville and the hamlet of Ruthven to the east and well marked. The greenhouse and garden supply company sprawls through twenty huge, interconnecting greenhouses in which you can buy anything from pansy seeds to wicker baskets. Owner Joe Colasanti loves birds and animals and has expanded his personal aviary and zoo so that the collection has become a tourist attraction in its own right. There's no charge to admire the rows of caged—and often rowdy—birds or to take your children into the petting zoo where they can feed a variety of gentle animals.

The greenhouses contain everything from exotic flowers to rare cacti, and the staff happily answer questions. It's a determined nonshopper who leaves empty-handed. Open daily year-round, Monday–Thursday 8:00 A.M. to 5:00 P.M., Friday–Sunday 8:00 A.M. to 7:00 P.M.; closed Christmas Day and New Year's Day. (519) 326–3287.

LUNCH: Colasanti's offers apple cider and freshly made donuts or a complete hot lunch. Sunday buffet 9:00 A.M. to 1:00 P.M.

Afternoon

Pelee Island Winery is on Highway 18 just east of Kingsville. Open daily May through December, tours at noon and 2:00, and 4:00 P.M. $3.00 charge ($2.00 for seniors) for tour and tastings, which take sixty to ninety minutes. (519) 733–6551 or (800) 597–3533.

The **John R. Park Homestead and Conservation Area** is on the shore of Lake Erie, 10 km (6 miles) west of Kingsville on Essex County Road 50. The showpiece is the 1842 Classical Revival home of John and Amelia Park. Costumed interpreters escort visitors through the house and also through a working sawmill operated by an 1885 steam engine, an operating blacksmith shop, a smoke house, an ice house, and two barns filled with farm tools of the last century. There are a gift shop, a video show, livestock in summer, a nature trail, a boardwalk on the beach, and a picnic area. Admission $3.00. During May through October, open Sunday–Thursday 11:00 A.M. to 4:00 P.M.; in November, January, and February, open Tuesday–Thursday 11:00 A.M. to 4:00 P.M. Call for hours during March and December. (519) 738–2029.

DINNER: The **Vintage Goose Restaurant** is in a 150-year-old former hardware store at 24 Main Street West. It has been restored to its original elegance, with stained-glass windows, brick walls, and wooden floors. You enter through the Piggery, a gift shop. The menu is creative and changes monthly, though there's always local fresh fish. Only wines from the five regional wineries are offered here. Complete dinners cost $19–$22. Open daily 11:00 A.M. to 9:00 P.M., closed Mondays. Reservations are recommended, and required on Friday and Saturday evenings. (519) 733–6900.

LODGING: The ninety-four-room **Pelee Days Inn** has an indoor pool, sauna and whirlpool, putting course, badminton court, table tennis, pool and video games, restaurant and lounge. $89–$99 per double. (519) 326–8646.

DAY 3

Morning

BREAKFAST: Sherman Station is an antiques-strewn eatery at 119 Erie Street North in Leamington. Their special—two pancakes, two eggs, two sausages, and two strips of bacon at $4.99—is popular. Open 7:00 A.M. to 10:00 P.M. Monday–Saturday and 8:00 A.M. to 8:00 P.M. Sunday. (519) 326–6745.

There are a heck of a lot more nature lovers out there than we think. More than half a million visit **Point Pelee National Park** annually—up to 80,000 a month during spring and fall migrations of birds and butterflies. They must be naturalists because there's precious little else to do besides admire nature in this park, which has the smallest dry land area of any national park in Canada. Pelee is a "day use" park and overnight camping is not permitted. There are many other rules, because the park is home to endangered species of plants and reptiles.

But there are picnic tables scattered around in idyllic settings, and if the weather is good, plan on a picnic lunch. (If you let them know the night before, the folks at Pelee Days Inn will provide a box lunch.) Also plan on guests at your lunch—chipmunks, squirrels, and some of the more adventurous birds will approach your table looking for a handout.

Point Pelee National Park is about 10 km (6 miles) east of Leamington; follow the signs. As you enter the park (and pay your $3.25 per adult admission fee or $8.55 family maximum) you'll be handed a visitor guide. Pull in at one of the parking areas and take a look at it so you'll have a better idea of what to look for. Then slowly drive 7 km (4 miles) to the end of the road and the **Visitor Centre** (519–322–2365), which is open 10:00 A.M. to 6:00 P.M. daily.

Along the way you're likely to see red flashes of cardinals or tanagers or the orange color of Baltimore orioles or American redstarts. You may also spot anything from a white pelican to a yellow-bellied sapsucker, and you'll be warned of a turtle crossing area—possibly the only highway warning sign of its kind in Canada.

At the center there are exhibits, slide shows, and an interested, knowledgeable staff to answer questions and offer advice on where you're most likely to find whatever flora or fauna you'd like to see; there are more than 700 species of plants. From the center you can take a propane-powered open-sided "train" to the tip of Point Pelee, the **southernmost point of the**

Canadian mainland. Well, almost to the very tip; you'll have to hoof it across sand for the last little bit.

In September this is the best place to see Monarch butterflies resting before they cross Lake Erie en route to winter in the Sierra Madre Mountains of Mexico, 3,350 km (2,000 miles) south. The park is touted as the best location in North America for bird-watching, particularly during migrations, and more than half of the half-million annual visitors come from outside Canada. The reason for such concentrations of birds and butterflies is that the Great Lakes act as a barrier to the migrants and V-shaped Point Pelee becomes a funnel into the lake.

The fragility of the park's environment is such that visitors are constantly urged to stay on the roadways, pathways, and boardwalks. There are seven walks in the park, and if you take them all you'll log 10.8 km (7 miles). One of the most popular is the 1.6-km (1-mile) **Marsh Boardwalk,** which makes a giant loop into a marsh and has a 50-foot-high viewing station at each end.

The most interesting animal in the park is *homo sapiens* in quest of ornithological sightings. You'll see them in outlandish garb from deer stalker hats to plus fours, bedecked with camera lenses the size of rocket launchers and clanking with binoculars, tape recorders, video equipment, and even CB radios (to learn the locations of bird sightings from other birders). If you're not a birder stay clear of this area during the May and September migration months.

And then you have that utterly boring drive back home on Highway 401, the most direct route.

LUNCH: For great home-style cooking at bargain prices, try **Miss Ingersoll Restaurant.** Take exit 218 north from Highway 401 and drive about 2 km (1.5 miles) into the town of Ingersoll. After you pass the first traffic light, start looking for a parking spot. The small restaurant is on your right at 107 Thames Street South, just before the next traffic light. Daily specials run $5.00–$7.00 with all the trimmings. (519) 485–1762.

SPECIAL EVENTS

April. Easter Celebration egg hunt. Colasanti's Tropical Gardens and Petting Farm, Ruthven.

May. Mother's Day Celebration. Colasanti's Tropical Gardens and Petting Farm, Ruthven.

Mid-June. Leamington Fair. Midway, livestock, arts and crafts, grandstand entertainment.

Mid-August. Leamington Tomato Festival. Tomato stomping, antique cars, parade, festival tent.

Late September. Ruthven Apple Festival. Parade, entertainment, arts and crafts booths, food booths, farmers' market.

Mid-October. Kingsville Migration Festival. Arts and crafts, parade, sportsmen's show at Jack Miner's Bird Sanctuary.

End of November to early January. Kingsville Fantasy of Lights. More than sixty glittering displays at Lakeside Park.

OTHER RECOMMENDED RESTAURANTS AND LODGINGS

Kingsville

Adams Golden Acres Motel, 1.6 km (1 mile) west of Kingsville on Highway 18. (519) 733–6531. A good-value accommodation—particularly for families. Half of the twenty-seven units are kitchenette suites and most units have refrigerators. The motel is fully booked for spring and fall bird migrations, but rates drop in nonmigratory periods.

Leamington

Thirteen Russell Steak House, 13 Russell Street. (519) 326–8401. In a lovely Victorian mansion whose rooms and antique furniture create intimate dining areas. Open for dinner daily. Reservations recommended.

Town 'n' Country Motor Inn, 200 Talbot Street East. (519) 326–4425. Just north of Leamington Mall. Outdoor swimming pool, refrigerators in the rooms.

Pelee Island

Westview Motel and Tavern, at West Dock. (519) 724–2072. Known for its local pickerel and barbecued chicken and ribs.

FOR MORE INFORMATION

Windsor, Essex County & Pelee Island Convention & Visitors Bureau, Suite 103, City Centre, 333 Riverside Drive West, Windsor ON N9A 5K4. (519) 255–6530.

Pelee Island Transportation Service (ferryboat company): information and reservations, (800) 661–2220.

Port Elgin and Southampton
EXPLORING LAKE HURON'S
BRUCE COUNTY COAST

1 OR 2 NIGHTS

Sun and sand • Swiss dining • Nuclear power
The world's biggest culvert

The mayor of Port Elgin calls his town of 6,200 people on the shores of Lake Huron, "one of the finest small towns in Canada," and His Worship is right. Nicknamed "Town of Maples," Port Elgin is a pretty, self-contained town of large, well-kept homes and prosperous-looking businesses.

It also has a lot of hometown spirit and friendliness it doesn't mind sharing with a sizable summer population attracted by fine beaches and good sports fishing. The town has spruced up its waterfront and has a 200-berth marina, benches along a landscaped boardwalk, and a miniature steam train for children to ride.

Port Elgin is the Ontario Weigh-in Centre for the World Pumpkin Confederation, a nonprofit organization whose objective is "to justly promote and keep open competition on a world level for the sport-hobby of growing giant pumpkins, squash, and watermelons." Countries in the southern hemisphere hold their weigh-in in March, and the northern hemisphere weigh-in is usually held in the fall.

The neighboring towns of Kincardine, 37 km (23 miles) south, and Southampton, 9 km (6 miles) north, also have fine, sandy beaches, good restaurants, and accommodations. All the attractions can be easily visited from a base in one of these three communities.

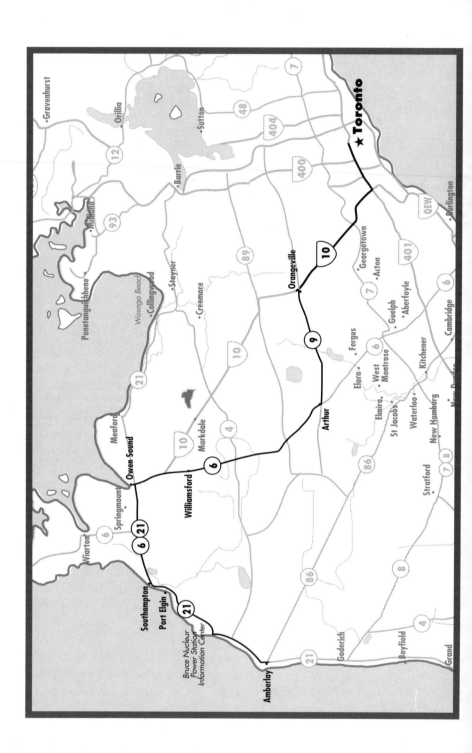

DAY 1

Morning

Take Highway 401 west to Highway 10 (exit 342) and Highway 10 north around Brampton 45 km (28 miles) to Orangeville. At Orangeville take Highway 9 west 39 km (24 miles) to Arthur and then Highway 6 north. Williamsford is 24 km (15 miles) north of Durham.

LUNCH: On your left as you enter Williamsford is **Cavanagh's Olde Stone House.** The 1880 gray stone building, formerly the Williamsford General Store, has been tastefully converted to a country-style inn where guests can enjoy fine dining. The atmosphere is comfortable, homey, unpretentious, and relaxing. The antiques on the walls of the single dining room don't scream to be noticed, nor do the framed pictures and stained-glass windows. There are an antique bar and original wood floors, and a woodstove spices the air when it's opened in cool weather to admit another log.

Lunch offerings are light, with a daily soup and sandwich choice, tossed or Caesar salad, and entrees like crab cheese melt, fettuccini primavera, and seafood crêpe. One popular lunch item, at $6.50, is Grey County Lamb Stew. Lunches cost $5.00–$8.50. (519) 794–0202.

Afternoon

Continue north on Highway 6 to Owen Sound. (There are many things to see and do in Owen Sound, covered in Southwestern Ontario Escape Eleven.) At Owen Sound turn left on Highway 6/21.

Local history, rare military uniforms, and locally made furniture are displayed at **Bruce County Museum and Archives** in Southampton, at 33 Victoria Street North. The new **Bruce Coast Marine Gallery** brings back to life the days of sail and steam on the Great Lakes. David Milne, an original member of the Group of Seven Canadian painters, was born and grew up here. During World War I he was hired by the Canadian government to chronicle battle scenes on canvas, and he produced more than 100 watercolors. Some of his works, and those of lesser-known local artists, are displayed in the museum's art gallery. Open weekdays 9:00 A.M. to 5:00 P.M. and Sunday 1:00 to 5:00 P.M.; in summer, also open Saturday 9:00 A.M. to 5:00 P.M. Admission by donation. (519) 797–3644.

In Port Elgin, ride the **Port Elgin and North Shore Railroad.** It's a twenty-four-gauge miniature steam train that runs on a 1.6-km (1-mile) track

Sailboats in the Kincardine marina.

around **Port Elgin Harbour.** The train runs Saturday and Sunday 11:00 A.M. to 8:00 P.M. in May, June, and September; daily 10:00 A.M. to 10:00 P.M. July through August. Rides are $2.00.

DINNER: The imaginative menu at **André's Swiss Country Dining** will satisfy the most demanding, and the dishes all have those extra touches that only European chefs seem able to pull off. André's is in the two large front rooms of a former home at 442 Goderich Street South, on the town's main street. The decor is basic and the menu is unabashedly Swiss. There's no nickel-and-diming: lunch and dinner entrees are accompanied by a vegetable garnish and choice of spaetzli, rice, or roesti potatoes, a Swiss potato pancake. The desserts are all made in-house and include items like apple strudel, Black Forest cake, chocolate mousse, and ice-cream sundaes. Dinners are $9.00–$14.00. (519) 832–2461.

LODGING: At the **Colonial Motel,** 235 Goderich Street South. Owners Bill and Sibyl Henderson have added nine posh units, a suite, an indoor pool, and a whirlpool spa. Full breakfasts are served. Rates $62–$102. (519) 832–2021.

DAY 2

Morning

BREAKFAST: At the Colonial Motel.

The following itinerary is for those who chose a one-night escape. Those staying another night may want to relax on the beach or explore the scenic countryside and pretty small towns and villages of Bruce and Grey Counties as well as see the following sights.

MacGregor Point Provincial Park is just south of Port Elgin and has a large **Visitor Centre** containing displays, an aquarium, a campers' library, and information on local communities and special events. Three nature trails and boardwalks through the pond enable visitors to see animals, birds, and insect-eating pitcher plants. No charge at a day-use area with sandy beach and picnic tables. In winter there are cross-country ski trails. For information or reservations, contact: Superintendent, MacGregor Point Provincial Park, R.R. 2, Port Elgin ON N0H 2C0. (519) 389–9055.

Sixteen km (10 miles) south of Port Elgin off Highway 11, just north of Tiverton, is one of the world's largest nuclear power installations. The **Bruce Nuclear Power Development** (BNPD) has eight Candu reactors that produce seven million kilowatts of electricity, or one-third of Ontario's requirements. The huge plant, whose stacks can be seen for miles, also produces heavy water for use in the reactors, cobalt 60 for medical and industrial purposes, and steam for agricultural and industrial applications in the adjacent Bruce Energy Centre.

One of the fringe benefits of BNPD are the **Bruce Brand Tomatoes** grown in an adjacent 7.5-acre greenhouse and sold across Southern Ontario. The tomatoes are grown hydroponically—in water carrying controlled amounts of nutrients—and the greenhouses use surplus heat from the energy center. Strict hygienic conditions preclude public tours.

What BNPD does, how it does it, and why, is all explained at a free **Information Centre** well marked from Highway 11. Displays explain how electricity is produced in a nuclear generating station, and there are films and a guided tour. The center has a cafeteria and picnic facilities. Open daily 9:00

A.M. to 4:00 P.M. mid-April through mid-October and Monday–Friday the rest of the year. For more information, contact: Bruce Nuclear Power Development Information Centre, Box 1540, Tiverton ON N0G 2T0. (519) 361–7777.

You may want to take a pass on this next attraction, and if you're heading straight home, take Highways 86, 87, 89, 9, 10, and 401 back to Toronto. But if you want to be one of the very few people in your hometown to have seen the **World's Largest Culvert,** continue south on Highway 21 to Amberley and turn left onto Highway 86 to Lucknow and Wingham. At Bluevale, 7 km (4 miles) past Wingham, turn left on Highway 87 to Harriston. There, take Highway 9 south to Teviotdale. In Teviotdale, take County Road 7 to Rothsay, then County Road 10 southwest 2 km (1.2 miles). The world's largest soil and steel bridge spans the Mallett River on Wellington County Road 10. The culvert spans 58 feet, ⁵⁄₁₆ inches across the river and is 24 feet, ⅔ inches high at its highest point.

Return to Rothsay, turn right on County Road 7, and then turn left on County Road 11. At Highway 9 turn right and go east to Orangeville, where you take Highway 10 south to Highway 401. Head east on 401 to Toronto.

THERE'S MORE

At Point Clark, 18 km (11 miles) south of Kincardine, marine artifacts are on display in the **Point Clark Lightkeeper's House Museum,** and you can tour the lighthouse. Turn right off Highway 21 at the hamlet of Amberley and follow the signs. The 87-foot-high tower, built in 1857 by artisans from Paris, France, is still in use. Open daily 10:00 A.M. to 5:00 P.M. late June through Labor Day. Admission $2.00 per adult, $6.00 per family. (519) 395–2494.

Midway between Kincardine and Point Clark, on the west side of Highway 21, you'll see the **Pine River Cheese Factory.** Visitors can watch the cheese-making process from an observation gallery and buy the product. Best viewing times are morning or very early afternoon. (519) 395–2638.

SPECIAL EVENTS

Late May. Spring Craft Festival, Southampton. Southampton Coliseum, Albert Street.

Late May. Fish Kincardine Salmon Derby, Kincardine. Station Beach.

Late July. Waterfront Art & Craft Festival, Port Elgin. Marina Park, Stevens Street.

Late July. Huron Shores Kinsmen Annual Arts and Crafts Festival, Kincardine. Kincardine Davidson Centre, 601 Durham Street.

Late July. Heritage Fair, Port Elgin. Natural heritage demonstrations, children's activities, guided hikes. MacGregor Point Provincial Park, Highway 21.

Mid-August. Craft Show, Tiverton. Tiverton Community Centre.

Mid-August. Lac Ac Heritage Walk, Kincardine. Tour heritage homes in Kincardine and learn the history of some of the oldest buildings.

Late August. Massed Bands in Victoria Park, Kincardine. Public corn roast, pipe band entertainment. Downtown in Victoria Park.

OTHER RECOMMENDED RESTAURANTS AND LODGINGS

Kincardine

Gilley's Bar and Grill, 832 Main Street. (519) 396–7423. A fun, informal dining spot with friendly staff, an excellent chef, and something for everyone on the menu.

Harbour Motor Inn, 249 Harbour Street. (519) 396–3311. It isn't fancy, but the rates reflect that and you get a nice view of Kincardine's lighthouse and marina. Large rooms with two double beds and refrigerator. Reservations are a must in summer.

FOR MORE INFORMATION

Port Elgin District Chamber of Commerce, 515 Goderich Street, Port Elgin ON N0H 2C4. (519) 832–2332 or (800) 387–3456.

Southampton Information Centre, 33 Victoria Street North (Bruce County Museum), P.O. Box 261, Southampton ON N0H 2L0. (519) 797–2215.

Stratford, St. Marys, and New Hamburg

FROM SHAKESPEARE TO CANADA'S LARGEST SWIMMING POOL

2 NIGHTS

Drama • Edison's close call • Opulent lodgings
Canada's largest outdoor swimming pool

When you see the original Stratford in England you can get some idea of how homesick early Canadian settlers must have been and how hard pressed they were to come up with names for their new communities. All the two towns would have had in common when Canada's Stratford was named was a river called Avon meandering through rolling countryside—not even similar countryside.

Now both cities have white swans swimming on the river and theaters performing works written by the original Stratford's most famous son, and both draw immense numbers of tourists throughout the summer season. Physician-journalist Dr. William "Tiger" Dunlop, who gave Goderich its octagonal layout, christened Canada's Avon River, but at that time Stratford was a hamlet called Little Thames. A few years later, in 1831, it was renamed "to honor English bard William Shakespeare."

Any connection with Shakespeare lay dormant until the early 1950s when Stratford-born journalist Thomas Patterson inspired the Stratford Festival. It started in 1953 in a huge tent with Sir Alec Guiness playing the lead in *Richard III*. The following year, musical programs augmented the Shakespearean

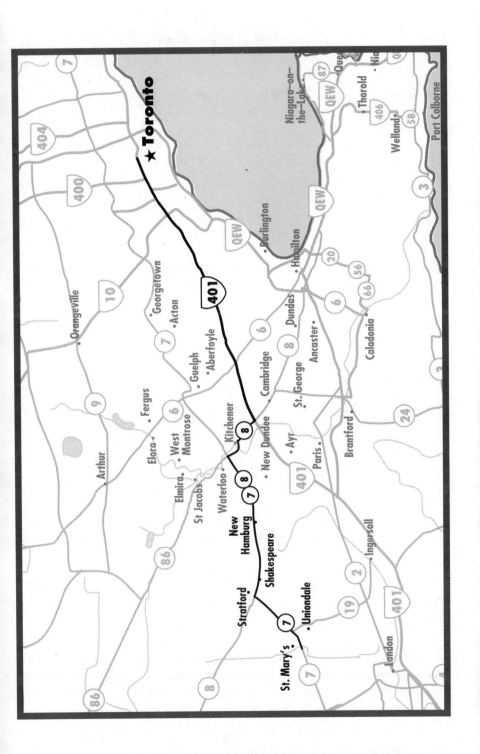

menu. It was a huge success, and the 1957 season opened in a permanent structure with seating for 2,262 people, none of whom is more than 65 feet from the stage, thanks to a revolutionary design conceived by British producer Tyrone Guthrie. Guthrie's "thrust" stage is surrounded on three sides by the audience, which sits in a steeply sloped amphitheater patterned after the classical Greek theater of Epidaurus.

The 1,107-seat Avon Theatre, built in 1901, became a partner in the festival in 1967, and the Third Stage, seating 410, opened in 1971. The Avon and Third Stage theaters offer music, opera, and contemporary drama to more than 400,000 people each year.

A number of programs have been developed to help visitors better understand what's involved in theater. There are question-and-answer sessions with actors and actresses from that evening's performance; moderated discussions with members of the acting company, production staff, or administrative staff; backstage tours; warehouse tours; workshops; readings of new plays; music concerts and recitals; open houses; and even an opportunity to share your ideas on seasonal themes and aspects of production at Talking Theatre in a session with the festival's education liaison officer and literary manager.

DAY 1

Morning

Take Highway 401 west to exit 278 and Highway 8 north to Highway 7, south of Kitchener. Follow Highway 7/8 west to Stratford, a total distance of 150 km (94 miles).

The hamlet of **Shakespeare** is on Highway 7/8, 12 km (8 miles) before you reach Stratford. It's just a wide spot in the road but it bristles with antiques and gift shops and a tearoom that bakes its own goodies.

Today Stratford is one of the gems of Ontario's tourism industry, drawing visitors from around the world to both its famous theater and its natural beauty. Many of the city's grand old buildings, like the **Perth County Court House** and **Stratford City Hall,** have been carefully preserved and are in mint condition.

Stratford Festival starts in late April, runs into November, and draws its audiences from around the world. Information on the festival's performances and special programs is in a free booklet available from Tourism Stratford, 88 Wellington Street, Stratford ON N5A 6W1; (519) 291–5140. Tickets can be ordered from the Festival Box Office, (519) 273–1600.

City Hall in Stratford.

Art in the Park is another adjunct of the festival. There are at least five art galleries in Stratford, but from June through mid-September on Wednesday, Saturday, and Sunday, regional artists display their wares under willow trees lining the Avon River near Island Bridge, within sight of Festival Theatre.

On Saturdays there's a **Farmers' Market** from 6:30 A.M. to noon at the Fairgrounds. In addition to fresh produce there are baked goods, fish, cheeses, flowers, and handcrafts.

LUNCH: If it's a fine summer Saturday, consider picking up fresh goodies at the Farmers' Market and picnicking along the banks of the Avon River beneath Festival Theatre. There are picnic tables and barbecue grills.

Or, head out to the historic hamlet of Millbank and **Anna Mae's Bakery and Restaurant** at 136 King Street, where you'll get down-home Mennonite country cooking at its finest. Broasted chicken is their signature dish, but they have potpies, roasts, schnitzels, sandwiches, salads, and impossible-to-resist pastries. Open Monday–Saturday 5:30 A.M. to 8:00 P.M. (519) 595–4407.

Afternoon

Take in a play at the Avon or Third Stage Theatre or browse Stratford's many gift shops and boutiques.

DINNER AND LODGING: For those who like to stay at historic hotels, Stratford has a dandy. The 1853 **Queen's Inn** has been fully restored to its original opulence. There's a nonsmoking lounge with full bar service, a white baby-grand piano often tinkled by customers, and eleven draft beers on tap, or you can visit the old downstairs bar room, the **Edinburgh Lounge.** Both serve pub grub. (The pub's name carries on a tradition started when Stratford went wet. It's attributed to the Duke of Edinburgh who, during a visit in 1959, complained about the city's archaic liquor laws.) The hotels' **Henry's at the Queen's** serves "middle of the road" fare—roast beef, steak, meat pies, fish and chips, and the like. Dinner entrees cost $6.00–$16.00. Room rates are $85–$225, the latter for a large new suite. For information contact: Queen's Inn, 161 Ontario Street, Stratford ON N5A 3H3. (519) 271–1400.

Evening

Attend Festival Theatre.

DAY 2

Morning

BREAKFAST: At Henry's at the Queen's.

Take Highway 7 southwest 14 km (9 miles) to **St. Marys.** A walk in any direction from downtown takes you past magnificent homes and stately buildings like the **1880 neo–Gothic opera house** at 20 Water Street South, the **1891 Romanesque town hall** at 175 Queen Street East, or the **1899 water tower** on the south side of Queen Street East, 3 blocks east of the town hall. The town is at the confluence of the Thames River and Trout Creek, a fact that caused planners of the Grand Trunk Railway a spot of bother as they pushed the rail line west from Toronto to Sarnia. Nor could St. Marys be bypassed, because in the late 1800s more wheat was shipped from St. Marys than from any other Canadian market.

The solution was two magnificent **stone viaducts**—the London and the Sarnia—still in use. The viaducts carry track across a span of more than 700 feet, 70 feet above the rivers. Automobiles cross the rivers at a lower level on double- and quadruple-span stone bridges, two of the six stone bridges still standing in Ontario.

A free guide is available from the town hall or by contacting Pam McGirr, Tourism Manager, Town of St. Marys ON N0M 2V0; (519) 284–2340.

Arthur Meighen, who headed the Conservative government as prime minister in 1920–21 and for a few days in 1926, was from St. Marys. An impressionistic statue of him by Montréal sculptor Marcel Braithstein was commissioned in 1967 and was not well received by Meighen's family. Prime Minister John Diefenbaker described it as "a cross between Ichabod Crane and Daddy Longlegs." The 9-foot-high statue was stored in an Ottawa warehouse until 1987, when local citizens effected its release and erected it at the corner of Church and Jones Streets.

It's a long and controversial story why, but St. Marys' first railway station was built a few kilometers outside town in the 1850s. Although it was declared a federal historic site in 1982, the stone building sits empty, preyed upon by vandals.

In 1863, Thomas Alva Edison was a night operator at St. Marys Junction Station. The lad who was to become a famous inventor was then sixteen or seventeen years old. To make sure night operators didn't sleep on the job, they were required to tap out the code for the word "six" every half-hour. Edison invented a device that automatically sent that code every time a crank was turned. He had the night watchman turn the crank every half-hour—while he slept.

His scam worked well—until the night a message came to hold a train in the passing track. Edison failed to relay the message. Fortunately the engineers saw each other's headlights in time to stop. During the subsequent investigation, Edison slipped away and went on to invent the phonograph and electric lightbulb and take out patents on 1,029 other inventions.

LUNCH: Damen's is in the old St. Marys post office at 17 Water Street, another magnificent stone building. Open daily for lunch and dinner and on Friday–Sunday evenings for a buffet with roast lamb, beef, and two other entrees. Sunday brunch 11:30 A.M. to 2:00 P.M. Lounge and outdoor patio. Reservations: (519) 284–3424.

Afternoon

St. Marys Museum is one of the better museums in Southwestern Ontario. It's in one of the town's oldest buildings, an 1850s limestone mansion at 177 Church Street South, and has ten rooms of exhibits and a barn filled with antique farm machinery. For children there's a Discovery Room where they're invited to touch things and try their knowledge with fun tests. Nature lovers will enjoy the Taxidermy Room. It has two stuffed passenger pigeons (an extinct breed), a stuffed albino raccoon, and excellent bird specimens. Open weekdays April 1 to May 30 and September 1 to December 15. In June, July, and August open daily. (Enter the museum grounds from the rear off Tracy Street; there's plenty of free parking.) Nominal admission. (519) 284–3556.

If you're visiting St. Marys in summer, you might want to have a dip in another superlative—**Canada's Largest Outdoor Swimming Pool.** The old limestone quarry is open for public swimming from the last weekend of May until Labor Day from 1:30 P.M. until dusk daily. There are lifeguards and changing rooms.

DINNER: If you've booked another performance at one of the theaters, you'll probably want to eat early or dine after the performance—in either case in Stratford. For a memorable dining experience outside Stratford, try the **Waterlot Restaurant** in New Hamburg. Take Highway 7/8 east to New Hamburg, 25 km (16 miles). The inn is at 17 Huron Street, behind the Royal Bank. In winter try for a table near the crackling fireplace; in summer try for one near the windows overlooking the scenic Nith River and Waterwheel Park.

The Waterlot is a primrose-yellow brick building whose architectural style doesn't fit handily into any category. It's mostly Victorian, but an elegant cupola gives it an Italian flavor. William J. Scott, a.k.a. Lord Campfield, built the house after he bought the community's first mill and the water rights. He went on to become the first postmaster, reeve of the township, and operator of a cloth factory, flour mill, sawmill, general store, and distillery.

The Waterlot's kitchen uses only fresh produce (local and organic when possible), sweet butter, nonfat skim milk, and whole-grain flour, as well as yogurt, fresh fruits, and herbs. The dinner menu has eight entrees; there are two daily specials, one of which is seafood. Trademark dishes are Dover sole and half-duckling. Entrees range $16–$28. Some of the most popular dessert items are sold in **The Waterlot Store** next door. Reservations: (519) 662–2020.

LODGING: The Queen's Inn.

DAY 3

Morning

BREAKFAST: Madelyn's Diner has a loyal clientele of locals drawn by the price, quality, quantity, and service of her breakfasts. From the Queen's Inn, drive west on Highway 7/8 (Ontario Street) and at the end of the street swing right at the Court House on Highway 8. Madelyn's is half a dozen blocks past the bridge, on your left at 377 Huron.

Return to Toronto by taking Highway 7/8 to Highway 401 east.

SPECIAL EVENTS

July to September. Festival Celebrated Writers Series, Stratford. Lectures, readings, and discussions by leading authors.

Early August. St. Marys Doll Show. Antique, reproduction and one-of-a-kind dolls, and doll supplies. St. Marys Community Centre, James Street South.

Early August. Kirkin' O' the Tartan, Stratford. Traditional Scottish service and historical ceremony, Knox Presbyterian Church.

Mid-August. Victorian Psychic Fair, Stratford. Psychics, mystics, clairvoyants, palmists, tarot readers, lectures, demonstrations, displays, psychic museum. Stratford Fairgrounds.

Mid-August. Teddy Bear Reunion, St. Marys. Categories to be judged, childrens' games, wagon and pony rides. St. Marys Recreation Centre, James Street South.

Mid-August. Children's Carnival, Stratford. Experience a day in an early twentieth-century classroom. Brocksden Country School Museum.

Late October. Stratford Coin Club Show and Sale. Kiwanis Community Centre, Lakeside Drive.

OTHER RECOMMENDED RESTAURANTS AND LODGINGS

New Hamburg

Festival Inn, 1144 Ontario Street. (519) 273–1150. Has a great weekend brunch smorgasbord for $11.95 per person.

The Waterlot, 17 Huron Street. (519) 662–2020. Upstairs are two guest rooms sharing a bathroom and a suite with bathroom en suite. Rates are $70 for the rooms, $90 for the suite.

St. Marys

Creamery Pub, 120 Parkview Drive. (519) 284–3891. Budget lunch or dinner on a licensed patio overlooking Trout Creek and the Thames River.

Westover Inn, 300 Thomas Street. (519) 284–2977. Another of St. Marys' fine stone buildings. Original structure has five guest rooms and a suite with whirlpool bath; an annex contains a dozen guest rooms, and Thames Cottage has a two-bedroom suite with living room. On nineteen acres overlooking the Thames River. Tennis courts, outdoor pool, and patio.

Stratford

Woods Villa Bed and Breakfast, 62 John Street North. (519) 271–4576. Owner Ken Vinen has tenderly restored the former home of Magistrate James Peter Woods to its original grandeur and rents five rooms, most of which have fireplaces. Vinen uses the public rooms to display restored player pianos and vintage juke and music boxes. Breakfast is served on an outside patio beside the swimming pool.

FOR MORE INFORMATION

Tourism Stratford, 88 Wellington Street, Stratford ON N5A 6W1. (800) 561–7926.

St. Marys Tourism, 206-22 St. Andrews Street North, St. Marys ON N4X 1C5. (519) 284–4174.

Collingwood, Owen Sound, Meaford, and Wasaga Beach

OUTDOOR FUN IN GREY AND

BRUCE COUNTIES

2 NIGHTS

Skiing in winter • Water slides in summer
Scenic caves • Lovely waterfalls

The Tobacco Indians, in whose former territory the town of Collingwood now sits, used to call the town site an "impenetrable swamp." And when Sir Sandford Fleming surveyed the area in the 1840s, he called Collingwood's bay "Hen and Chickens" because of its offshore islets. Despite these impediments to both settlement and navigation, Collingwood has 12,000 residents and a distinguished history of shipping and shipbuilding.

The 1929 Collingwood Terminal Elevator, a landmark that can be seen 45 km (30 miles) away, attests to the continuing shipping industry here. Shipbuilding ended in 1986 and now condominiums are sprouting around Nottawasaga Bay and on Blue Mountain, southern Ontario's biggest ski center. City dwellers from the south use them for year-round getaways and retirement homes.

At any time of the year you may want to try one of the many packages offered by Blue Mountain Resort. But this chapter presumes you just want to enjoy a quick escape and tells you what there is to see and do in Collingwood and Owen Sound.

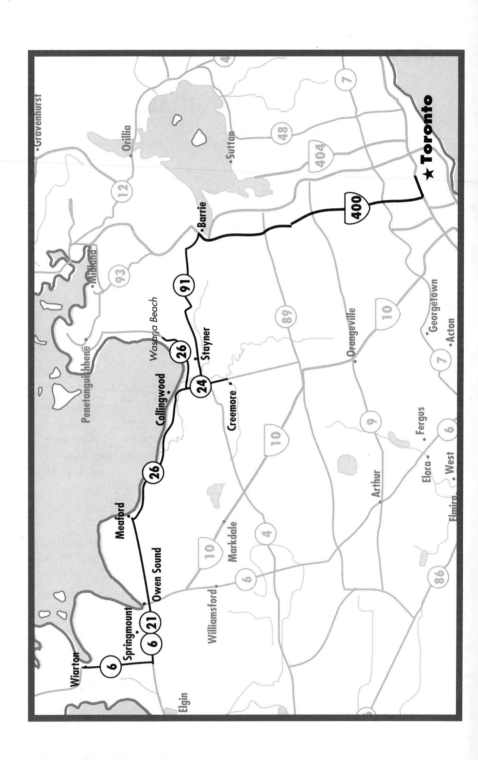

DAY 1

Morning

From Toronto take Highway 400 north to Barrie, exit 98, and follow Highway 26 through Stayner to Collingwood.

Collingwood's story is told at **Collingwood Museum** on the site of the old railway station at Memorial Park on St. Paul Street. Displays start in Petun Indian times and include the shipbuilding era and the story of the Simcoe Huron Railway. Open late June to Labor Day, Monday–Saturday 10:00 A.M. to 5:00 P.M., Sunday noon to 4:00 P.M. During the rest of the year, open Wednesday–Sunday noon to 5:00 P.M. Admission $2.00. (705) 445–4811.

Blue Mountain Pottery has been made here since the 1950s, and the factory on Highway 26 just west of Collingwood offers free daily tours. From July 1 to Labor Day the factory is open 9:30 A.M. to 8:00 P.M., the rest of the year 9:30 A.M. to 5:00 P.M. (705) 445–3000.

The **Georgian Triangle Information Centre and Tourist Association** office is on Highway 26 west of Collingwood, and their free pamphlet guides you on a walking tour of downtown Collingwood.

LUNCH: At the **Blue Mountain Resort,** 11 km (7 miles) west of Collingwood off Highway 26. Try to get a table overlooking the ski hill to watch the skiers swish down the slopes. In summer, watch people getting rear-ended on the **Great Slide Ride.**

Afternoon

The Blue Mountain Resort draws more than 300,000 skiers and more than 600,000 visitors each year. With 720 feet of vertical rise, the ski area now has twenty-seven trails (six lighted for night skiing), serviced by fourteen lifts. On the lower slopes are a 100-room five-star resort hotel and hundreds of condo units and chalets. There are bars, lounges, and fast food outlets; a ski school and ski shop; a day-care center; squash, racquetball, and tennis courts; a sauna, whirlpool, and indoor swimming pool; and an exercise room.

To lure summer traffic, Blue Mountain built the **Great Slide Ride,** the **Slipper Dipper Water Slide,** and the **Tube Ride.** The Great Slide Ride is two asbestos-cement tracks that weave 3,000 feet down the hillside. Riders take a chairlift to the top, sit in a plastic sled with an efficient braking system, and hurtle down the mountain at whatever speed traffic allows. The Slipper Dipper has three fiberglass flumes carrying sliders to a splashdown pool. Move quickly there, because there's always somebody behind you! The Tube Ride is a tad more sedentary. Blue Mountain also has five indoor tennis courts and an eighteen-hole, par-72 golf course. (705) 445–0231.

Nearby, off Highway 26 on Mountain Road, at the top of Blue Mountain, is the **Collingwood Scenic Caves Nature Preserve.** The caves plunge hundreds of feet into the hillside, revealing interesting rock formations. If you can squeeze through **Fat Man's Misery** and get to the cave below, snow and ice remain there through the summer and the air-conditioning is a welcome relief on a hot day. Open daily mid-May through mid-October, weather permitting. Admission $7.50. (705) 446–0256.

If you have time, the village of Creemore 24 km (16 miles) south, and slightly east, of Collingwood rates a visit. The village is tucked into the valley of the Mad and Noisy Rivers amid rolling farmland. For years Tweed, Ontario (north of Belleville), boasted it had **North America's Smallest Jail.** Then the folks at Creemore measured theirs and found it was smaller. Its outside dimensions are 20 feet, 2 inches by 15 feet, 2 inches. Each of the three cells measures 7 feet by 5 feet, 4 inches. The jail was built in 1892 and its first prisoner was a black cow. It's at the corner of Jane and Caroline Streets. Open daily 9:00 A.M. to 5:00 P.M. May through October.

Creemore is also home to **Creemore Springs Brewery,** housed in an 1889 hardware store. The brewers will take you on a dry tour of the premises year-round. Groups are preferred and arrangements must be made in advance: (705) 466–2240.

If you're using Owen Sound as your base, stay on Highway 26 west through the pretty apple-growing region and delightful communities of Thornbury and Meaford.

DINNER: In Owen Sound, for dining at its finest with commensurate prices, try **Louis' Steak and Seafood House.** The old brick mansion is a couple of kilometers east of town on Highway 26. Reservations recommended: (519) 376–4430.

LODGING: Owen Sound's five-star property, **Best Western Inn on the Bay,** could easily be mistaken for a fortress. The two-story, gray stone building was designed so each of its fifty-six rooms and four suites has an unobstructed view across the mouth of the harbor, and in some cases to downtown Owen Sound and the hills beyond. The lobby is of Italian marble and has a cathedral ceiling and quiet corners where guests can have a pre- or postmeal drink. The **Lumina Cafe** overlooks the harbor and serves international-style cuisine.

The 1898-vintage Creemore Springs Brewery.

There's a patio and rooftop terrace for summer dining. Rates are $100–$190. At 1800 2nd Avenue East. (519) 371–9200.

DAY 2

Morning

BREAKFAST: Try the eggs Benedict at **Boot and Blade,** a fun eatery with a hockey theme at 1135 2nd Avenue East. The walls are covered in antique hockey and lacrosse sticks and old team photos. Open at 6:00 A.M. Monday–Friday, 7:00 A.M. Saturday, and 8:00 A.M. Sunday. (519) 372–2222.

Owen Sound has a nice, comfortable feeling. It's a city, but as you wander its tree-lined streets you'll realize it's really a small town; just notice how many people greet each other and stop to chat.

The town site is like a pie with one narrow slice cut out of it. The missing wedge is Owen Sound, the deep bay off the south side of Georgian Bay. Stately old homes rise street by street, overlooking the bay. Geography makes Owen Sound a compact site, and its distance from a major city makes it more independent, or more self-dependent, than most Ontario towns of only 20,000 people.

The city is the seat of Grey County and the regional commercial center for an increasing number of people escaping southern cities for weekends, vacations, or retirement. The variety of goods and services reflects the demands of the newcomers. There are more than 100 shops, stores, and boutiques where you can enjoy a big-city selection with small-town service.

This is fishing and hunting country, and when the snow melts there's water for everything from whitewater canoeing to sailing or motorboating. When the snow lies deep in the woods—and they measure it here by the meter—there are hundreds of kilometers of snowmobile and cross-country trails.

Owen Sound also launched many ships. When that industry was at its zenith, it was known as "Liverpool of the North." The first ship, the *Ann McKenzie*, was launched in 1848. Some ships were immense, like the 303-foot SS *Manitoba*. The shipbuilding era is recalled in the **Owen Sound Marine and Rail Heritage Centre,** in the former Canadian National Railway station at 1165 First Avenue West. There's a gallery with old photographs of ship launchings and of the men who built the ships. Another area is devoted to the corvette HMCS *Owen Sound,* built in nearby Collingwood. More than 1,600 ships were launched before the industry died in the 1960s. Open June through September, Tuesday–Saturday 10:00 A.M. to noon and 1:00 to 4:00 P.M., Sunday 1:00 to 4:00 P.M. Admission by donation. (519) 371–3333.

The **County of Grey and Owen Sound Museum** is at 976 6th Street, opposite Holiday Inn. It's surrounded by a small village of pioneer buildings. Open July through August, Monday–Saturday 9:00 A.M. to 5:00 P.M., Sunday 1:00 to 5:00 P.M. Admission $4.00. (519) 376–3690.

LUNCH: Norma Jean's at 243 8th Street is very popular for lunch. The cuisine in this always-busy place is salads, quiche, and finger foods. You soon meet the folks at the next table because tables are only inches apart.

Afternoon

World War I flying ace William Avery "Billy" Bishop grew up in Owen Sound and is buried here. He was officially credited with destroying seventy-two enemy aircraft and after the war formed the Royal Canadian Air Force as a separate brigade. His boyhood home at 948 3rd Avenue West is now **Billy Bishop Heritage,** a repository of World War I memorabilia. Open May 24 to July 1 and Labor Day to mid-October, 1:00 to 4:00 P.M. weekends only; open July and August, daily 1:00 to 4:00 P.M. Admission free; donations welcome. (519) 371–0031.

Owen Sound's centennial project was the handsome **Tom Thomson Memorial Art Gallery,** which draws visitors from around the world. Thomson, a local artist and woodsman, is credited with forming Canada's Group of Seven painters. The museum at 840 1st Avenue West has more than 100 items by Thomson and the Group of Seven as well as works by other Canadian artists. Admission by donation. Open June through August, Monday–Saturday 10:00 A.M. to 5:00 P.M., Sunday noon to 5:00 P.M.; September through May, Tuesday–Saturday 10:00 A.M. to 5:00 P.M., Sunday noon to 5:00 P.M., and Wednesday evenings 7:00 to 9:00 P.M. Admission by donation. (519) 376–1932.

Three waterfalls in three different rivers tumble down the edge of the escarpment surrounding Owen Sound. The beauty of each has been maintained by its inclusion in a small park.

Inglis Falls on the Sydenham River has picnic tables around the small lake formed by the dam above the falls. Below the falls is 100-acre **Harrison Park** with tennis courts, wading and swimming pools, playgrounds, a campground, picnic areas, minigolf, paddleboats, nature trails, and a restaurant.

Indian Falls is on the Indian River within the thirty-acre **Indian Falls Conservation Area.** It's a pretty, horseshoe-shaped waterfall with water dropping 49 feet off a limestone ledge into a steep-walled canyon. The falls are a kilometer from the parking area.

Jones Falls is a 39-foot cataract on the Pottawatomi River. It's reached by a short trail that starts at the Grey-Bruce Tourist Association Office and Information Centre north of the intersection of Highways 8, 21, and 70 at the village of Springmount, 5 km (3 miles) west of Owen Sound. The center is open mid-June through mid-September, Monday–Saturday 9:00 A.M. to 9:00 P.M., Sunday 10:00 A.M. to 5:00 P.M.; during the rest of the year, open Monday–Friday 9:00 A.M. to 5:00 P.M. Phone toll free from area codes 519, 416, and 705: (800) 265–3127. From other area codes, call (519) 371–2071. Or contact Owen Sound Tourism, listed under "For More Information" at the end of this chapter.

DINNER AND LODGING: Best Western Inn on the Bay.

DAY 3

Morning

BREAKFAST: At Best Western Inn on the Bay.

Wiarton and **Meaford,** each 28 km (18 miles) on either side of Owen Sound on adjoining bays, are both pleasant places to visit. Wiarton, northwest on Highway 6 and Colpoy Bay, is the home of **Wiarton Willie,** Canada's answer to Pennsylvania's Punxsutawney Pete. (You may have seen either groundhog on TV newscasts looking for its shadow in February.) A few years ago Wiarton earned the questionable distinction of having Ontario's record annual snowfall: 618.5 centimeters, more than 6 meters, or 20 feet.

Meaford, on Nottawasaga Bay and on your way home, is a pretty town of 4,400 with a marina, antiques shops, and boutiques. It's surrounded by rolling countryside covered with apple orchards. **Meaford Museum** has a notable collection of early clocks. Open Monday–Saturday 9:30 A.M. to 5:00 P.M. and Sunday 12:30 to 5:00 P.M., June through September. In July and August **Meaford Opera House** offers straw-hat theater, and a horse-drawn surrey with a fringe on top takes visitors on tours. To find out what's playing and when, call the Georgian Theatre Festival, (519) 538–3569.

LUNCH: At the mouth of Bighead River at 12 Bayfield Street is a British pub as a British pub ought to be. The dining room and motel annex are called the **Fisherman's Wharf Restaurant and Motel,** but the pub is **St. Vincent Arms Pub,** reflecting a bit of Meaford's history. (The community was named for Meaford Hall, the Staffordshire estate of Admiral Sir John Jervis, Earl St. Vincent, after whom the surrounding township of St. Vincent is named.)

St. Vincent Arms Pub is a social center where locals and visitors play darts or board games and swap lies about their skiing prowess in winter or the big one that got away in summer. The dining room and a deck overlook the river and harbor. (519) 538–1390.

Afternoon

The resort town of **Wasaga Beach** is 20 km (14 miles) away around the south end of Nottawasaga Bay. A long stretch of light-brown sandy beach causes the permanent population of 4,600 to increase many times over during the summer. The beach is 14 km (9 miles) long and touted as the **longest freshwater beach in the world.**

At the mouth of that river is **Nancy Island Historic Site,** formed by the schooner *Nancy*. The *Nancy* was originally a trading ship belonging to the North West Company, but during the War of 1812 she was commandeered by the British Navy and outfitted for war. In 1913, during a naval battle with three American ships, the *Nancy* sought refuge in the Nottawasaga River. She ran aground and burned. Silt and sand built up around the charred hulk and formed a small island. In 1925 the *Nancy* was dug up and displayed beside a museum that electronically depicts the War of 1812.

Nancy Island Historic Site is in **Wasaga Beach Provincial Park** on Mosley Street and 3rd Street off Highway 92. Open May 24 to June 24 on weekends and June 24 to Labor Day daily 10:00 A.M. to 6:00 P.M. Vehicles $6.00, walk in free. (705) 429–2516.

Wasaga Beach Provincial Park is open year-round for day use and has 350 acres of beachfront with areas for picnicking, tennis, bicycling, cross-country skiing, ice skating, and snowmobiling.

Wasaga Beach calls itself the **Snowmobile Capital of Ontario,** and the Wasaga Snowmobile Club maintains 130 km (81 miles) of groomed trails. Their clubhouse is on Klondike Park Road just off Powerline Road. To contact them write to: The Wasaga Snowmobile Club Inc., P.O. Box 67, Wasaga Beach ON L0L 2P0.

Wasaga Waterworld on Highway 92, on the east side of town, has four slides, paddleboats, a thermal whirlpool, a children's adventure playground, and a wave pool. Open daily from the end of June to Labor Day, 10:00 A.M. to 7:00 P.M. Adults are $14.99; a family pass is $39.99. (705) 429–4400.

Wasaga Landing, on the beach between 1st and 2nd Streets, has four 350-foot flumes and a minigolf course. Open daily mid-June to Labor Day. An adult all-day pass costs $14.99; a family pass is $39.99. (705) 429–4400.

SPECIAL EVENTS

Mid-July. Wasaga Beach Craft Fair. Oakville Community Centre, Mosley Street.

Mid-July. Georgian Bay Air Show, Meaford. Canadian Forces Training Centre.

End of July. Waterfront Art & Craft Show, Owen Sound. Outdoor juried craft show. Kelso Beach Park, Eddy Sargent Parkway.

Mid-September. Creemore Oktoberfest. German food, auction, craft marketplace, German music, bands and dancers, Kinderfest for children. Creemore Recreational Centre.

Mid-September. Owen Sound Pratie Oaten. Potato harvest celebration, traditional Celtic food made from potatoes, demonstrations of Celtic crafts, Celtic music and dancing, horse-drawn wagon rides. County of Grey–Owen Sound Museum.

Mid-October. Autumn Around the Sound, Owen Sound. Tour of artists' studios.

Mid-November to mid-January. Festival of Northern Lights, Owen Sound. Eleven km (7 miles) of Christmas light displays throughout the downtown area.

OTHER RECOMMENDED RESTAURANTS AND LODGINGS

Collingwood

Blue Mountain Resorts Ltd., 11 km (7 miles) west of Collingwood off Highway 26. (705) 445–0231. Offers all kinds of package deals year-round. Indoor pool, licensed deli, and three lounges, at least one of which has live music nightly. There's a nursery that accepts children ages two to five.

Meaford

Ted's Range Road Diner, a few kilometers west of Meaford off Highway 26 (turn right on Range Road and the diner is in an old Quonset hut about a kilometer along on your left). (519) 538–1788. Menu runs from pastas to burgers to buffalo stew, and the place is popular with soldiers from a nearby military base.

Owen Sound

Marketside Food Shop and Cafe, 813 2nd Avenue East, opposite City Hall. (519) 371–7666. Reasonably priced exceptional-quality natural foods, including fresh fish from Georgian Bay.

Wasaga Beach

Dyconia Resort Hotel, 381 Mosley Street. (705) 429–2000. Thirty-five rooms, most with fireplaces and double Jacuzzi tubs. Most units overlook the Nottawasaga River. Outdoor pool, sauna and whirlpool, gym, games room, and babysitting service. Sweetwater Lounge and the Dinner Bell Lounge also overlook the river.

FOR MORE INFORMATION

Owen Sound Tourism, 1155 1st Avenue West, Owen Sound ON N4K 4K8. (519) 371–9833 or (888) 675–5555.

Georgian Triangle Tourism Association, 601 1st Street, Collingwood ON L9Y 4L2. (705) 445–7722.

Bruce County Office of Tourism, P.O. Box 180, Southampton ON N0H 2L0. (800) 268–3838.

Grey-Bruce Tourism Association, R.R. 5, Owen Sound ON N4K 5N7. (800) 265–3127.

Penetanguishene, Midland, and Orillia

WORLD-CLASS HUMOR AND HURON INDIAN HISTORY

3 NIGHTS

A literary shrine • A religious shrine • A great marsh
A spectacular casino

The pretty towns of Midland and Penetanguishene (pronounced "pen-et-ang-wish-een") have their own special corner of Ontario and everything that a self-contained little kingdom ought to have—except a king and a castle. The towns are in an area called Huronia, part of northern Simcoe County, 30 by 60 km (20 by 40 miles), and the scene of some of the most dramatic and grisly episodes in North American history. Huronia is bounded on the west by Nottawasaga Bay, on the north by Georgian Bay and the Severn River, and on the southeast and south by Lake Simcoe and Kempenfelt Bay.

Each town is at the foot of a deep bay off a larger bay off Georgian Bay; Penetanguishene is at the foot of Penetang Bay and Midland is situated on Midland Bay. They are snug, safe, beautiful harbors. Both towns and the peninsula on which they are located are steeped in history and have a wealth of unique historic attractions.

Surrounding Tiny Township and the villages of Lafontaine and Perkinsfield were settled in the 1840s by Québecers attracted by cheap, fertile land. Penetang—as it's called by locals—is the natural market and meeting place for these people, and the last census determined that 16 percent of them still have French as their mother tongue. The towns are seldom mentioned on news-

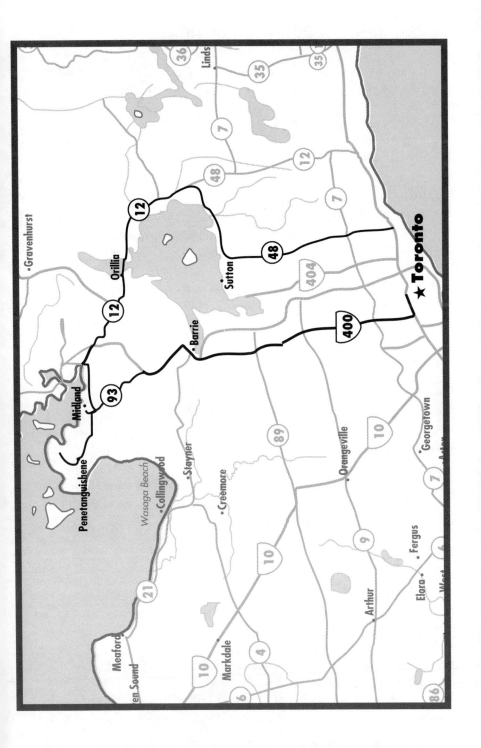

casts because there are no huge manufacturing plants to announce layoffs or strikes and there are no raging controversies. Midland, population 15,000, is 51 km (32 miles) northwest of Barrie and Orillia. Penetanguishene has 8,000 residents and is 5 km (3 miles) west of Midland.

DAY 1

Morning

Take Highway 400 north past Barrie to exit 121, and Highway 93 to Penetang. As you enter town you'll pass the **Penetanguishene Angels.** The "Portals to Huronia" were erected on either side of Penetanguishene Road (Highway 93) at the entrance to town during tercentenary celebrations in 1921. The angels, each blowing a long trumpet, are a symbol of the town's dual heritage, noted by the inscription QUÉBEC on one and ONTARIO on the other. For tourist literature or to book seats for a performance at the **Stage Company** this evening, drive to the dock and the **Chamber of Commerce** office.

LUNCH: The directions may sound complicated, but they aren't. You're just following the coastline. From the town dock, facing the Main Street hill, turn left on Beck Boulevard and go to its end, then turn left on Fox Street, right on Broad Street, and left on Jury Drive. **Captain Robert's Table** is in a square-timbered building, and the dining room and outdoor patio overlook the bay, where three tall ships come and go on excursion trips. Full-course daily specials cost $6.00–$10.00 but you might want to try the fresh Arctic char plate at $15.00. The char comes from nearby Victoria Harbour, and Cedarbrook Farms is so far the only place successful at raising char south of the Arctic Circle. (705) 549–8064.

Afternoon

From the town dock the **MS *Georgian Queen*** takes up to 200 passengers on three-hour tours of the **Thirty Thousand Islands** and local attractions like **Champlain's Landing, Discovery Harbour, Beausoleil Island, Whiskey Island,** and **Giant's Tomb.** The *Queen* has a snack bar and there's free parking at the dock. The boat sails from the end of June to Labor Day and has a sunset jazz cruise July through August. Admission $14.00 for adults, $12.00 for seniors, $6.00 for children. (705) 549–7795 or (800) 363–7447.

The little frame **St. James On-The-Line Anglican Church**, built in 1836, is believed to be named after the "line," or communication road, from

Toronto to Penetang. It has an unusually wide aisle permitting soldiers to march into church four abreast, and the pews are all different. Soldiers were ordered to make the pews, which each did in his own way. The oldest stone in the adjoining cemetery is from 1831, and the church is still in use.

There are fifteen reconstructed and furnished buildings at **Discovery Harbour,** the original site of Canada's only combined British naval and military base. Costumed interpreters offer guided tours, dramas, and drills, and in the harbor are working replicas of the two-masted schooners **HMS** *Bee,* **HMS** *Tecumseth,* and **HMS** *Perseverance.* On the premises are a gift shop, snack bar, and picnic facilities. Admission is $5.50 for adults, $3.50 for seniors and students. Open daily 10:00 A.M. to 5:00 P.M. Victoria Day weekend to Thanksgiving. (705) 549–8064.

The 1875 **Carl Beck General Store** is part of **Penetanguishene Centennial Museum,** a collection of everything from farm implements to Victoriana. Beck, who owned the sawmill, provided the store for his employees, who were paid partly in cash and partly in Beck Tokens, redeemable only at his stores. The museum, near the dock, is open daily Victoria Day to Labor Day, 9:30 A.M. to 4:30 P.M.; closed Sunday the rest of the year. Admission $2.50. (705) 549–2150.

DINNER AND LODGING: Best Western Highland Inn is the biggest and best accommodation center for miles around. The inn's dining room is recommended. All of their food is prepared from fresh supplies and there's a wide range of entrees and luscious desserts. Entrees are $11.00–$20.00.

The 122 rooms range from standard motel rooms to suites with heart-shaped bath tubs, hot tubs, Jacuzzis, fireplaces, round beds, and mirrored ceilings. One of the three dining rooms shares an immense glass atrium with a pool and whirlpool. At Highway 12 and King Street, Midland's main street. Rooms cost $79–$109, suites $149–$249. (705) 526–9307 or (800) 461–4265.

DAY 2

Morning

BREAKFAST: Try **The Daily Perk** in downtown Midland, about halfway down Main Street on the left as you face the harbor. Their home-baked croissants, muffins, cookies, and other goodies are enormously popular. Gourmet coffees are also a specialty of the house.

In their zeal to save the souls of the Huron Indians, Jesuit missionaries built a mission near Midland in 1639, which they called **Sainte Marie** and which was Canada's first inland settlement. The Jesuits preached Christianity, and the Hurons, also known as Wendat, taught the missionaries how to survive in the harsh climate. The Jesuits planted gardens and imported livestock from Québec, and by 1648 the mission was home to one-fifth of the European population of New France. Ontario's first hospital, farm, school, and social service center were at Sainte Marie, and a canal system was built at the site from the nearby Wye River.

But all did not go well. Cultures and ideologies came into conflict, and the French brought with them influenza, dysentery, measles, and smallpox, which proved fatal to some Indians. And the traditional rivalry between the Wendat and Iroquois escalated. In 1648 the Iroquois attacked the nearby mission of St. Joseph, and Father Antoine Daniel was killed. The following year Fathers Jean de Brébeuf and Gabriel Lalémant, along with hundreds of Hurons, were captured, tortured, and killed.

The people of Sainte Marie waited tensely for an attack, which never came. Later that year they burned their village and traveled by canoe to nearby St. Joseph Island (now called Christian Island). There they established Sainte Marie II, a well-fortified community. But after a winter of ghastly hardships the Jesuits abandoned the mission.

Today's visitor can wander around a complete reconstruction of Sainte Marie, called **Sainte-Marie Among the Hurons.** Twenty-two structures are faithfully reproduced, based on the scientific excavation of the site 5 km (3 miles) east of Midland. The canal works again, and staff in period costume hand-saw timber, repair shoes, sew clothes, and grow vegetables. In the non-Christian area are an Indian longhouse and wigwam, and guides carry on the daily chores as they were handled in the early 1600s. Visitors in July and August can, for an added charge, help paddle a 21-foot canoe on the Wye River and view the palisaded mission from the water, as the seventeenth-century adventurers saw it.

You'll enter Sainte Marie through an interpretation center with two theaters in which films set the mood for a trip 350 years back in time. There's a museum of artifacts excavated at the site, a gift shop, and a restaurant open daily from 10:00 A.M. to 5:00 P.M. The site is open daily mid-May to Thanksgiving 10:00 A.M. to 5:00 P.M. with special events on some winter weekends. It's just off Highway 12, about 5 km (3 miles) west of Midland. Admission $9.75 for adults, $6.35 for seniors and students. (705) 526–7831.

The **Wye Marsh Wildlife Centre** driveway leads off the road to Sainte Marie. The nonprofit facility is open year-round. From the interpretation center, nature walks fan out through a marsh teeming with wildlife. There are floating boardwalks, viewing platforms, an underwater window, a theater, a gift shop, and a display hall. Open daily. Admission $6.00 for adults, $4.00 for seniors and students. (705) 526–7809.

Across Highway 12 from the Wye Marsh/Sainte Marie road is **Martyr's Shrine,** a twin-spired stone cathedral built in 1928 to honor the eight missionaries martyred in Huronia. In 1930 five of those priests were canonized by the Roman Catholic Church. There are crosses, fountains, gardens, shrines, and the outdoor altar erected for the 1984 visit of Pope John Paul II. Admission is $2.00. (705) 526–3788.

If you can handle another Indian village museum, **Huron Indian Village and Huronia Museum** in Midland has interesting exhibits. The museum houses the best artifacts from several hundred archaeological excavations in Huronia. The village behind the museum is a full-scale replica of a sixteenth-century Huron Indian village that would have been occupied by about 100 people. The Hurons built some of North America's earliest apartment houses, called longhouses, and there's one in the village that has been left unfinished so visitors can see the construction techniques. The Hurons believed in advertising: Outside the village are totems identifying the inhabitants by their physical skills. The features of the totems are grossly exaggerated, and their colors indicate the particular skills of each family. Be sure to look into the shaman's hut, filled with totems and masks. The center is in **Little Lake Park,** and entrance is $6.42 for adults. Open May 24 to Thanksgiving.

Take Highway 12 to Orillia and head for downtown. Orillia is on Lake Couchiching (actually a long bay off Lake Simcoe), and its main street, Mississauga Street, runs down to the lake.

LUNCH: In Couchiching Park, just off Mississauga Street, are the **Ossawippi Express Dining Cars.** There are eight of the gaily painted, flower-bedecked cars, and four are dining rooms overlooking the beach and lake. The signature dishes have names like Brakeman's Plate or Conductor's Special; the latter is salmon in champagne sauce with a Super Salad at $16. Everything is cooked on-site, including the tiny loaves of bread. If you want just a light lunch, they have soup and sandwiches. Licensed and open daily Monday–Friday 11:00 A.M. to 9:00 P.M. and Saturday and Sunday noon to 10:00 P.M.

The **Champlain monument** is also in Couchiching Beach Park. The impressive bronze statue to Samuel de Champlain commemorates the Québec founder's visit in 1615 in the company of an armed party of Huron Indians.

Afternoon

Follow signs to **Stephen Leacock Memorial Home.** Disciples of Canada's greatest humorist will recognize Orillia as Mariposa, the "little town" Stephen Butler Leacock described in his classic humorous novel, *Sunshine Sketches of a Little Town.* Its population of 24,000 is four times larger than it was when Leacock built his first cottage in 1908 on a point of land in Lake Couchiching. He named the area Old Brewery Bay because the ruins of a stone brewery stood there. Today Orillia is a summer resort with 21 km (13 miles) of waterfront.

Leacock wintered and worked in Montréal for forty years, twenty-eight of them as chairman of the Department of Economics and Political Science at McGill University. But he loved his long summers at Old Brewery Bay, where he rose early and wrote for several hours in a room over his boathouse. After Leacock's death in 1944, the house stood empty for years until it was purchased by the town of Orillia in 1957 to be a literary shrine.

Leacock's book about Orillia has been called "the most Canadian book ever written," and although the author protested it was written about "70 or 80 towns," his writings didn't fool anyone. Indeed, in the original handwritten manuscript, most of the characters are referred to by their real names. Upstairs there's a gallery called the **Mariposa Room,** and in it the book's characters are matched with the Orillia residents who inspired the lampooning.

Old Brewery Bay is loaded with 30,000 artifacts of Leacockiana, many of them original manuscripts and old photographs. This is one of few museums in which interest is growing. Curator Daphne Mainprize says attendance has rocketed from 6,000 in 1990 to 46,000 in 1995. "It's not unusual to welcome people from China, Japan, Germany, New Zealand, or Australia who have tears in their eyes because they're at the site of the lifetime pilgrimage they have always wanted to make," she says. Open daily mid-June to Labor Day, 10:00 A.M. to 7:00 P.M., and daily Labor Day to mid-June, 10:00 A.M. to 5:00 P.M. Admission $7.50 for adults. (705) 329–1908.

The 1895 **Orillia Opera House** at 20 Mississauga Street West is home to the **Sunshine Festival Theatre Company,** which has dedicated itself to preserving the turn-of-the-century ambience of the building and its traditions. The company presents musicals, comedies, and special children's shows

Summer home of Canada's most famous humorist, Stephen Leacock.

year-round. Late June through Labor Day, costumed guides conduct tours for a nominal fee. For a program of what's playing, call (705) 326–8011.

The most exciting thing to hit the Orillia area in years is **Casino Rama,** Canada's largest casino. The 195,000-square-foot facility opened last summer, creating 6,000 jobs. The casino is a partnership of Ontario's 131 First Nations, and the philosophy behind its design was to give patrons an atmosphere of excitement twenty-four hours a day, 365 days a year. That translated into such spectacular sights as a huge waterfall fountain, the Circle of Nature Laser Light Show and Art Wall, and a 37,000-square-foot mural of Chippewa Indian legends and personalities using 450 panels of aboriginal artwork. There are three restaurants, a gift shop, and a lounge with live entertainment for the 14,000 patrons daily. From Orillia, take Highway 12 east to Rama Road North and follow signs to the parking lots. (705) 329–3329.

DINNER AND LODGING: The Downing family has been dishing out fun and hospitality at **Fern Resort** since 1895. The place is now a major resort with 102 rooms in modern buildings, plus duplex and single cottages on the shore of Lake Couchiching. All but seventeen of those rooms have wood-burning fireplaces. The resort prefers to sell all-inclusive packages for two or more nights, and cancellations are about the only way you can get a one-night package. Rates are $100–$175 per person and include three meals per day. Fern Resort is off Rama Road, 4 km (2.5 miles) north of Atherley, just east of Orillia on Highway 12. (705) 325–2256.

DAY 3

Morning and Afternoon

Spend the day enjoying all that Fern Resort has to offer. There's an indoor pool with saunas and whirlpool, but the resort's trademark is an 8-foot-wide open-air hot tub. Be sure to try it! In summer there are facilities for all water sports and games, as well as jogging and nature trails, and in winter there are groomed cross-country trails, a floodlit rink, a ski equipment sales and rental shop, and cross-country ski instructors. There are continuous movies on an in-house TV channel, pool and Ping-Pong tables, and an exercise room. The resort has children's programs so parents can leave the kids at 9:00 A.M. and not see them again until lunch, return them after lunch, and know they'll be supervised and entertained until 5:00 P.M. All three meals are included in the price of your room.

DAY 4

Morning

BREAKFAST: Mariposa Market is on your left about halfway up the first block of Mississauga Street going away from the lake. It's a rustic general store/gift shop/bakery/cafe. They bake bread, croissants, and pastries, and for lunch they even *bake* sandwiches.

There's a **Kids Store** inside the large emporium, and the stores on either side are the **Scent Shop** and **Seasons Shop,** the latter selling lawn and home decorations and Christmas items.

Start for home on Highway 12, which will take you around, and provide occasional glimpses of, the east side of Lake Simcoe. Take Highway 48 to

Sutton. If you still have a warm glow from the good humor you soaked up at Stephen Leacock's home, you might want to visit his very pretty gravesite. He's buried in the family plot of **St. George's Anglican Church** near Sibbald's Point on the south shore of Lake Simcoe. His grave is sheltered by a rare umbrella elm planted about 1848. Canadian novelist Mazo de la Roche is buried in the same cemetery.

LUNCH: Just down the lakeshore drive from the cemetery is one of Canada's most historic and prestigious resorts. **The Briars** at Jackson's Point was built as a manor house in 1848 for a Napoleonic War veteran who came to Canada to serve on the Great Lakes. Stephen Leacock was a frequent guest when the property was owned by Frank Sibbald, whose descendants have tastefully expanded the huge estate into an elegant resort that can accommodate 150 guests. The Briars is a full pension resort, but nonguests are welcome for lunch or dinner, which are served in the bright and airy **Garden Court Dining Room,** just off the manor house in three adjacent dining rooms, or in the **Drinkwater's Lounge** (light fare ranges from $3.75–$8.95). During the summer months, try the buffet lunch ($15.25) in the **Summer Dining Room**. At 56 Hedge Road. (416) 493–2173 or (800) 265–2376.

From Jackson's Point take Highway 48 south 50 km (31 miles) to Highway 7 and home, or 60 km (38 miles) to Highway 401.

SPECIAL EVENTS

May. Midland District Model Railway Show. At Midland Centennial Arena.

Mid-May. Sawfest, Penetanguishene. Log-sawing demonstrations, old-time music, lumberjack shows at Waterfront Park.

First three weekends of June. Orillia Artfest. Exhibition and sale of work by local artists. Sir Samuel Steele Art Gallery.

Mid-June. Christmas in June, Orillia. Boats decorated for Christmas cruise the shoreline of Couchiching Beach; evening lighted boat parade.

Mid-July. Library Garden Tours, Penetanguishene. Self-guided tour of sixteen gardens and landscaped properties.

End of July. Leacock Festival of Humor, Orillia. Children's games, entertainment, face painting, fortune-telling at Leacock Museum.

Mid-October. Orillia Thanksgiving Art Show. Celebration of local artists, perennials on sale, gardening tips at Leacock Museum.

Mid-October. Images Thanksgiving Tour, Barrie and Orillia. Self-guided tour of art studios in area.

Mid-October. Wye Marsh Festival, Midland. Items handcrafted in glass, wood, leather, paper, ceramics. At Sainte-Marie Among the Hurons.

OTHER RECOMMENDED RESTAURANTS AND LODGINGS

Midland

Rev Bistro, 249 King Street. (705) 526–9432. Greek and Canadian cuisine. The reasonably priced menu choices are tempting and numerous. Murals display scenes from the owners' homeland. Open daily for dinner.

Orillia

Frankie's Restaurant, 83 Mississauga Street. (705) 327–5404. Easy to find—the purple-painted building leaps out of the historic streetscape. The interior decor is modern, comfortable, funky. Pasta and other Italian dishes at reasonable prices are offered daily for lunch and dinner.

Highwayman Inn, just outside Orillia off Highway 11, at 10 Woodside Drive. (705) 326–7343. Eighty-six units, indoor pool, sauna and whirlpool, licensed lounge, and dining room.

Comfort Inn by Journey's End Motel, 75 Progress Drive. (705) 327–7744. Eighty units.

Sundial Inn, 600 Sundial Drive, off Highway 11. (705) 325–2233. Ninety-four units, indoor pool, and licensed dining room.

FOR MORE INFORMATION

Midland Chamber of Commerce, 208 King Street, P.O. Box 158, Midland ON L4R 4K8. (705) 526–7884 or (800) 263–7745.

Orillia and District Chamber of Commerce, 150 Front Street South, Orillia ON L3V 4S7. (705) 326–4424.

Toronto

A VIBRANT METROPOLIS

AS MANY NIGHTS AS YOU CAN SPARE

Galleries • Gardens • Shopping • Museums
Unique restaurants

Any Torontonian over fifty will remember how Toronto used to be: no Sunday movies, no games in city parks on Sundays, no alcohol, and no Sunday shopping. But the city has changed dramatically over the last few decades and made good on its name, which means "meeting place" in the Huron language. More than eighty ethnic groups speaking more than fifty-two languages have met up here. The flood of immigration has diluted the stodgy puritanism and made Toronto Canada's largest and most cosmopolitan city.

On January 1, 1998, the six munipalities that used to make up Metropolitan Toronto—the cities of Toronto, Etobicoke, York, North York, and Scarborough and the borough of East York—were all merged into a single "megacity." Toronto is now one of the largest urban centers in North America (after New York and Los Angeles). The Greater Toronto Area (GTA), which includes the surrounding regions of Halton, Peel, York, and Durham, is home to 4.3 million people—15 percent of the population of Canada. Despite its new "mega" status, Toronto isn't all concrete and brick. It is a green city with 9,772 acres of parkland, much of it beachfront property on Lake Ontario.

And let's get the pronunciation right: Torontonians pronounce only one of the o's in the name. It's T'ronna, and you can always spot visitors, particularly Americans, by the way they pronounce all the o's slowly and carefully: "Toe-ron-toe."

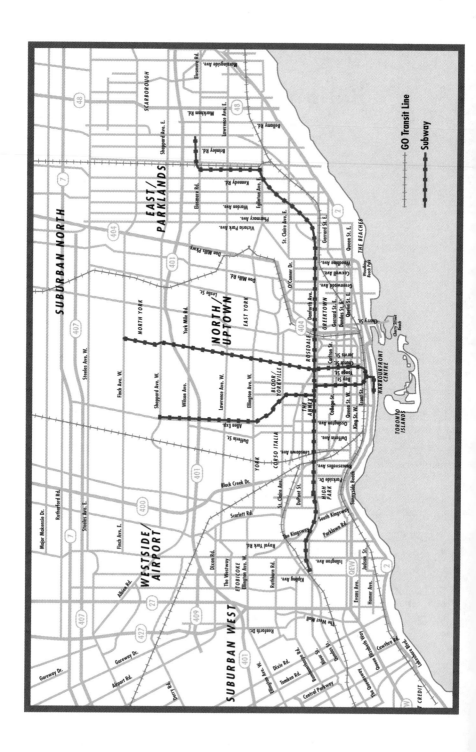

GO Transit Line
Subway

SOUTHWESTERN ONTARIO

Toronto can vie with any city for things to see and do—top entertainment, big-name sports, arts, fashion, culture, and glittering nightlife. Whereas thirty years ago Torontonians looking for excitement fled to the American border cities of Buffalo and Detroit, the traffic pattern is now reversed. Americans come to Toronto, the safest and cleanest city of its size in the world, and a vibrant, modern, ever-changing metropolis.

While Toronto has become enormous, its planners avoided the pitfall that has occurred in so many large American cities. The downtowns of those cities are places where human beings are seen only between 8:00 A.M. and 5:00 P.M., after which storefronts are barricaded by steel bars that could repel guided missiles. Despite high land costs, tens of thousands of people live in downtown Toronto. There are shopping meccas such as Eaton Centre, as well as theaters, parks, concert halls, marinas, play areas, and a bicycle path along the waterfront. Those invitations to downtown city living were inevitably followed by an explosion of restaurants, bistros, bars, outdoor patios, fast-food stands, variety stores, street vendors, and nightclubs.

There are two Toronto escapes in this book. This one is for those who want to explore historic Toronto and enjoy some of its ethnic areas, including restaurants. The second, "Toronto with Kids," tells you where to stay and eat and what to see and do to entertain your kids. Unlike other chapters in the book, neither Toronto chapter leads you through your visit meal by meal, morning by afternoon by evening, simply because there's such an extensive smorgasbord of things to see and do and not everybody will want to follow the same itinerary. The major attractions are listed alphabetically in the categories of Special Sites, Historic Buildings and Museums, Theaters, Out-of-Town Attractions, and Spectator Sports.

At the end of the chapter is a list of accommodation options and suggested venues for breakfast, lunch, and dinner, from economical to very expensive. A wealth of free information is available from Tourism Toronto, listed under "For More Information" at the end of this chapter.

GETTING AROUND

The prospect of driving in downtown Toronto can be intimidating if you're used to the slower pace of a small town, and parking can be expensive and difficult to find. (It can cost you $12–$20 per twenty-four-hour period, so it's worth asking before booking reservations at a hotel whether the rate includes free parking.) If you plan to drive and don't know your way around, get a city map. This will show you the limited-access highways that can get you quickly to different areas of the city. Yonge, the main street, runs north from the lake, roughly bisecting the city. (Yonge Street is also the **world's longest street.** It starts in the heart of Toronto and ends in Rainy River on the Minnesota border, 1,900 km [1,187 miles] northwest.)

You'll save money, time, and frustration by using the excellent public transportation system. Locals call it the **TTC (Toronto Transit Commission),** and it is annually recognized as the safest, cleanest, and most efficient public transportation system in North America. Three interconnecting subway routes and the **Scarborough Light Rail Transit System** link the extremities of the city, and a bus and trolley system operates on surface routes covering almost 4,000 km (2,500 miles).

Buses and streetcars will take you wherever the subway won't, anywhere in the city for the same single fare (but remember to get a transfer when you pay). Drivers don't carry change, so have the exact fare ready or buy tokens or tickets from vendors in the subway station. Or, you can buy a daily pass for two adults and up to four children for $6.50. For more information call the TTC at (416) 393–4636, 7:00 A.M. to 11:30 P.M.

GO (Government of Ontario) commuter trains run from Union Station on Front Street West to Hamilton, east to Whitby, and north to Richmond Hill, Georgetown, and Bradford. For GO information, call (888) 438–6646. Union Station is the main terminal for national and international train travel. **VIA Rail** passenger service information is available at (416) 366–8411. There is regular bus service every twenty minutes from selected downtown hotels to Toronto's **Lester B. Pearson International Airport.** Buses to the airport also leave from Islington, York Mills, and Yorkdale subway stations. For information, call Airport Express at (905) 564–3232.

There's also no problem getting comfortably around Toronto during freezing or otherwise rotten weather. There is a huge city underneath the sidewalks—more than 12 km (7.5 miles) of walkways along which you can shop, be entertained, have your hair cut, get a drink or a gourmet meal—all without having to wear a coat or boots.

The underground network starts at **Union Station,** which is an attraction in its own right. The cavernous structure, opened in 1927, has a monumental facade of 38-foot-high, 75-ton Bedford limestone pillars. The inside, which is larger than a 747 airline hangar, has an 86-foot-high ceiling of Italian marble. The station connects to the **Royal York Hotel,** which has thirty-five shops and restaurants in its basement; from there you can walk to the **Royal Bank Plaza,** which has sixty-five more dining spots and shops. It connects to the **Toronto-Dominion Centre** and its sixty-eight shops, which connect to the **Commerce Centre Mall** and so on . . .

Afraid of getting lost? **Toronto Underground City Tours,** 7433 Yonge Street, Suite 714, offers personalized two-hour walking tours beneath the financial or theater districts on Tuesday and Wednesday at 1:30 P.M. Admission $15, $10 for seniors. (905) 886–9111.

Despite its size and ever-changing skyline, Toronto is an easy city in which to find your way, thanks to the grid system and such points of reference as Lake Ontario and the CN Tower. But as with any big city, it helps to get an overview. Consider taking an organized tour that hits the high spots; then you can decide which ones you want to look at more closely.

GETTING AN OVERVIEW

By Air

National Helicopters Inc., Toronto City Centre Airport, Toronto, offers aerial views of Toronto from Queens Quay (next door to the Westin Harbour Castle Hotel). They'll fly you around Toronto pointing out the sights, or extend the tour to Niagara Falls or the Muskokas. (416) 361–1100.

By Water

At least eight companies operating more than fifteen boats offer tours of the waterfront and Toronto islands, from one-hour quickies to many-hour trips with entertainment, dining, and dancing. Rates for harbor cruises aboard the 96-foot-tall schooner *Challenge* are typical: $10 per adult for a one-hour cruise; $15 per adult for a two-hour cruise. (416) 260–6355. The options for water tours are all presented in *Toronto Visitors Guide,* available from Tourism Toronto (listed at the end of this chapter).

By Land

Numerous companies operate bus, minivan, and walking tours of the city. You can even be pulled around downtown in a rickshaw. Most companies will pick you up and return you to your hotel. Greyhound has a dozen different tours, each of which spends time at one or two specific attractions. (416) 594–0343.

The CN Tower.

A Taste of the World Neighborhood Bicycle Tours and Walks, Inc. takes you on a culinary and cultural tour of Chinatown, which includes visits to an herbalist and a noodle factory. (416) 463–9233.

From a Tower

If a trip to the top of one of the world's tallest free-standing structures is on your list, use the view from **CN Tower** to get yourself oriented to Toronto. The tower is 1,815 feet, 5 inches high. The highest spot the public can get to is the **Space Deck** at 1,465 feet, which is high enough for most—especially on a windy day. . . since the tower sways.

That sway is no surprise to students of physics, but it can be unnerving to those who don't like heights in the first place! You ride up in one of four glass-fronted elevators in less than a minute. The architects say their masterpiece won't blow over unless winds reach 400 km/h (260 mph), and the highest gust yet recorded was a mere 182 km/h (114 mph).

From the Space Deck you can look straight down through sloping windows. It's a strange feeling to look down on aircraft taking off and landing at **Toronto's Island Airport.** On a clear day you can see mists rising from Niagara Falls, 90 km (56 miles) south. The view is particularly interesting during a thunderstorm, since the tower is struck by lightning an average of 200 times a year.

Horizons Bar is at the 1,136-foot level and, just above it, there's the **360 Revolving Restaurant,** which makes a complete revolution every seventy-two minutes. Entrees cost $21–$35; for reservations call (416) 362–5411. At the base of the tower is **The Marketplace at the Tower**, a complex of stores, and the licensed Horizons Cafe, which serves grilled meats and pasta.

CN Tower is open 10:00 A.M. to 10:00 P.M. September through June; from July through August it's open 9:00 A.M. to midnight Monday–Saturday and to 10:00 P.M. on Sunday. It's located at 301 Front Street. For information call (416) 868–6937.

SPECIAL SITES

Allan Gardens. The Allan Gardens Tropical Plant Collection is in a park in the center of the city surrounded by Jarvis, Gerrard, Sherbourne, and Carlton Streets. There's a large collection of tropical plants and succulents. The Palm House was built in 1909 in the tradition of the great Victorian glass greenhouses. Free admission. Open Monday–Friday 9:00 A.M. to 4:00 P.M.; Saturday, Sunday, and holidays, 10:00 A.M. to 5:00 P.M. (416) 392–1111.

Art Gallery of Toronto. Fifty recently renovated galleries contain one of North America's largest and finest collections, including the world's largest public collection (893 pieces) of works by English sculptor Henry Moore. **The Grange,** a Georgian manor that was the gallery's first home (and is Toronto's oldest remaining brick building), is behind the new gallery, furnished to the 1830s era. Admission to both is $7.50 for adults. Located at 17 Dundas Street West. (416) 979–6648.

Bay of Spirits Gallery. A dramatically designed gallery offering a fine collection of Canadian native arts and crafts from the Pacific Northwest. At 156 Front Street West (across from the Metro Toronto Convention Centre). Open Monday–Friday 10:00 A.M. to 6:00 P.M., Saturday 10:00 A.M. to 5:00 P.M. Free admission. (416) 971–5190.

Eaton Centre. This is state-of-the-art shopping. Within a nine-level self-contained city along Yonge Street between Queen and Dundas there are 330 shops and services from banks to pubs to a seventeen-screen movie theater. If that isn't enough choice, Simpson's flagship department store is linked to the Centre by a walkway across Queen Street.

Eskimo Art Gallery Inc. Toronto's largest collection of contemporary Inuit art and carvings. Open Monday–Friday, 10:00 A.M. to 7:00 P.M., Saturday and Sunday 10:00 A.M. to 6:00 P.M. Free admission. At 12 Queen's Quay West. (416) 366–3000.

Harbourfront Antique Market. Canada's largest permanent antiques market has 100 exhibitors during the week and 150 on weekends, with an additional market open May through October. Open Tuesday–Sunday, free admission. At 390 Queen's Quay West. (416) 260–2626.

Harbourfront Centre. Toronto's lakefront area has been transformed, and it's worth a visit. At the heart of Harbourfront is **Queen's Quay Terminal,** a two-level courtyard and arcade with ninety-nine boutiques and cafes. No two shops sell the same thing, and nationalists will be delighted to find only Canadian-made products. Stretching over 100 acres are mixed yachting slips, parks, restaurants, high-rise condos, playgrounds, office space, hotels, cafes, theater and dance facilities, and art displays. From Harbourfront you can charter an ersatz Mississippi paddle wheeler or a genuine Chinese junk for sightseeing or dinner cruises. Open daily year-round except Christmas Day. Free admission. At 410 Queen's Quay West. (416) 973–3000.

Isaacs/Inuit Gallery. Contemporary sculpture, prints, drawings, and wall hangings by Inuit artists; prehistoric Inuit artifacts; and early North American Indian art and artifacts. Open Monday–Saturday 10:00 A.M. to 6:00 P.M. Free admission. At 9 Prince Arthur Avenue. (416) 921–9985.

Kensington Market. The whole area is a market; there are outdoor booths with all kinds of foodstuffs and shops and boutiques with used clothing, records, and antiques. You'll also find some great cafes, bistros, and small restaurants. The area is west of Spadina Avenue, between College and Dundas, and it's in full swing starting in the early hours, Monday–Saturday.

Ontario Parliament Buildings. That's their proper name, but Ontarians call the complex of huge pink sandstone buildings **Queen's Park.** They were built between 1886 and 1893 after an international competition among architects, which was won by a young Briton living in Buffalo, New York. The buildings are Romanesque, but look closer and you'll find Moorish, Victorian, and Gothic influences. Inside are long hallways lined with paintings of dour-looking, self-important politicos and Canadian scenes, and there's also a display of minerals. Tickets (free) are required to enter the Visitor's Gallery to watch the Legislative Assembly in session. There are free tours year-round. (416) 325–7500.

Toronto City Hall. The architecture of this building at Bay and Queen Streets symbolized the drastic changes in Toronto during the mid-1960s. The twenty- and twenty-seven-story clam-shaped towers now are dwarfed by nearby skyscrapers, but the futuristic buildings astonished some Torontonians when Finnish architect Viljo Revell's masterpiece opened in 1965. The towers look down on the white dome of the council chambers and a large plaza with reflecting pools that become skating rinks in winter. Free tours are available Monday–Friday, 8:30 A.M. to 4:30 P.M.; closed weekends and holidays. At 100 Queen Street West. (416) 392–7341.

HISTORIC BUILDINGS AND MUSEUMS

Bata Shoe Museum. Yes, it's all about shoes. Four permanent and rotating themed exhibitions are devoted to the footwear of all cultures, from ancient times to the present. There are more than 10,000 artifacts. Open Tuesday–Saturday 10:00 A.M. to 5:00 P.M. (until 8:00 P.M. on Thursday), Sunday noon to 5:00 P.M. Adults $6.00. At 327 Bloor Street West. (416) 979–7799.

Campbell House. Sir William Campbell, sixth chief justice of Upper Canada, built this Georgian mansion in 1822 at the corner of Queen and University. Costumed guides show visitors through the furnished home and chat about the Campbells. There are special events during the Christmas season. Open Monday–Friday 9:30 A.M. to 4:30 P.M., Saturday and Sunday noon to 4:30 P.M. Adults $3.50. At 160 Queen Street West. (416) 597–0227.

Colborne Lodge. One of Toronto's earliest architects, John Howard, built this grand, Regency-style house at the south end of High Park after the turn of the last century. It contains what may have been the first indoor toilet in Upper Canada. Howard was also a surveyor, engineer, and artist, and many original furnishings are on display. Closed January through March. Guided tours Tuesday–Friday noon to 4:00 P.M., Saturday and Sunday noon to 5:00 P.M. Adults $3.50. (416) 392–6916.

Gardiner Museum of Ceramic Art. This $25 million collection of rare European ceramics and the building in which it is displayed were given to Ontario by financier George Gardiner and his wife. It is the only specialized ceramics museum in North America and houses a fine collection of Italian majiolica, English delftware, and Meissen harlequin figures. At 111 Queen's Park. (416) 586–8080.

Gibson House Museum. David Gibson was a supporter of William Lyon Mackenzie and fled with him to the U.S. after the abortive Rebellion of 1837. When they returned in 1849, Gibson built this house on the ashes of his former home, which had been burned by government supporters. It is restored to its mid-eighteenth-century elegance, and there are guided tours and demonstrations of baking and pioneer crafts. Open Tuesday–Friday 9:30 A.M. to 5:00 P.M.; Saturday, Sunday, and holidays noon to 5:00 P.M. Adults $2.75. At 5172 Yonge Street. (416) 395–7432.

Gooderham Building. It's also called the **Flatiron Building,** and it was built in 1892 for a distilling company, to fit the sharp V between Front and Wellington Streets where they meet Church Street.

Holocaust Education and Memorial Centre. Dedicated to the memory of six million Jews murdered during twelve years of Nazi genocide. Two audiovisual presentations. Open Monday–Friday 9:00 A.M. to 3:00 P.M., Sunday 11:00 A.M. to 4:30 P.M. Free admission. At 4600 Bathurst Street. (416) 631–5689.

Hummingbird Centre for the Performing Arts. This is the home of the **National Ballet of Canada** and the **Canadian Opera Company,** and since it opened in 1960 it has been played by everybody who's anybody in the world of theater or the performing arts. It's at 1 Front Street and has a preshow dining room. (416) 372–2262.

Mackenzie House. Toronto's first mayor, William Lyon Mackenzie, was a fiery character who was so opposed to the incumbent government of Upper Canada that he led an abortive armed rebellion in 1837, after which he fled to the U.S. with a price on his head. He was able to return in 1849 and was elected to the Legislative Assembly. When he retired in 1858, his supporters bought him the house at 82 Bond Street, which is now furnished to the 1860 era and operated as a museum. There is a re-created nineteenth-century print shop and gallery. Open in winter Tuesday–Friday 10:00 A.M. to 4:00 P.M., Saturday and Sunday noon to 5:00 P.M. In summer, open Tuesday–Sunday noon to 5:00 P.M. Adults $3.50. (416) 392–6915.

Montgomery's Inn. Irish immigrant Thomas Montgomery, a militia captain, built this Georgian-style inn in 1830. Staff in period costume demonstrate early baking techniques and crafts. Guided tours are provided each afternoon, and tea is served 2:00 to 4:30 P.M. year-round. Open Tuesday–Friday 9:30 A.M. to 4:30 P.M., Saturday and Sunday 1:00 to 5:00 P.M. At 4709 Dundas Street West, at Islington Avenue. Adults $3.00. (416) 394–8113.

Museum for Textiles. The museum focuses on traditional textiles from all parts of the world and has a gallery dedicated to contemporary Canadian textiles. There are changing exhibitions in twelve of the galleries. Open Tuesday, Thursday, and Friday 11:00 A.M. to 5:00 P.M.; Wednesday 11:00 A.M. to 8:00 P.M.; and Saturday and Sunday noon to 5:00 P.M. At 55 Centre Avenue. Adults $5.00. (416) 599–5321.

Old City Hall. When it opened in 1899 this city hall caused as much of a stir as the new one, but it still took a heck of a fight by citizens' groups to keep the wrecking ball away in the late 1960s. It's at 60 Queen Street West, facing down Bay Street, and it houses provincial courts. As you enter, there are a great stained-glass window and marble columns. The wooden floors are from Georgia, and the city's coat of arms is stamped into many of the doorknobs. Outside, under the eaves, are carvings and gargoyles, the latter said to be caricatures of city councillors of the day and of architect James Lennox.

The Pier. One of Toronto's newest attractions (it opened in the summer of 1998), this museum is housed in a two-story warehouse dating back to the 1920s. The Pier traces the marine history of Toronto and its waterfront. One of many maritime exhibits is the 1932 steam-powered tug *Ned Hanlan,* named for a famed rowing champion of the 1870s. There are also wooden boat building demonstrations. 245 Queens Quay West. For hours and fees, call (416) 392–1765.

Redpath Sugar Museum. This free museum has a fun twenty-minute film called *Raising Cane,* and you can browse through related industry artifacts. At 95 Queen's Quay East, several blocks east of the island ferry dock. Open weekdays 10:00 A.M. to noon and 1:00 to 3:00 P.M. (416) 366–3561.

Scadding Cabin. This log cabin is the oldest remaining house in Toronto. It was built in 1794 and later moved to the Canadian National Exhibition (CNE) grounds. It is preserved as an example of a late eighteenth-century pioneer residence. It's open during the CNE (last half of August) and admission is by donation. (416) 494–0503.

Scarborough Historical Museum. The museum is housed in four historic buildings: the 1858 Cornell House, furnished to period; the McCowan Log House depicting pioneer life in the 1850s; the Hough Carriage Works, a typical nineteenth-century carriage shop; and the Kennedy Display Annex. The museum is in Thomson Memorial Park at 1007 Brimley Road. Open April through June and September 4 through December 22, Monday–Friday 10:00 A.M. to 4:00 P.M.; July through Labor Day, Wednesday–Sunday and holiday Mondays, 10:00 A.M. to 4:00 P.M. Adults $2.00. (416) 431–3441.

Sigmund Samuel Building. Antiques lovers could swoon in this museum of Canadian room settings, furnishings, and glassware. In one gallery there's a wood-paneled room from 1820 Québec. At 14 Queen's Park Crescent West. Open daily. Free admission. (416) 586–5549.

Spadina House. This magnificent estate of financier James Austin contains elegant furnishings and fine art and was the site of Toronto's finest Victorian/Edwardian gardens. In winter open Tuesday–Friday noon to 4:00 P.M., Saturday and Sunday noon to 5:00 P.M. In summer open Tuesday–Sunday noon to 5:00 P.M. Adults $5.00. At 285 Spadina Road. (416) 392–6910.

Roy Thomson Hall. It may look like an oversized, upside-down dog's dish with mirrored sides, but the acoustics are excellent and it's the city's best concert venue. The hall at 60 Simcoe Street is home to the **Toronto Symphony** and the **Toronto Mendelssohn Choir,** and the annual list of special guest performers is impressive. Tours Monday–Saturday. (416) 872–4255.

St. Lawrence Market. This market comes in two sections. The newer building has permanent food shops, a Saturday farmers' market, and a Sunday antiques and collectibles market. The other building, which was Toronto's first city hall, has two floors of market goods and spices, teas, coffees, and cheeses from around the world. They're both within the block bordered by King, Front, and Jarvis Streets, which has been the city's market site for almost 200 years.

Todmorden Mills Heritage Museum. At 67 Pottery Road, just off the Bayview Avenue Extension, historic buildings have been preserved at a mill site on the Don River. They include two pioneer homes, an 1821 brewery, an 1825 paper mill, and the Old Don Railway Station, which houses a railway museum. Open May through September, Tuesday–Friday 10:00 A.M. to 4:30 P.M.; Saturday, Sunday, and holidays 11:00 A.M. to 4:30 P.M.; October through December, Monday–Friday 10:00 A.M. to 4:00 P.M. Closed December 25 and 26 and Victoria Day. Adults $2.25. (416) 396–2819.

Toronto Police Museum. This interesting collection of Toronto police crime artifacts and displays never closes. The hours listed are 9:00 A.M. to 9:00 P.M. but since it's at Police Headquarters, 40 College Street, there's usually a tolerant desk sergeant who will let you browse among the displays at any hour of any day. A gift shop with souvenirs and police-related kitsch is open Monday–Friday 11:00 A.M. to 3:00 P.M. Donations accepted. (416) 808–7020.

THEATERS

Elgin and Winter Garden Theatres. The world's only active "stacked" theaters opened in 1913 and reopened in 1989, after $29 million had been spent to restore them to their original magnificence. The 1,500-seat Elgin is downstairs, the 1,000-seat Winter Garden is upstairs, and the shows offered—usually musicals or plays—are just as impressive as the theaters themselves. For tickets call (416) 872–5555.

Pantages Theatre. This theater's first opening was in 1920 as a vaudeville house, and it reopened in 1990 after Cineplex Odeon spent $18 million restoring it to its original grandeur. At 244 Victoria Street or 263 Yonge Street across from Eaton Centre. (416) 872–2222.

Royal Alexandra Theatre. Department store tycoon Ed (Honest Ed) Mirvish saved this 1907 theater in 1962, restored it, and has kept most of the 1,500 seats filled ever since by booking top entertainment. (416) 872–1212.

OUT-OF-TOWN ATTRACTIONS

Kortright Centre for Conservation. Located on 800 acres, the center encompasses a wildlife marsh, lush meadows, thick forests, and more than 18 km (12 miles) of walking trails. Open year-round 10:00 A.M. to 4:00 P.M. Adults $5.00. Many seasonal activities. (905) 832–2289.

McMichael Collection. Even if you don't care for art, the physical setting of this collection of more than 5,000 Canadian works is worth the twenty-minute drive north of Toronto. The collection is housed in a magnificent complex wrapped around pine-clad hills outside the village of Kleinburg. In addition to works of the Group of Seven, there are galleries of sculpture and Native and Inuit art. Adults $7.00. Follow signs from Major MacKenzie Drive, off Highway 400. Open daily year-round, closed on Mondays November through April. (905) 893–1121.

Parkwood Estate. The Oshawa mansion of Canadian automobile tycoon R. S. McLaughlin is furnished with antiques and art treasures, and you can stroll through the beautiful gardens surrounding it. Open daily June through Labor Day, except nonholiday Mondays; from Labor Day through mid-December and April through May, open Tuesday, Friday, and Sunday. Adults $5.00. (905) 433–4311.

Sharon Temple. The **Temple of the Children of Peace** at Sharon, 50 km (31 miles) north of Toronto, has no architectural equal in the world. Construction on the three-story frame building started in 1825 and was completed seven years later. Each of the windows, doors, and stairways symbolizes aspects of the sect's beliefs, and the quality of the carpentry is without parallel in the region. Volunteer guides in period costume show visitors through the temple and an adjoining museum of pioneer artifacts. **Music at Sharon,** which started in 1980, is held in July and features such groups as the Amadeus Ensemble, the Elmer Iseler Singers, and the Gabriel Quartet. Sharon is between Holland Landing and Mount Albert, just south of Queensville. The easiest way to find the hamlet is to take Highway 11 (Yonge Street) north from Toronto. Turn right at the sign for Holland

Landing, and the 3-km (2-mile) route to Sharon is well marked. Open daily except Friday from May through October; open daily in July and August. (905) 478–2389.

Thomas Foster Memorial Temple. This miniature of the Taj Mahal, located in the middle of farm fields 13 km (9 miles) north of Uxbridge, looks out of place, to say the least. It's a private mausoleum that's open on the first and third Sundays of the month, June through September.

Uxbridge-Scott Museum. Just west and north of Uxbridge on Concession Road 6, six historic buildings hold pioneer exhibits, including a Quaker display. Open May 24 through late October, Wednesday–Sunday and holidays. (905) 852–5854.

SPECTATOR SPORTS

Mohawk Raceway. At Campbellville, 45 km (30 miles) west of Toronto at Guelph Line and Highway 401. There's harness racing most nights, and the **Terrace Dining Room** overlooks the track. (905) 675–7223 or (800) 268–9967.

Woodbine Race Track. Day and evening Thoroughbred and Standardbred action on three tracks at Highway 27 and Rexdale Boulevard. (416) 675–3993 or (800) 268–9967.

DINING

There are more than 5,000 restaurants in Toronto, so if you're in town for more than a few days you'd do well to invest in one of the many available dining guidebooks. Or you may want to ask the natives—they're usually delighted to refer you to some special spot they've found. Here is just a sample of what you'll have to choose from in Toronto.

Barberians, 7 Elm Street. (416) 597–0335. Probably the best steak in town— they've been perfecting the art since 1959 in a historic building filled with art treasures.

Ed's Restaurants, 270 King Street West. (416) 593–6676. A Toronto institution that just keeps on expanding. There were five Ed's restaurants at last count, each specializing in a different type of cuisine. Ed's Warehouse! is for steaks and roast beef, and when you ask for rare you get rare. There's also

Ed's Italian!, Ed's Seafood!, Old Ed's!, and Ed's Chinese! For entertainment and dancing, there's Ed's Folly.

Lighthouse, One Harbour Square. (416) 869–1600. The revolving restaurant on the thirty-sixth floor of the Westin Harbour Castle Hotel gives the diner a better view of the city than CN Tower's 360 Revolving Restaurant does. They have good lunch buffets and a fine continental dinner menu. In addition, prices are lower than at the CN Tower and the food is better.

The Old Mill, in the Humber Valley at 21 Old Mill Road. (416) 236–2641. It's lovely, it's expensive, and it's the sort of place for a memorable lunch or dinner of continental cuisine, preferably on an expense account. The **Old Mill Tea Room** opened in 1914, and dining rooms have been added over the years.

The Old Spaghetti Factory, 56 The Esplanade. (416) 864–9775. Choose this old favorite for a reasonably priced meal amid greenery, stained glass, and an incredible collection of memorabilia. Not only the spaghetti is excellent; there's a full range of Italian fare. It's in a downtown area in which you'll find other great wining and dining spots and a number of busy outdoor patios.

Sai Woo, on the second floor at 130 Dundas Street West. (416) 977–4988. Who cares about decor when the Cantonese food is this good and this inexpensive? The crowds of Chinese diners are tacit testimony to the superb cuisine.

LODGINGS

From mid-November through March, most major Toronto hotels participate in a marketing program in which hotel rates are cut in half for stays of two nights or longer. Guests are asked to mention when reserving that they are participating in the program, and they are given an **Adventure Passport** of discount coupons for shopping, dining, and attractions. Check with Tourism Toronto for details. (See For More Information at the end of this chapter.)

The **Novotel Toronto Centre** has modest, modern rooms right downtown and was created in 1987 by a French company that has more than 200 hotels in forty-two countries. The hotel's slogan is "The Soul of Europe in the Heart of Toronto," and while that may sound Madison Avenue glib, the property lives up to the claim without artifice. At 45 The Esplanade near the Westin Harbour Castle and the Royal York, but Novotel snagged the best location among the boutiques, outdoor gardens, cafes, and a dozen fun restaurants—places like the Old Fish Market, the Spaghetti Factory, Muddy York, Scotland Yard, and the Organ Grinder. The hotel's own **Cafe Les Arcades** is great for lunches and pre- or post-theater dinners. The hotel is also within walking distance of O'Keefe Centre and the St. Lawrence Centre for the Performing Arts. Double rooms are $115–$165. You'll need a reservation. (416) 367–8900.

The huge old **Royal York Hotel** has probably seen more deals cut in its bars, cavernous lobby, rooms, and suites than any other building in the city. If you're booking ahead, request one of the "new" rooms. Sauna, swimming pool, and whirlpool. Weekend rates from $129. (416) 368–2511 or (800) 441–1414.

SPECIAL EVENTS

Early June. Market Fair. Street festival, face painting, pony rides, petting zoo, farmers' market, live entertainment. On Dundas and Keele Streets.

Mid-June. Metro International Caravan. A travel adventure of fifty pavilions representing the cultural capitals of the world and Toronto's cultural diversity, with entertainment, food, crafts at various locations.

Mid-June. International Dragon Boat Race Festival. Dragon boat races, multicultural entertainment, crafts, food. At Centre Island.

Mid-June to early July. Benson and Hedges Symphony of Fire. International musical fireworks competition at Ontario Place.

Mid-June to July. Du Maurier Ltd. Downtown Jazz Festival. Over 1,500 international jazz artists in every jazz style, daily performances, workshops and films, street performances, and ticketed concerts at fifty venues, most in downtown Toronto.

Late June. Gay and Lesbian Pride Week. A week of celebrations including a parade and free downtown street party.

Late June. Fort York Festival. Over 100 British, Canadian, and U.S. War of 1812 soldiers reenact the Battle of Fort York. At Fort York.

Late June. Cheers, Scarborough. A showcase of contributions made by cultural groups to Scarborough. Highlights include dancers, musicians, fashion show, art exhibits, cultural cuisine. At Scarborough Civic Centre.

Late June to early July. Taste of Toronto. Festival featuring forty of Toronto's top restaurants. Chefs prepare their specialties while patrons are entertained by top adult and children's performers. Free. Along Front Street between Simcoe Street and Blue Jay Way.

End of July and early August. Caribana. Caribbean music, art, culture, food, and parade.

Early August. Olde Tyme Picnic Games, Scarborough. Croquet, badminton, ring toss, horseshoes, ice cream made the old-fashioned way. At Scarborough Historical Museum.

Early August. Simcoe Day celebrations. Military reenactment with Gov. John Graves Simcoe and Elizabeth Simcoe, outdoor artisans show and sale, children's activities, heritage showcase, local cultural and environmental groups. At Todmorden Mills Heritage Museum and Arts Centre.

Early August. Simcoe Day at Fort York. Military and drill reenactments, guest speakers, and tours of the birthplace of Toronto, Fort York.

Mid-August to early September. Canadian National Exhibition. Oldest and largest annual exhibition in the world, with a pavilion devoted to cultural diversity, The New Kids' World, entertainers, air show, casino, Inuit Pavilion. At Exhibition Place.

Early September. Canadian International Air Show with the Snowbirds, Misty Blues, and Northern Lights. Stationary display at the Canadian Airlines hangar at Pearson International Airport; Canadian National Exhibition show over Lake Ontario.

Early September. Cabbagetown Festival. Community festival, fashion show, music, crafts, parade, tour of homes, street entertainment, children's activities. At Parliament and Carlton Streets.

Early September. International Film Festival. Now ranked as one of the top five film festivals in the world, features 300 films from forty countries at various locations.

Early October. Harvest Fair. Traditional fall fair on the grounds of a nineteenth-century home, with music, dance, children's games, and activities. At Colborne Lodge, High Park.

Late November. Canadian Aboriginal Festival. Celebration of native heritage and culture, over 1,000 dancers in full North American native regalia, drum/singing groups, crafts, food, variety show. At Skydome.

FOR MORE INFORMATION

Tourism Toronto, 207 Queen's Quay West, Suite 509, P.O. Box 126, Toronto ON M5J 1A7. Call (416) 203–2600, or (800) 203–1990.

ESCAPE FOURTEEN

Toronto with Kids

URBAN FUN FOR THE YOUNGER SET

AS MANY NIGHTS AS YOU CAN AFFORD

A huge zoo • Amusement parks • IMAX theater
Hands-on science museum • Sports • Laser tag

There are two Toronto escapes in this book, and this one is for parents who are looking for places to take their children for entertainment, education, or just plain fun. Information about getting a Toronto overview, city tour, or harbor tour and an explanation of the city's public transportation network are included in Southwestern Ontario Escape Thirteen.

Because there are so many things to see and do with kids in Toronto and not everybody will want to follow the same itinerary, this chapter does not lead you through a prescribed itinerary meal by meal, morning to evening. The major attractions are listed alphabetically in the categories of Special Sites, Historic Buildings and Museums, Theaters, Out-of-Town Attractions, and Spectator Sports.

At the end of the chapter are lists of accommodation options and suggested venues for breakfast, lunch, and dinner for all budgets.

SPECIAL SITES

Black Creek Pioneer Village. There are more than forty buildings, most from the mid-1800s, in this village at Jane Street and Steeles Avenue, a half-hour northwest of downtown. Staff in period costume perform old-time chores from horse-shoeing to baking. Gift shop, dining, village-made crafts, and seasonal events. Open daily May through December, 10:00 A.M.

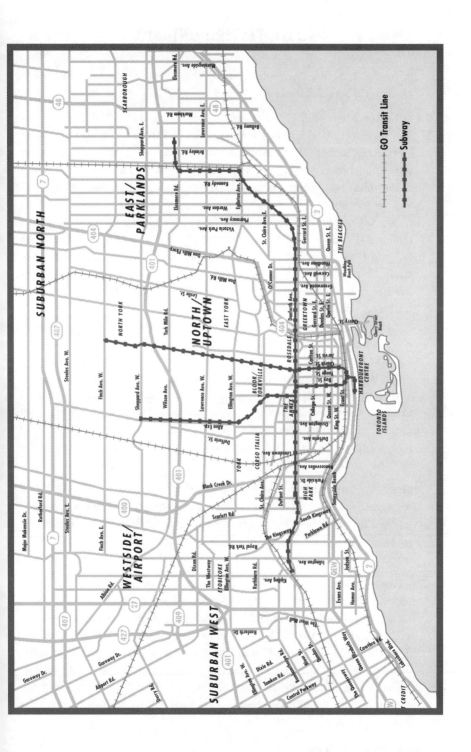

GO Transit Line

Subway

to 5:00 P.M. Adults $9.00, children $5.00. At 1000 Murray Ross Parkway, Downsview. (416) 736–1733.

Casa Loma. After the CN Tower and Skydome, Casa Loma has to be the easiest place to find in Toronto. It rears up from Davenport Hill, a couple of kilometers north of the lake, and dominates everything around it. On your tour of this incredible ninety-eight-room castle you'll walk about 2 km (1.25 miles) and go up and down 370 stairs, so be sure you and the kids wear comfy shoes.

Canadian financier and military officer Sir Henry Mill Pellatt started building his castle in 1911 so that visiting royalty would have a place to stay and Torontonians would have a fine permanent building of which they could be proud. (That was his story, anyway.) Sir Henry and Lady Pellatt lived at Casa Loma—which translates to "castle on the hill"—from 1913 until Lady Pellatt died in 1924.

Thereafter, Sir Henry spent most of his time at his country estate near King, north of Toronto. In the 1930s his stockbrokering fortunes reversed and the city took Casa Loma over for taxes. It stood empty until 1937, when the Kiwanis Club of West Toronto opened it as a tourist attraction. The rooms and hallways are magnificent, and many contain period furniture. There are exhibitions of special interest for military buffs and Girl Guides (Girl Scouts in the U.S.). Open daily in summer 9:30 A.M. to 4:00 P.M.; winter hours are 10:00 A.M. to 4:00 P.M. Adults $8.00, children $4.50. At 1 Austin Terrace. (416) 923–1171.

Centreville Amusement Park. A turn-of-the-century town with rides, restaurants, shops, and games on Centre Island in the Toronto Islands, reached by ferryboat. Open daily May through September. An all-day ride pass costs $16.78 for adults and kids over 4 feet tall, $11.79 for kids under 4 feet; a family pass for four is $55.16. (416) 203–0405.

CN Tower. Toronto's most visible landmark has undergone a $26 million renovation, and several new family-oriented attractions have been added to the world's loftiest building. There are virtual games (dinosaur chasers, a snowboarder, and the like) that small fry can play in a themed arcade. They can also "go on" a simulator ride on a stomach-lurching roller coaster, or "take" the more gentle easy-glide Canadian Panorama simulator ride that gives them an aerial tour of Canada. Showing at the movie theater is a film entitled *Momentum,* which highlights Canada and the

Canadian way of life. Admission $15 adults, $12 children. The CN Tower is at 301 Front Street West, Toronto ON M5V 2T6. (416) 868–6937.

Children's Own Museum. This fun, hands-on kid's museum opened recently in the old McLaughlin Planterium building. There are eighteen activity areas, including a miniature vet's "clinic" (for stuffed animals!) and a forty-seat theater, with racks of costumes for budding actors. Open daily, year-round, Tuesday 10:00 A.M. to 8:00 P.M., Wednesday–Saturday 10:00 A.M. to 5:00 P.M., Sunday noon to 5:00 P.M. (416) 542–1492. The museum is at 90 Queen's Park, Toronto ON M5S 2C5. Admission is $3.75. No charge for children under two.

Fantasy Fair. Ontario's only indoor amusement park, inside Woodbine Shopping Centre. There are a Victorian town with rides, games, restaurants, and a children's play area. Open daily year-round. Adults $10.95, children $7.95. At 500 Rexdale Boulevard, Rexdale. (416) 674–5437.

Funstation Funpark. Two eighteen-hole railway-themed minigolf courses, batting cages, bumper cars, carousel, patio restaurant. Open daily April through October, 10:00 A.M. to midnight, weather permitting. Adults $5.25, children $4.75. At 4150 Jane Street, Downsview. (416) 736–4808.

High Park. Bison, West Highland cattle, yaks, deer, llamas, and swans may be viewed in this unusual park in the middle of a major city. There are also sports facilities, a summer theater featuring the works of Shakespeare, a summer music festival, and self-guided walking tours of oak savannah restoration plots. The park is open daily year-round, and there's no admission charge. Between Queensway and Bloor Street West on the west side of Parkside Drive. (416) 392–1111.

Ontario Place. Wear comfortable shoes: This family playground is spread across ninety-six acres on three connected islands in Lake Ontario, and it's a long hike to the gate just from the parking lot. In Children's Village, children are supervised while they slide, run, jump, crawl, bounce, and scream in an environment where everything is padded and designed to be roughly handled.

For music lovers, there's the 16,000-seat Molson Amphitheatre. Shows range from ballet to rock, classical to jazz. While the kids are beating up on the toys in Children's Village, you might want to visit Molson Canadian Waterfall Showplace, a 150-seat club surrounded by rock faces and waterfalls. When the club's stage isn't in use it's behind a curtain of water that cascades 21 feet into a reflecting pool.

Inside Ontario Place's trademark geodesic dome, Cinesphere IMAX seats 800 people facing a six-story-high screen. There are lots of restaurants, snack bars, and picnic areas, and visitors can bring their own food and (nonalcoholic) drinks. Through the season there are special events, from fireworks to daredevil acts to the Dragon Boat Race Festival and the Benson & Hedges Fireworks Competition. Open mid-May to Labor Day. At 955 Lakeshore Boulevard West. (416) 314–9900.

Ontario Science Centre. This hands-on fun place opened in 1969, and it's been delighting kids of all ages ever since. You can't go past any of the 800 exhibits without learning something and having a good time while you're at it. There are fifteen minitheaters with short film or slide shows and no tours because the object of the whole place is discovery. Watch a chrysanthemum frozen in liquid oxygen shatter into thousands of icy shards, walk through a steaming tropical rain forest, or make an exhibition of yourself in a shadow tunnel. (Don't try this one on a tight time budget.) Open daily except Christmas Day, 10:00 A.M. to 6:00 P.M. Adults $8.00, kids five to sixteen $5.00. At 770 Don Mills Road, North York. (416) 696–3127.

Paramount Canada's Wonderland. A 150-foot-high "mountain" made of steel, wire mesh, and concrete is the focal point of this theme park located northwest of Toronto, near Maple. More than two million people visit the 300-acre theme park each summer to see its 160 attractions, including Canada's largest wave pool (32,000 square feet), and choose among its fifteen thrilling rides. They're also drawn to its themed areas: International Street, International Festival, Medieval Faire, The Grande World Exposition of 1890, Hanna Barbera Land (the Flintstones and gang), Smurf Forest, and White Water Canyon.

There are concerts and international food and drink. Open weekends in May and fall and daily late May to Labor Day. Opening time is 10:00 A.M.; closing times vary. Located in Vaughan on the west side of Highway 400, between Rutherford Road and Major MacKenzie Drive. (905) 832–7000.

Royal Ontario Museum (ROM). The collecting hasn't stopped since the ROM opened in 1912, and there are now more than six million items . . . so budget your time accordingly! There are a fantastic dinosaur exhibit, a complete Ming tomb, and a Jamaican limestone bat cave. The

European Musical Instruments Gallery contains more than 1,200 instruments, and in other areas you'll find suits of armor, mummies, ancient Greek gold jewelry—the list goes on and on, as do the galleries. The ROM has just completed an $80 million expansion that makes it the continent's second-largest museum after New York's Metropolitan Museum of Art. Open Monday–Saturday 10:00 A.M. to 6:00 P.M., Thursday 10:00 A.M. to 8:00 P.M., Sunday 11:00 A.M. to 6:00 P.M. Adults $10.00, children $5.00, family $22.00. At 100 Queen's Park Crescent. (416) 586–8000.

Toronto Islands. The three connected islands are reached by ferries departing the foot of Bay Street every fifteen minutes in summer. Centre Island is where the action is (see Centreville Amusement Park, p. 146). There are an antique carousel, a hollow log ride, a miniature railroad, haunted barrel works, or, for romantics, a ride across a lagoon in a white swan. You can rent a canoe, bicycle, or pedal boat. There are formal gardens and a licensed dining room with a great view of the city's skyline. Hanlan's Point Island and Ward's Island are pleasant places to get away from the hectic pace of the city. You can walk for miles amid the huge old trees and along the boardwalk. Hanlan's Point has free tennis courts. Round-trip ferry fare is $4.00 for adults, $1.00 for children fourteen and younger. Ferry service information: (416) 392–8193.

Toronto Zoo. It would take the average person about four days to see everything since the site covers 710 hilly acres. Wear comfortable shoes, plan to spend the whole day, and study the map you get when you pay your admission to decide which of the 5,000 inhabitants in seven pavilions you want to see. A good overview is available from the Zoomobile monorail, which has a taped commentary. Open daily except Christmas, 9:00 A.M. to 7:30 P.M. in summer and 9:30 A.M. to 4:30 P.M. in winter. At the northeast edge of the city, 2 km (1.25 miles) north of Highway 401 on Meadowvale Road. (416) 392–5900.

HISTORIC BUILDINGS AND MUSEUMS

Historic Fort York. One of the bloodiest battles of the War of 1812 was fought on these grounds in the spring of 1813, when 1,750 invading U.S. troops trounced 700 defenders and then burned all the community's public buildings except the fort. There are tours, displays, and military demonstrations. In summer the Fort York Guard marches to fife and drum. Open in summer Monday–Friday 10:00 A.M. to 5:00 P.M., Saturday and Sunday noon to 5:00 P.M.; in winter open Tuesday–Friday 10:00 A.M. to 4:00 P.M., Saturday and Sunday noon to 5:00 P.M. Free admission. Near Harbourfront and the foot of Bathurst Street at 100 Garrison Road. (416) 392–6907.

Hockey Hall of Fame. In this shrine to the national sport, its ultimate treasure, the 1893 Stanley Cup, is displayed. It is the oldest North American professional sports trophy. You'll also see "significant" hockey sticks and sweaters, videos of major games, goalie masks . . . and, of course, Wayne Gretzky's feet cast in bronze! Open Monday–Friday 10:00 A.M. to 5:00 P.M., Saturday 9:30 A.M. to 6:00 P.M., Sunday 10:30 A.M. to 5:00 P.M. Adults $10.00, children $5.50. At BCE Place, 30 Yonge Street. (416) 360–7735.

OUT-OF-TOWN ATTRACTIONS

Canadian Automotive Museum. Just east of Whitby at Oshawa, this fine collection of antique autos fills two large floors at 99 Simcoe Street South. There are some real gems—a Rolls-Royce custom-built for Lady Eaton, an 1898 Fisher electric, and some fascinating one-of-a-kinds. Open daily year-round. Admission $5.00 adults, $4.50 students twelve to eighteen, $3.50 kids six to eleven. (905) 576–1222.

Cullen Gardens and Miniature Village. This is one of those marketing gimmicks that have become tourist attractions in their own right. There's an enormous barn just north of Whitby, a half-hour east of Toronto, where you can shop your heart out on three floors. But many go to see the twenty-five acres of gardens and the miniature village, which has 140 historic or famous buildings from southern Ontario replicated to one-twelfth scale. During the seasons different flowers are featured and from mid-November to early January there's a Festival of Lights. There are also a theater and two restaurants. Adults $8.99, children $3.99. Open daily. (905) 686–1600.

The Farm Museum. West of Toronto, take exit 320 near Milton to this collection of more than thirty buildings and displays, all of which have an agricultural theme. It's well worth the visit. Adults $4.50, children $2.25. Open daily mid-May through September. (905) 878–8151.

Making friends at the zoo.

SPECTATOR SPORTS

Immediately west of the CN Tower is the world's first domed stadium with a retractable roof. This temple to the big business of professional sports, known as the **SkyDome,** has more than 50,000 seats and is the home of the Toronto Blue Jays baseball team and the Toronto Argonauts football team. Fans attending games don't even have to miss the advantages of TV coverage—the Sky-Dome has the world's largest video replay screen and scoreboard. The roof is capable of opening or closing in twenty minutes, and there's room inside for a thirty-one-story building on enough acreage to accommodate a thirty-two-home subdivision. There are nine restaurants, souvenir shops, cafes, lounges, and a 278-room hotel. Seventy of those rooms and suites overlook the playing field. Subject to scheduled events, tours of SkyDome are 9:00 A.M. to 6:00 P.M. daily. (416) 341–2770. Following is information on the two teams that play at the SkyDome:

Toronto Argonauts Football Club. The "Argos" compete in the North Division of the Canadian Football League between June and November. Tickets are $15–$41. (416) 341–5151.

Toronto Blue Jays Baseball Club. A member of the American League Eastern Division, the Jays play eighty-one home games at SkyDome. Tickets are $6–$40. (416) 341–1000.

The Toronto Raptors Basketball Club no longer plays at the SkyDome. The team moved, along with the Toronto Maple Leafs Hockey Club, to the new **Air Canada Centre**, a sport and entertainment complex within walking distance of the SkyDome, at 20 Bay Street. (416) 214–2255. The Raptors have a forty-five game schedule October through April. The new phone number for tickets is (416) 815–5600 and tickets are $25–$120.

DINING

Casey's Grill House & Beverage Co., Sherway Gardens, Queen Elizabeth Way and Highway 27. (416) 626–2626. Kids get coloring sheets and crayons and their drink in a neat plastic cup with a conical lid and straw they may keep. There are chicken nuggets, grilled cheese, burgers, pasta, and hot dogs, all with fries and soup. The kids' meal prices of $3.99–$4.99 include drink and cup, ice cream, and a lollipop. Adult entrees: $7.98–$16.37.

Pickle Barrel, Atrium on Bay, 312 Yonge Street. (416) 977-6677. Huge "pickle people" murals inspire kids to color one of the most extensive kids' menus in town. All meals cost $3.79 and include pop, milk, or juice. Adult entrees: $4.99–$15.99.

Mövenpick Marché, 42 Yonge Street, BCE Place. (416) 366-8986. A series of self-serve stations where kids can see it all happening: penne coming out of a pasta maker, sausages on the grill, juice being squeezed. Adult entrees: $8.00–$22.00. Children's portions approximately half-price.

LODGING

The **Radisson–Don Mills** is on Don Mills just south of Highway 401. There are free parking and an indoor pool, and all rooms have two double beds. Room rates are $99 and discounted tickets to area attractions are available at the front desk. **Cafe Bellevue** has casual family dining. (416) 449–4111.

SPECIAL EVENTS

See the Special Events section in Southernwestern Ontario Escape Thirteen for a list of events of interest to both children and adults. The following events are specifically geared to kids:

Early May. Forsythia Festival, Toronto. Annual community event for children, children's parade, kids' costume contest, local entertainers. Wellesley Park.

Mid-May. Annual Milk International Childrens' Festival, Toronto. International performers for young people, cultural activities at Harbourfront.

FOR MORE INFORMATION

Tourism Toronto, 207 Queen's Quay West, Suite 509, P.O. Box 126, Toronto ON M5J 1A7. (416) 203–2600 or (800) 203–1990.

EASTERN
ONTARIO
ESCAPES

Brockville, Prescott, and Athens

TRAVELING ALONG THE ST. LAWRENCE

2 NIGHTS

Prehistoric monsters • Fort Wellington • Murals
A village-size museum

Brockville is a peaceful, prosperous, and dignified city of 22,000 people, with beautiful old public and private buildings of locally quarried limestone. The town's first settler, William Buell, built a home on the St. Lawrence River in 1784. The place was first known as Buell's Bay and then as Elizabethtown, but after the War of 1812—during which there was an inconclusive naval battle at Brockville—the name was changed to honor General Sir Isaac Brock, who died defeating American invaders at Queenston Heights.

Brockville is at the foot of the Thousand Islands of the St. Lawrence River between the international bridges at Ivy Lea and Johnstown. At one time it was a playground for the rich and famous and it is said to have had more millionaires per capita than any other place in Canada. The Gloria Vanderbilt story, *Little Gloria: Happy at Last,* was filmed in Brockville, taking advantage of the town's stately mansions, elaborate fountains, and impressive architecture. Many of the city's historic buildings play a role in **Symphony of Lights,** a glittering tableau of more than 25,000 tiny white lights that outline major landmarks and trees. The lights twinkle from late June through August and at Christmastime.

One of the light-bedecked buildings is the 1842 County Court House and Jail set in a village green laid out in 1809. Connecticut-born Buell donated part of his Crown land grant for the site. Buell obviously had influence on the land's use: Brockville is the only municipality in Ontario with a New

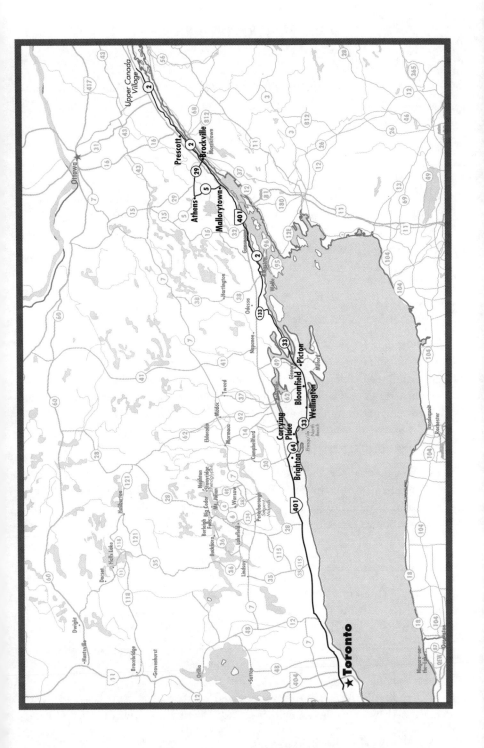

England–style town square surrounded by a courthouse green and a church on each corner. The region was the earliest-settled part of Ontario, and the architecture of the communities included in this escape reflect that history.

DAY 1

Morning

It's 340 km (213 miles) to Brockville from Toronto on Highway 401. For a break from the four to six lanes of truck-cluttered traffic, take exit 509 through Brighton to Carrying Place, then Highway 33 across Prince Edward County, through Wellington, Bloomfield, Picton, and Glenora. Take the (free) ferry from Glenora to Adolphustown on the mainland, and at Millhaven take Highway 133 north to Highway 401 at exit 593. The pastoral sights of Prince Edward County and the short ferry trip will help you cope with the last hour from exit 593 to Brockville.

LUNCH: The **River Walk Mill** is in a beautifully restored and renovated century-old mill in the heart of downtown Brockville at 123 Water Street West at St. Paul Street. There are fine dining upstairs and a comfortable bar/lounge on the ground floor. The lunch menu offers sandwiches, fish and chips, and pasta dishes ranging from $5.50 to $10.00. (613) 345–7098.

Afternoon

Brockville has made the most of its waterfront location with a major park development, the **Armagh S. Price Park** and **Brockville Municipal Harbor and Marina.** Owned by one of many Thousand Island cruise boat companies, the steamboat replica *Spirit of Brockville* uses the marina as a base for cruises through the islands.

In the park is the south end of the **oldest railway tunnel in Canada.** The tunnel was controversial when proposed in the early 1850s. Many felt the rail line being built to provide access to the riverfront could go around the western end of the town "at half the price in half the time." But the 1,730-foot tunnel under the town was completed in 1860. In 1954 the last steam locomotive capable of negotiating it was scrapped and the doors of the tunnel were closed. You can walk a few steps inside it and admire the vaulted stone ceiling.

Brockville Arts Centre was erected in 1858 as a town hall and then taken over by a citizens' group that formed **Brockville Opera House Com-**

pany and added a theater. For schedules, prices, or reservations, contact: The Brockville Arts Centre, 225 King Street West, Brockville ON K6V 5V5. (613) 342–7122.

Brockville Museum at 5 Henry Street is in a building constructed in two stages during the early 1800s. The rear part is one of the earliest remaining structures in the city. Open daily in summer and on afternoons the rest of the year. Small admission fee.

Brockville has had a **farmers' market** since 1833. It's next to City Hall on Market Street West and opens at 7:00 A.M. on Tuesday, Thursday, and Saturday mornings. **Sheridan Mews** is reached through a wagon way from King Street West, and the historic buildings around it house an antiques shop, art gallery, tearoom, and craft shop.

A few kilometers northeast of Brockville on Highway 2 is the village of Maitland, just outside of which is **Homewood,** the 1800 home of Solomon Jones. Jones was a busy doctor but found time to act as district judge and as a member of the Legislative Assembly of Upper Canada. Seven generations of the Jones family lived at Homewood through 1972. In the 1880s one of Solomon's descendants, Harold Jones, developed an experimental fruit orchard later designated as the **St. Lawrence Fruit Station of the Dominion Experimental Farm.** In 1900 Harold developed a variety of snow apple, the Jones Red Fameuse, that won medals and for a time threatened to displace the McIntosh as Ontario's favorite. In addition to period furnishings, much of Solomon's medical paraphernalia is on display along with artifacts of the apple business. Open 10:00 A.M. to 4:00 P.M. Monday–Friday March through November, and also on weekends in July and August. (613) 348–3560.

DINNER AND LODGING: Brockville's five-star property is the **Royal Brock,** where the **St. Lawrence Room** offers one of the finest dining experiences between Montréal and Toronto. Tuxedoed waiters serve French cuisine on Wedgwood china with Marlboro silver atop damask linen cloths. All dishes are finished at your table. *Wine Spectator* magazine of California ranks the hotel's wine list as one of the finest in the world, and SOPEXA (the marketing arm of the French government) rates the Brock's sommelier as Ontario's finest. Dinner is $25–$50 per person. The hotel's **Greenery Restaurant** offers a more relaxed atmosphere. Reservations recommended.

Guests staying at the hotel can enjoy the indoor pool, sports club, whirlpool, sauna, squash courts, fitness center, bar/lounge, and disco. Rooms cost $120–$135; suites $247. At 100 Stewart Boulevard. (613) 345–1400 or (800) 267–4428.

DAY 2

Morning

BREAKFAST: At the Royal Brock.

Take Highway 2 northeast along the St. Lawrence River toward Prescott. Several miles before reaching this pretty town of 4,600, you'll come to the **Blue Church** on your left. The small wooden chapel painted pale blue was built in 1845 to replace an earlier structure that burned. It's the burial place of Irish-born Barbara Heck, who immigrated to New York with her husband, Paul, and founded the first Methodist Society and the first Wesleyan Church in America. After the Revolutionary War she and her husband moved to Canada, settling near the church in 1785. In Canada she again formed a pioneer Methodist Society. She died in 1804.

Prescott was a major transshipment point on the St. Lawrence River between Montréal and Toronto. Cargoes were transferred from lake boats to river vessels in Prescott until 1847, when a canal permitted uninterrupted navigation from Montréal to Lake Ontario. The story of the forwarding trade is told at **Forwarders' Museum,** an 1812 stone building on the waterfront at Water and Centre Streets. It's open daily June through August. Admission $1.00. (613) 925–5788.

Prescott's premier tourist attraction is **Fort Wellington,** the second fort to stand guard over the St. Lawrence River at that site. Because it was never attacked and has been fully restored, it is one of the best forts for getting a feel for Canadian military life of the mid-nineteenth century.

The first fort was built by the British in 1813 to protect goods and troops moving between Montréal and Upper Canada after the outbreak of the War of 1812. The war showed the British military the vulnerability of the St. Lawrence frontier, and in 1826 construction started on the Rideau Canal between the Ottawa River and Kingston, to bypass the St. Lawrence in time of war. When that waterway was completed in 1832, Fort Wellington was no longer a military necessity and was abandoned.

In 1837 rebellion broke out in Upper and Lower Canada. A force of Canadian rebels attempting to free the colony from British rule was defeated and fled to the United States. The British were forced to reinforce their border defense system and in 1838 built a new and stronger Fort Wellington on the ruins of the former fort.

While they were building the second Fort Wellington, Canadian rebels and their American sympathizers invaded Canada at Prescott with a force of 190 men in two schooners. They tried to land at Prescott but withdrew when the customs inspector sounded an alarm. In the confusion, one schooner ran aground off Windmill Point several kilometers downriver. To lighten the ship and float her off, men and equipment were landed and a large stone windmill became their fortress. Local men mustered in militia units, backed up by British regulars from Prescott and Kingston, and surrounded Windmill Point. A violent and bloody battle raged for four days before the rebels surrendered.

The buildings at Fort Wellington have been furnished to the 1846 period. The top two stories of the central blockhouse were used as barracks for the men, who lived there with their wives and children in appallingly crowded and unsanitary conditions. From the top-floor barracks, low doorways opened onto a machicoulis, an overhang of the third story from which defenders could fire through trapdoors in the floor at any enemy that had breached the palisaded walls. Another interesting feature of the fort is the caponniere. Reached by a passage under the earthworks, this bombproof chamber allowed defenders a safe position from which to fire down both sides of the front of the fort at attackers who had reached the ditch between the palisades and the inner wall of the fort.

The fort is open daily mid-May to mid-October, 10:00 A.M. to 5:00 P.M., and Monday–Friday the rest of the year, 10:00 A.M. to 5:00 P.M. by appointment. It's on Highway 2, 5 km (3 miles) west of International Bridge. Admission $2.25. (613) 925–2896.

Ontario's oldest barracks building, built in 1810, is 1 block west of Fort Wellington and is open daily only in July and August as both a museum and a luncheon facility. Lunches are available at **Stockade Barracks and Hospital Museum** from 11:30 A.M. through mid-afternoon and feature historical menus including soups, salads, stews, and more. By prior arrangement, groups can have five- or six-course dinners of 1812-style dishes served by mess waiters in military uniform. Contact Paul Fortier, Stockade Barracks & Hospital Museum, P.O. Box 446, 356 East Street, Prescott ON K0E 1T0. (613) 925–4894.

LUNCH: The **Bridgeview Restaurant,** 5 km (3 miles) east of Prescott on Highway 2 east, offers family dining with a full menu and brunch on Sunday. The dining room overlooks the marina. Lunches cost $7.00. Open daily.

Afternoon

Continue east on Highway 2 or Highway 401 and watch for signs to **Prehistoric World**. This unique theme park is immediately west of **Upper Canada Village;** take exit 758 off Highway 401. You guide yourself on a kilometer-long (0.6-mile) path through fern-carpeted forest past displays of more than forty life-size replicas of prehistoric animals, from the ferocious tyrannosaurus to the docile woolly mammoth. Children can dig in a giant sandbox "salted" with replica dinosaur teeth, bones, and eggs. Admission $6.50 adults, $4.25 children. Open daily May 24 through Labor Day, 10:00 A.M. to 4:00 P.M., and weekends same hours until mid-October. (613) 543–2503.

Just east of Upper Canada Village off Highway 2 is **Upper Canada Migratory Bird Sanctuary,** a 3,500-acre refuge popular with birders during spring and fall migrations. There are 6 km (4 miles) of trails, an observation tower, and an interpretation center. Open April through November.

Eight villages disappeared under rising waters when the St. Lawrence Seaway opened in 1959, but the best of their historic buildings were moved to a new village, Upper Canada Village. Newfangled things like radios and tape players are banned in this throwback to the days of United Empire Loyalists and other settlers of Eastern Ontario. The St. Lawrence Parks Commission operates Upper Canada Village and has hired local people and dressed them in clothing typical of the early 1800s. The village occupies part of the 2,000-acre **Crysler's Farm Battlefield Memorial Park,** a site that figured prominently in the War of 1812.

Upper Canada Village contains three mills, two farms, two churches, two hotels, and twenty-five other buildings originally used as homes or workshops. A leisurely tour takes three to four hours. Adult admission is $12; with it you get an illustrated map with thumbnail sketches of major points of interest. Your best bet is to locate a shady bench, study the map to see what most interests you, and then plan your route accordingly.

If you don't feel like walking the whole way, hop onto one of the horse-drawn "carry-alls" at any of the many designated stops. There is regular return transportation between Cook's Tavern and the Tenant Farm at the east end of the village. You can also take a cruise in the horse-drawn bateau. The docks are behind Cook's Tavern and the Tenant Farm.

Every artifact in the village is in working order. The 1830 woolen mill turns out the products sold in the village outlets, and the sawmill produces all the lumber needed for village building or repairs. The village is primarily agricultural, with fruit and vegetable gardens and farm animals on the two farms.

A millpond at Upper Canada Village.

The **Village Store** is open year-round and has a wide selection of Canadian crafts and village-made bread, cheese, and flour. The **Garden Snack Bar** provides a picnic area. At **Willard's Hotel,** lunches, full-course meals, and teas with a historic flavor are served. The **Harvest Barn Restaurant** offers cafeteria-style lunches, snacks, and refreshments. Both places are licensed for beer and wine. Open daily mid-May through mid-October and weekends in winter. At Crysler Farm Battlefield Park, Highway 2. Adults $12.50, children $6.00. (613) 543–3704 or (800) 437–2233.

DINNER AND LODGING: Ramada Inn has a 110-room motel with indoor pool, sauna and whirlpool, licensed lounge, and dining room. It's at 805 Brookdale Avenue, exit 789 from Highway 401 to downtown Cornwall or the Seaway International Bridge to New York State. (613) 933–8000.

DAY 3

Morning

BREAKFAST: At the Ramada Inn.

Take Highway 401 westbound to exit 696 and Highway 29 west through Tincap to Forthton. At Forthton take Highway 42 to **Athens.** This village of just under 1,000, situated 25 km (16 miles) northwest of Brockville, got itself on the tourist maps of Ontario by painting the town, a promotional gimmick initiated some years ago in Chemainus, British Columbia. The scenes are on the sides of buildings around town and range in size from 26 by 12 feet to 96 by 26 feet. There are twelve now and there's talk of more. The murals are eye-catching and almost force the visitor to park and wander around the pretty village for a leisurely look. For a brochure, contact: Village of Athens, P.O. Box 159, Athens ON K0E 1B0. (613) 924–2044.

Take County Road 5 past Graham Lake back to Highway 401 just east of Mallorytown. Return to Toronto on Highway 401, or alternate that tedium with sections of scenic, two-lane Highway 2.

SPECIAL EVENTS

End of April to early May. Multicultural Festival, Brockville. Ethnic displays, dancing, singing, drumming, food, folk art. At Brockville Memorial Centre.

End of June to first week of July. Riverfest, Brockville. Festival on the waterfront, arts and crafts, entertainment, children's activities, water events, family picnic. At the waterfront on Water Street.

Mid-July. Festival under the Stars, Morrisburg. An evening of homegrown and Eastern Ontario entertainment to make you laugh, sing, and dance. At Riverside Cedar Park.

Third week of July. Loyalist Days, Prescott. An 1812 reenactment, heritage displays, Loyalist events, artisan shows, entertainment. At Fort Wellington National Park, Leo Boivin Community Centre, and Prescott waterfront.

Early August. Automotion, Brockville. Souped-up cars, trucks, and antique vehicles. Blockhouse Island.

Mid-August. Cornfest, Athens. Sidewalk sales, art and crafts, shows, entertainment, corn roast, parade, antique steam engines. On Main Street.

Mid-August. Shadows of the Fort, Prescott. Evening tours include encounters with spirits from the fort's past. At Fort Wellington National Historic Site.

OTHER RECOMMENDED RESTAURANTS AND LODGINGS

Brockville

Days Inn, 160 Stewart Boulevard (exit 696 from Highway 401). (613) 342–6613. Fifty-six units, with a dining room, lounge, and swimming pool.

Cornwall

Best Western Parkway Inn, 1515 Vincent Massey Drive. (613) 932–0451. Ninety-one-unit motel with outdoor pool, whirlpool, and sauna.

Holiday Inn Express, 1625 Vincent Massey Drive. (613) 937–0111. A 112-room facility.

Days Inn, 1541 Vincent Massey Drive. (613) 937–3535. A sixty-unit motel.

FOR MORE INFORMATION

City of Brockville, P.O. Box 5000, 1 King Street West, Brockville, ON K6V 7A5. (613) 342—8772.

EASTERN ONTARIO

The Kingston Area

TOURING THE THOUSAND ISLANDS

2 NIGHTS

Hockey museum • Art • Historic fort • Cruises
Nineteenth-century architecture • Wild animals • Pubs

Kingston has been impressing visitors with its buildings since 1673. That was when LaSalle chose the city's future site for a meeting between Governor Frontenac and the Iroquois Indians. Before the meeting, Frontenac built a stockaded fort to impress the Indians in the hope of tapping into the fur trade. His marketing strategy was successful and a grateful Louis XIV appointed LaSalle commandant of the fort and gave him the surrounding land and islands in the St. Lawrence River as a seigneury.

There followed a succession of forts that were burned, blown up, or otherwise destroyed until the present-day Fort Henry was built between 1832 and 1836. The site on Point Henry was a natural for protection of the lucrative fur trade and so was the site of Kingston just across the mouth of the Cataraqui River, now also the mouth of the Rideau Canal.

Kingston, now a city of 141,200, is at the extreme eastern end of Lake Ontario where the lake empties into the St. Lawrence River. It was incorporated as a town in 1838 and as a city in 1846, and from 1841 to 1844 it was the capital of the Province of Canada. In anticipation that it would remain the capital, a city hall of magnificent classical design was built, which stands to this day and impresses the modern-day visitor.

Kingston is a compact, well-organized city with a downtown that invites strolling. Care has been taken with the development—and redevelopment—of the waterfront, and many of the city's nineteenth-century limestone build-

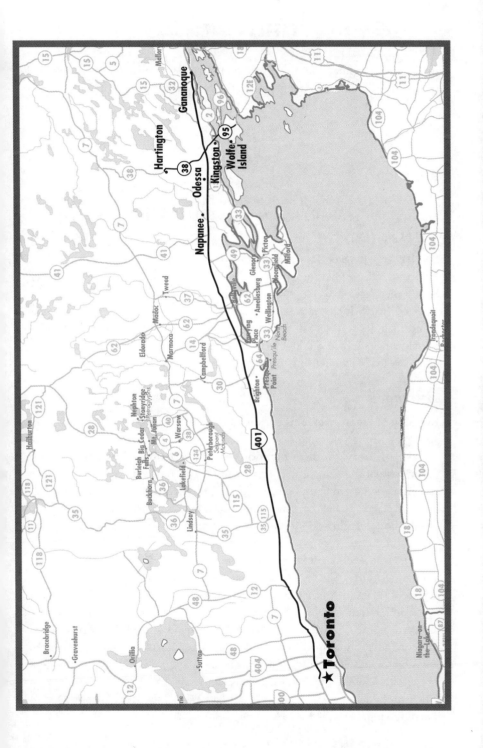

ings remain in mint condition. Even the federal penitentiary is an architectural gem—though visitors are not permitted to wander the grounds or photograph it.

DAY 1

Morning

It's 260 km (162 miles) from Toronto to Kingston, and you can do it all on Highway 401 or alternate on stretches of Highway 2 for a break from the tedium and heavy truck traffic.

LUNCH: Try the **Sax Restaurant,** downtown near the Inner Harbour. Exit Highway 401 on Division Street, and after 5 km (3 miles) turn left on Queen Street, then left on Wellington Street, and drive 2 blocks to 288 Wellington. The red-brick duplex was built in the late 1800s as a private residence. The menu includes steaks, veal, chicken, and pasta, with a wide range of desserts. Lunch will cost you $5.00–$10.00 per person. Open for lunch and dinner Monday–Friday, dinner only on Saturday; closed Sunday. (613) 549–4254.

Afternoon

Kingston has more museums per capita than any other place in Ontario. Take your pick of the following:

The **Military Communications and Electronics Museum** presents the history of the Canadian Forces Communications and Electronics Branch and all aspects of military communications. Fourteen minimuseums and galleries display flags, heliographs, Aldis lamps, Verey pistols, and a vast collection of telephones. Follow Highway 2 about 2 km (1.5 miles) east of downtown to the Vimy Gate. Turn right and follow signs to the rear of the Forde Building. Open in summer 8:00 A.M. to 4:00 P.M. Monday–Friday, 10:00 A.M. to 4:00 P.M. Saturday, Sunday, and holidays. During the rest of the year open 8:00 A.M. to 4:00 P.M. Monday–Friday. Free admission. (613) 541–5395.

Several hundred dolls and children's toys and other memorabilia of childhood are housed in **Polliwog Castle Antique Doll and Toy Museum,** a turn-of-the-century mansion 2 km (1.5 miles) north of Highway 401 on Division Street. Take exit 617 from Highway 401 or follow Division Street out of the city. Modest admission charge. Open daily 10:30 A.M. to 5:00 P.M. in July and August and weekends only May 24 to July 1 and Labor Day to Thanksgiving. (613) 548–4702.

Murney Tower Museum is in one of four martello towers built at the time of the Oregon Crisis in 1846 to bolster the city's defenses. (Martello towers are small, circular forts with massive walls usually erected on a coast to prevent enemy landings.) The walls of Murney Tower are 12 feet thick at the top and 15 feet thick at the base. Since 1925 it has housed military and social artifacts from nineteenth-century Kingston. It's at King and Barrie Streets. Admission $2.00. Open daily May 20 to September 4, 10:00 A.M. to 5:00 P.M. (613) 544–9925.

All you ever wanted to know about steam engines and their history is on display in the **Pump House Steam Museum,** a restored water pumping station at 23 Ontario Street. All exhibits run on steam and the collection is believed to be the world's largest. The 1849 pump house is an elegant Victorian building. Models range from miniatures to an 1897 Toronto-built engine with a nine-ton flywheel, 16 feet in diameter. A twenty-train model railroad operates Canadian, American, and European trains on 1,200 feet of track. Admission $3.95. Open daily 10:00 A.M. to 5:00 P.M.; closed Monday except for holidays. From mid-June to Labor Day all steam-powered displays are operating. (613) 546–4696.

The **Miller Museum of Geology and Mineralogy** shows the geology and fossils of the Kingston area, including dinosaur exhibits and an operating seismograph. No admission fee. On Queen's University campus at Union and Division Streets. Open Monday–Friday, 8:30 A.M. to 4:30 P.M. (613) 545–6767.

The history of Canada's century-old center of military education and some of the exploits of its graduates are told in exhibits in **Fort Frederick Martello Tower** at the **Royal Military College of Canada Museum.** The museum also contains the **Douglas Arms Collection,** which includes the small-arms collection of General Porfirio Diaz, president of Mexico from 1886 to 1912. On the grounds of Royal Military College off Highway 2 just east of Kingston. No admission charge. Open daily from last weekend in June through Labor Day, 10:00 A.M. to 5:00 P.M. (613) 541–6000 ext. 6664.

Kingston is the birthplace of organized hockey; the first league game was played here in 1885. In the **International Ice Hockey Federation Museum** there are displays of equipment, photographs, and "hockeyana." The museum shows the game's development from 1885 to the present and honors 200 hockey greats. At the corner of York and Alfred Streets, 1 block north of Princess Street (Highway 2). Admission $2.00. Open daily 10:00 A.M. to 5:00 P.M. mid-June through mid-September, and weekends 2:00 to 5:00 P.M. the rest of the year, or by appointment. (613) 544–2355.

A tour through the **Marine Museum of the Great Lakes at Kingston** comes in two parts. First is a rambling display area with artifacts, model ships, photographs, audiovisual presentations, charts, and paintings and sketches relating to Great Lakes shipping since 1678. The museum is at the former Kingston Drydock, itself a historic site.

The second part of the tour is aboard the 210-foot retired icebreaker *Alexander Henry.* Large numbers have been placed around the ship so visitors can take a self-guided tour. In summer you can rent a stateroom and sleep aboard (see Other Recommended Restaurants and Accommodations at the end of this chapter). Admission to museum, $3.95; admission to museum and ship, $5.45. At 55 Ontario Street. (613) 542–2261.

The **Kingston Archaeological Centre** documents the 8,000-year history of the area's human habitation. Admission is by donation. At 370 King Street West. Open Monday–Friday 9:00 A.M. to 4:00 P.M. (613) 542–3483.

The collection at the **Agnes Etherington Art Centre** has more than 7,500 paintings, sculptures, and graphics by major Canadian artists; European old master paintings; Inuit prints and sculpture; antique silver and glass; heritage quilts; European graphics; and African art. Agnes Etherington bequeathed her red-brick Georgian house to Queen's University as a permanent art center. On Queen's Campus at the corner of University Avenue and Queen's Crescent, with direct access from Highway 401 via Division Street exit. Open Tuesday–Friday 10:00 A.M. to 5:00 P.M., Thursday evenings until 9:00 P.M., Saturday and Sunday 1:00 to 5:00 P.M.; closed July through August and on statutory holidays. Nominal admission fee. (613) 545–2190.

Locals nicknamed the house at 35 Centre Street "Tea Caddy Castle," "Molasses Hall," and "Pekoe Pagoda," but Canada's first prime minister, who lived there for a year, called it **Bellevue House** because of its view over the St. Lawrence River. Sir John A. Macdonald's name for the Italianate villa-style house outlasted the nicknames. Today the house, with its proliferation of delicate balconies and three-story central tower, is a National Historic Park restored to the period when it was occupied by its most famous tenant.

It was built in 1840 by grocer Charles Hales, and Macdonald rented it in 1848, hoping its quiet seclusion would improve the chronic ill health of his wife, Isabella. At the time, Macdonald had been a member of the provincial cabinet and was a rising star in the Conservative party, though that party was not then in power. The move didn't help Isabella's health, Macdonald's law practice wasn't doing well, and after a year the couple moved to less pretentious quarters. Isabella died in 1857 and Macdonald threw himself into pub-

Kingston's Marine Museum of the Great Lakes.

lic life, eventually becoming Canada's first prime minister and receiving a knighthood.

The house is furnished with antiques, sketches, paintings, and all the social trappings of the era. Admission $2.75. Open April 1 to May 31 and Labor Day to October 31, 10:00 A.M. to 5:00 P.M. daily. From June 1 to Labor Day, open 9:00 A.M. to 6:00 P.M. daily. Closed Good Friday and Easter Monday. (613) 545–8666.

Kingston City Hall is the gorgeous domed limestone building on Ontario Street dominating the city's downtown and facing a riverfront park. There are tours Monday–Friday in summer, but you can wander into the lobby area anytime.

Kingston claims Canada's oldest **Farmers' Market.** It was created by the Crown in 1801 and continues on the same open-air site behind City Hall.

Open 6:00 A.M. to 6:00 P.M. on Tuesday, Thursday, and Saturday. A large craft market, also open Sundays, offers handcrafts, clothing, jewelry, and art.

Your feet will let you know how massive **Fort Henry** is. It was built during the War of 1812 to repel a possible American invasion that never came. It is operated by the St. Lawrence Parks Commission, and in summer students in period military costume guide visitors around the fort and hold parades. In July and August the Officer of the Day's Parade is held daily at 2:00 P.M., and the Sunset Ceremony is on Monday, Wednesday, and Saturday evenings, usually at 7:30 P.M. but days and times may change without notice. There are a number of museums within this museum—including one of Canada's largest collections of military arms, equipment, uniforms, and accoutrements. On Highway 2 at the intersection of Highway 15, in the east end of the city. Open daily May 20 to October 7, 10:00 A.M. to 5:00 P.M. (613) 542–7388.

DINNER: The **Kingston-1000 Islands Cruise Company** operates three-hour dinner cruises aboard their 300-passenger *Island Queen*, a triple-deck paddle wheeler. There's reserved seating, and table settings are china on linen with table service. The meal includes a prime rib beef buffet and salad bar. The cruise costs $42. New this year is a dinner cruise and theater package. Passengers dine during a two-hour cruise through the islands to Gananoque, docking at the **Thousand Island Playhouse** for a theatrical production. After the show a limo returns theater-goers to Kingston. The dock is at the foot of Brock Street. (613) 549–5544.

LODGING: You'll get a sense of Kingston's age and history at the **Queen's Inn.** It's an 1839 limestone and brick landmark rejuvenated by the Mitchell family with twenty-four light and airy guest rooms. **Coppers Good Eats Restaurant** serves salads, burgers, and steaks and has an outdoor patio. Daily specials and dinner entrees are $6.00–$14.00. Also in the hotel is **The Sports,** with free popcorn, a wide-screen TV, and a pub grub menu. Rooms cost $65–$99. At 125 Brock Street. (613) 546–0429.

DAY 2

Morning

BREAKFAST: At the Queen's Inn.

Take Highway 2 east for 16 km (10 miles) to Grass Creek and the **MacLachlan Woodworking Museum.** The two-story log house was built in 1853. Everything you ever wanted to know about wood and its uses is explained, and there's a bewildering array of woodworking tools. The collection includes the almost-perfect wooden mousetrap! (613) 542–0543.

Continue east on Highway 2 to Gananoque and the **Gananoque Historic Museum** at 10 King Street East. The collection in the former 1863 Victoria Hotel is a strange mix: There are a Link trainer (simulated aircraft cockpit), a Victorian parlor, a pioneer country kitchen, Native artifacts, pioneer tools, old Canadian money, and a photo collection that reminds the visitor that this quiet town of 5,000 was once a bustling industrial center nicknamed "Birmingham of Canada." Open June through September, Monday–Saturday. (613) 382–4024.

Skydeck is 16 km (10 miles) east of Gananoque. It's a 400-foot tower from which you can see 50 km (31 miles) on a clear day. It's near the Ivy Lea Bridge, which spans four islands while crossing the St. Lawrence River to New York State. It has a restaurant, gift shop, and cheese and ice-cream shop.

LUNCH: The **Prince George Hotel** is an "in" spot you'll already have noticed while rushing from museum to museum yesterday. The 1809 gem is across the street from City Hall and its restaurants are popular. **Tir na n'og** ("Land of Youth" in Irish Gaelic) is a lively spot. Musicians play Celtic and East Coast music every night during the summer. Pub fare and menu staples such as salmon, chicken, and mussels. **Monte's**, which has the same menu, is an oh-so-trendy cigar lounge.

Afternoon

Take Highway 2 or Highway 401 west 20 km (14 miles) to Odessa and the **Historic Babcock Mill.** It was built in 1856 and is a fully operational water-powered sawmill where "Better Baskets by Babcock" are made and sold during summer. Small admission charge; tours offered July 1 to Labor Day, Thursday–Monday 10:00 A.M. to 4:00 P.M. (613) 389–8314 or (613) 386–7363.

Continue west to Napanee and the **Allan Macpherson House.** Macpherson was a mill owner, merchant, postmaster, publisher, commander of the militia, and justice of the peace. His Georgian-style house was built in 1826 and is furnished to period. On Wednesdays, June through August, there's a Scottish cream tea from 2:00 to 4:00 P.M. Gift shop, gardens, and picnic area overlooking the Napanee River. (613) 354–5982.

Head back toward Kingston and take Highway 38 north for 30 km (20 miles). Five km (3 miles) northwest of **Hartington**, geologists studying aerial photographs of the Canadian Shield discovered an immense crater in 1955. It's 2.5 km (1.6 miles) in diameter, 800 feet deep, and believed to have been caused by a meteorite crash 500 million years ago. It's marked by a plaque on the Babcock farm on Holleford Road. Note: The crater is surrounded by privately owned land and accessible only by permission of owner Irwin Babcock, who can be reached at (613) 372–2736 or (613) 372–2786.

Return to Kingston.

DINNER: The popular **Chez Piggy** is a unique eatery in one of Kingston's oldest buildings, constructed circa 1810. It was built as a livery stable and has an outdoor garden court patio. Dinner is served daily 6:00 to 9:30 P.M., and the "international home cooking" menu offers dishes like rack of lamb *au jus des olives*, aged rib steaks, and two daily special entrees. Dinners cost $15–$20. At 68R Princess Street, at the corner of King Street. (613) 549–7673.

LODGING: The Queen's Inn.

Evening

If pubs are your thing, Kingston has them! Try the **Royal Oak** (British), 331 King Street East, (613) 542–3339; the **Pilot House** (neighborhood pub), 265 King Street East at Johnson Street, (613) 542–0222; **Kirkpatrick's** (Irish), 76 Princess Street, (613) 544–1974; the **Toucan** (lively), down the alley at 76 Princess Street, (613) 544–1966; **Stages** (dance club—seven bars on five levels, sunken dance floor, laser show), 390 Princess Street, (613) 547–5553; the **Wellington Pub** (Irish, live blues Monday, jazz Thursday, and Irish music weekends), 207 Wellington Street, (613) 544–8526; and **Kingston Brewing Company** (Ontario's first brewery restaurant and Canada's first wine pub), 34 Clarence Street, (613) 542–4978.

DAY 3

Morning

BREAKFAST: At the Queen's Inn.

Head for home on either Highway 401 if you're in a hurry or Highway 2 if you want a more relaxed pace.

THERE'S MORE

The Kingston-1,000 Islands Cruise Company offers **lunch cruises** aboard the 300-passenger *Island Queen*. The three-course hot menu varies from day to day and the cost of the cruise plus lunch is $29.95. The company also operates the *Island Belle,* which offers one-hour **island and harbor cruises** on the hour at $16.80 from the company's dock at the foot of Brock Street. (613) 549–5544.

If you'd like to see for free most of what the *Island Belle* tour shows you, take the **Wolfe Island Ferry.** The Kingston terminal is at the intersection of Ontario Street and Barrack Streets and the ferry operates year-round, weather permitting. Frequent sailings from 5:45 A.M. to 2:00 P.M. and passage is free to passengers and vehicles. A one-way trip takes twenty minutes and provides a fine view of Kingston, Old Fort Henry, and the martello towers at Royal Military College. From Wolfe Island a ferry links to Cape Vincent, New York, May through October.

Wolfe Island is low and flat with quiet farms and peaceful roads wandering through woods and meadows, but there's an excellent dining spot 1 block from the ferry dock. The **General Wolfe Hotel** has three dining rooms and a bar/lounge, and large windows overlook the St. Lawrence River. The inviting dining room features linen tablecloths, comfortable furniture, and gracious service. Steaks and crêpes are flambéed at your table. (613) 385–2611.

Frontenac County Schools Museum at 5 Clergy Street East is in an 1853 limestone building that housed the County Grammar School, which was formed in 1792. Small admission fee. Open Monday–Friday, 9:00 to 12:00 A.M. and 1:00 to 4:00 P.M.; closed statutory holidays. (613) 544–9113.

The restored **Kingston Mills Blockhouse** on the Rideau Canal is operated by Canadian Parks Service and depicts the lifestyle of a soldier in the 1839 era. It's on Kingston Mills Road at Kingston Mills Lock Station, just north of Highway 401 from exit 619 or 623. No admission charge. Open daily May 18 to September 3 except August 20–23 and 27–30. (613) 359–5377.

SPECIAL EVENTS

Early June. Sandvisions, Kingston. Beach and grass volleyball tournaments, horse show and tournament, children's festival and playground, pony rides, dunk tank, barbecue, pancake breakfast. At Woodbine Park.

Late October. Gem, Mineral, and Craft Sale, Kingston. Handcrafted jewelry, gemstones, fossils, crystals, children's mine, rock-working demonstrations, crafts.

OTHER RECOMMENDED RESTAURANTS AND LODGINGS

Casa Domenico, 35 Brock Street. (613) 542–0870. Mediterranean cuisine overlooking Kingston's historic Market Square. Great antipasta, fresh salads, pasta, seafood, and veal dishes.

Lone Star Cafe, 251 Ontario Street. (613) 548–8888. Loaded with ambience. Tex-Mex Food. Southern BBQ, mesquite-grilled chicken, and hot spicey fare that goes well with an ice-cold beer. .

Wooden Heads, 192 Ontario Street. (613) 549–1812. Thin-crust pizzas from a wood-burning oven and Mediterranean-style tapas (finger-food snacks). Heated courtyard patio.

The Grizzly Grill, 395 Princess Street. (613) 544–7566. Fresh seafood, grilled meats, pastas, wood-oven pizza, and appetizers ranging from grilled alligator to spring rolls.

Ramada Inn, 1 Johnson Street. (613) 549–8100. Indoor pool.

Holiday Inn Kingston Waterfront, 1 Princess Street. (613) 549–8400. Indoor pool.

FOR MORE INFORMATION

Kingston Area Economic Development Commission, 209 Ontario Street, Kingston ON K7L 2Z1. (613) 548–4415 or (888) 855–4555.

Ottawa and Hull, Québec
THE NATION'S CAPITAL

2 NIGHTS

The Hill • The world's longest skating rink
Pageantry • Cruises • Museums

As befits the national capital, Ottawa has a wealth of delights, from museums and beautiful natural scenery to lovely historic buildings and the finest in dining and entertainment. It's a city that impresses foreigners and instills a massive dose of national pride in visiting Canadians.

Queen Victoria chose Ottawa as the capital for five reasons, all valid at the time. The site was politically acceptable to both Canada East and Canada West; it was centrally located; it was remote from the then-hostile United States, it was industrially prosperous, and it had a beautiful setting at the confluence of the Ottawa and Rideau Rivers.

Thanks to the efforts of the National Capital Commission (NCC), Ottawa has remained beautiful. The NCC works with all municipalities within the 3,000-square-kilometer National Capital Region—including a big chunk of Québec—to coordinate development in the best interests of the region. Nothing may be erected or altered within the region without NCC approval.

The result is a profusion of beautiful parks, bicycle paths, jogging trails, and the world's longest skating rink, a 6-km (4-mile) stretch of the Rideau Canal kept cleared and smooth and serviced by heated huts, food concessions, and skate-sharpening and rental services. Skating the Rideau by day or night is one of the must-do things in Ottawa, and don't be surprised if you spot briefcase-toting bureaucrats and businessmen skating to and from their offices.

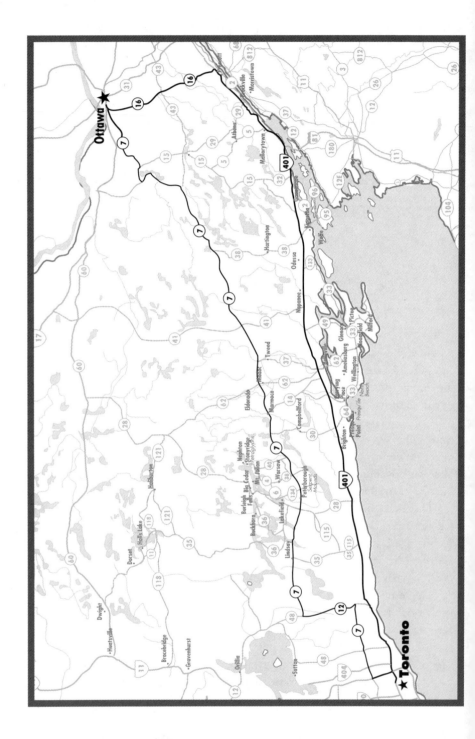

Ottawa's population is only 314,000, but it's a tricky city for the visitor to negotiate by car, and parking is at a premium. One wrong turn, it seems, and you're on one of five bridges across the Ottawa River to Hull, Québec. Prepare for your visit with a free information kit from Ottawa Tourism and Convention Authority, listed under For More Information at the end of this chapter.

DAY 1

Morning

It's 400 km (250 miles) from Toronto to Ottawa and you can do it in five-plus hours on Highway 7 or four-plus hours on Highways 401 and 16.

LUNCH: For a lunch break, see Eastern Ontario Escape One or Two, or try **Anthony's** in Gananoque. Take exit 645 and you'll find it on the river side of the main street at 37 King Street East. It's a cozy place with ambience, good service, daily specials in the $4.50–$6.95 range, and an extensive menu. A couple can usually be slipped in during high season, but four or more people should make a reservation even for lunch because it's popular with locals or travelers in the know. (613) 382–3575.

Afternoon

In Ottawa, the rule of thumb about first taking a city tour and then returning on your own to places that piqued your interest is particularly true. Tour buses and vans can get you to many places you can't take your own car. They can also slow to a crawl while passing the **prime minister's residence,** the **Centre Block,** and other points of interest. After you've taken a tour and heard the tour guide's spiel, you can do much of the rest of your sightseeing on foot.

Gray Line offers a two-hour, 50-kilometer (31-mile) **National Capital Tour** daily April through October from Wellington Street near your lodgings, or they'll pick you up at your hotel. (613) 725–1441.

Capital Double-Decker Trolley Tours offers on-and-off privileges at all major attractions, including the **Museum of Civilization** in Hull, and has free hotel pickup and a coupon that will give you discounted admission to museums. Adult fare is $20. (613) 729–7444.

The **Ottawa Riverboat Co.** offers daily ninety-minute **boat tours** on the Ottawa River and dinner and brunch tours. Departure points are at the foot of the Rideau Locks (between The Hill and the Chateau, where you'll be staying) or at Jacques Cartier Park in Hull. Ticket kiosks are in Confederation Square and Jacques Cartier Park. The company uses the 280-passenger *Sea Prince II* and the smaller, more elegant *Senator*. Fares are $14, $12 for seniors. (613) 562–4888 or (613) 778–2092.

DINNER: The **Courtyard Restaurant** is tucked into a courtyard at 21 George Street. Here fine French cuisine is served in dining rooms on two levels of a lovely old limestone building steeped in Ottawa history. The forerunner of today's elegant dining establishment was a log tavern built in 1827, likely inspired by construction of the Rideau Canal, then the largest construction project in North America. The humble log tavern was replaced by the Ottawa Hotel a decade later, and the building saw a variety of uses until it fell into disuse in 1912. Before the turn of the century, Canada's last military public hanging was held in the restaurant's courtyard. The chef uses all market-fresh meats and vegetables for traditional and innovative dishes. Daily specials for lunch and dinner. (613) 241–1516.

LODGING: There's only one **Chateau Laurier Hotel** and it's in Ottawa, so if you're here to get to know the city, it's the place to stay. The "Chateau," one of Canada's great railroad hotels, was built in 1916 with 425 rooms, an indoor pool, and a variety of dining rooms, lounges, and bars. It overlooks the Rideau Locks and is steps away from everything you'll want to see. There are more expensive hotels and certainly less expensive ones, but the Chateau is part of the Ottawa experience. Room rates vary daily based on occupancy levels, and the hotel has many package deals. Room rates are $249–$409, the latter price for a suite. For information contact: Chateau Laurier Hotel, 1 Rideau Street, Ottawa ON K1N 8S7. (613) 241–1414. Reservations: (800) 441–1414.

DAY 2

Morning

BREAKFAST: At the Chateau Laurier Hotel.

As with London's Buckingham Palace, the visitor moving around Ottawa has to pass the striking **Parliament Buildings** whether he or she plans to visit them or not, but they're usually at the top of the must-see list for any Canadian on a first visit to the capital. Free tours year-round except on Christmas and New Year's Days. Following the tour, visitors may go up the **Peace Tower** (except after the last tour of the day). To avoid waiting in the busy summer period, visitors may make same-day tour reservations at

Canada's Parliament Buildings.

Infocentre (613–239–5000 or 800–465–1867), 90 Wellington Street, close to the Chateau, or in summer at **Infotent,** a large white tent between Centre and West Blocks.

You can get a free, outdoor self-guiding booklet of the site and have questions answered by staff. At the allotted hour of their tour, visitors enter Centre Block through the **Visitor Welcome Centre.** (Allow fifteen minutes for security screening and an orientation exhibit.) When Parliament is in session you can get a pass to sit in the public galleries of the **Senate** or **House of Commons** to listen to debates. In the House of Commons galleries a recorded message tells visitors about the activities and artwork in the chamber. Question Period takes place in both chambers.

There's lots of room to stand and no charge to watch the **Changing of the Guard** ceremony, which takes place daily at 10:00 A.M. June 27 to August 29, weather permitting. The Ceremonial Guard brings together two of Canada's oldest regiments, the **Canadian Grenadier Guards,** who have white plumes on their towering black busbies (beaver fur hats) and the **Governor General's Foot Guards,** who have red plumes. They form ranks at **Cartier Square Drill Hall** at 9:30 A.M. and march to The Hill for a 10:00 A.M. appearance.

In 1869, Sir John A. Macdonald authorized the firing of a **noon gun** to regulate the postal service. (The cannon doesn't seem to do much for mail service, but the ceremony still interests tourists.) The nine-pound, muzzle-loading ship's cannon is fired weekdays at noon, and at 10:00 A.M. on Sunday and holidays. It's in Major's Hill Park off Mackenzie Avenue. In the same park there's a monument to Col. John By, who helped build the Rideau Canal.

The **Royal Canadian Mint** no longer makes coins, but you can watch tokens, medals, commemoratives, and bullion investment coins being made at the 1908 mint at 320 Sussex Drive (Canadian circulating coinage has been made in Winnipeg since 1976). Tours of the mint are free but by appointment only. Available year-round on weekdays except holidays, 9:00 A.M. to 4:30 P.M. (613) 993–8990.

Rideau Hall is an 1838 stone mansion that has been the residence of the governor general of Canada since 1865, and it's where visiting heads of state and members of the Royal Family stay while they're here on official visits. Free walking tours of the grounds are conducted year-round, but days and times change frequently. The tour route is wheelchair-accessible and free wheelchairs and strollers are available. (613) 998–7113 or (800) 465–6890.

Sentries of the Canadian Grenadier Guards and the Governor General's Foot Guards are posted outside the main gate of Rideau Hall from late June through August. The guard changes hourly, 9:00 A.M. to 5:00 P.M.

The **National Gallery of Canada** is a magnificent temple to art and a mirror in granite and glass of the **Parliamentary Library.** The gallery contains a huge collection of Canadian art, including many works by the Group of Seven. Inside is the reconstructed **Rideau Convent Chapel,** a classic example of nineteenth-century French Canadian architecture that has the only neo-Gothic fan-vaulted ceiling on the continent. There are three restaurants and a bookstore. Daily tours are given at 11:00 A.M. and 2:00 P.M. Admission charged every day except Thursday. Located at 380 Sussex Drive. (613) 990–1985.

War buffs will enjoy the sort of displays you'll find in the **Canadian War Museum**—torpedoes, tanks, guns, uniforms, military vehicles and planes, a World War I trench, and artifacts from as far back as the days when Canada was a French colony. It's the largest collection in Canada. At 330 Sussex Drive;

open daily except Christmas Day, 9:30 A.M. to 5:00 P.M. Small admission fee, except on Thursday; Canadian veterans are admitted free. (613) 776–8600.

Follow Sussex Drive past Rideau Hall to the Rockcliffe Driveway, then follow the signs for 4 km (2.5 miles) to the **National Aviation Museum** at Rockcliffe Airport. There are more than 100 aircraft in the collection, from a replica of the Silver Dart that made the first powered flight in Canada to World War I Sopwiths and the nose section of an Avro Arrow. There are air-oriented video games and four theaters. Small admission charge, except on Thursday. Free parking. (613) 993–2010 or (800) 463–2038.

Don't plan on rushing through the **National Museum of Science and Technology.** There are permanent displays of printing presses, antique cars, steam locomotives, and agricultural machinery, plus ever-changing exhibits, many of which are hands-on. All of the exhibits focus on Canadian accomplishments and the transformations they have caused in Canada. There are exhibits on marine and land transportation, astronomy, communications, space, and computer technology. Take the St. Laurent Boulevard South exit from the Queensway. The entrance is 1.6 km (1 mile) south, off Lancaster Road, and there's free parking. Small admission fee, free on Thursday. (613) 991–3044.

The dinosaur collection at the **Canadian Museum of Nature** is fabulous and so are the stuffed birds and animals in simulated habitats. Modest admission fee, free on Thursday. At McLeod and Metcalfe Streets. (613) 566–4700 or (800) 263–3344.

The scouting movement and the life of Lord Baden-Powell, its founder, are chronicled in photos, books, artifacts, and displays at the **Museum of Canadian Scouting** at 1345 Baseline Road. Follow Queen Elizabeth Driveway southwest past Dows Lake and turn right off Baseline Road. Open weekdays 9:00 A.M. to 4:30 P.M. Free admission. (613) 224–5131.

Ottawa claims it is the only national capital with an operating farm within its downtown area, and the **Central Experimental Farm/Agricultural Museum** is not just a token effort. You can see the best of the country's cattle and swine, take a ride on a horse-drawn wagon, or visit the gigantic arboretum. Researchers produce thirty-five to forty new plant varieties here each year; this is where "peaches and cream" corn was developed. It's on Experimental Farm Driveway. Follow Queen Elizabeth Driveway southwest past Dows Lake and turn right at the traffic circle. Free parking and admission. Open daily 9:00 A.M. to 5:00 P.M. except Christmas and New Year's Days. (613) 991–3044.

LUNCH: A stroll away from the Chateau is **Le Cafe,** which advertises itself as the place "where locals take their guests." In warm weather dine on barbecued fare outside next to the Rideau Canal. Lunches start at $9.75. At 58 Elgin Street at Confederation Square. (613) 594–5127.

Afternoon

All the ancestors of the plastic credit card are at the **Currency Museum**— including bracelets made from elephant hair, cowrie shells, and whale's teeth. You'll also find what may be the world's largest coin and, of course, the most complete collection of Canadian notes and coins. At 245 Sparks Street. Free admission. (613) 782–8914.

Ottawa's oldest building houses the **Bytown Museum,** a collection of Colonel By and Ottawa memorabilia at the Rideau Locks between The Hill and the Chateau. By built the stone building in 1826 as his commissariat for payroll monies and supplies during construction of the canal. Small admission charge. (613) 234–4570.

The **Canadian Museum of Civilization** is in the Province of Québec, but since it's part of the Ottawa scene (literally), it's included here. You can see this immense, modern building on the Québec shore of the Ottawa River from a number of points around The Hill. Galleries, displays, films, lectures, theaters, and exhibitions chronicle thousands of years of Canadian history. In the Grand Hall there are six Native longhouses and towering totem poles, and you can travel through time with the help of life-size reconstructions of Canadian historical scenes. There are special exhibitions (for an additional fee) at Cinéplus, the first theater to use the IMAX and OMNIMAX systems. Admission charge, museum free on Thursday. At 100 Laurier, Hull. (613) 776–7010.

In 1943, Princess Juliana of the Netherlands fled the German invasion and took refuge in Ottawa. When her baby was born, the Dutch flag was flown on the Peace Tower and Parliament declared a portion of the hospital to be Dutch territory, thus entitling the "Dutch born" Princess Margriet to ascend the Dutch throne. A grateful Holland sends thousands of tulip bulbs to Ottawa each year. More than three million bulbs now bloom during the **Canadian Tulip Festival** each year, 250,000 of them in Commissioner's Park.

Don't try parking near 24 Sussex Drive, **home of Canada's prime minister.** (Security is extra tight since one night several years ago, when a man wandered past the Royal Canadian Mounted Police security guard into the bedroom of the prime minister's wife.) Your best view of the mansion is from a tour bus, which slows as it passes the gates, but all you get is a glimpse of a couple of roof gables and some expensive-looking landscaping. **Stornoway** is home of the Leader of the Opposition and security there is just as tight, but you can see a bit more of the mansion as you pass.

In 1949 the **Supreme Court of Canada** became the ultimate court of appeal in the land. Its nine judges sit in three sessions and hear an average of 120 cases a year in their stately Art Deco building on Wellington Street, just below The Hill. Public tours daily May through August, 9:00 A.M. to 5:00 P.M. Free admission. (613) 995–5361.

The **Mile of History** runs from The Hill to Rideau Hall, and on Sussex Drive north of Rideau Street a streetscape of nineteenth-century buildings has been restored to re-create one of Ottawa's most historic neighborhoods. There are boutiques, restaurants, galleries, cafes, fountains, and sculptures in the five Sussex Courtyards running from George Street to Patrick Street, a short distance from By Ward Market.

DINNER: The **Mill Dining Lounge.** From its position west of The Hill, close to Portage Bridge, this restored stone lumber mill overlooks the Ottawa River and offers continental cuisine. Roast prime rib and seafood are specialties. Great place for Sunday brunch. (613) 237–1311.

DAY 3

BREAKFAST: At the Chateau Laurier Hotel.

You haven't had time to see more than a fraction of what Ottawa has to offer so you may want to stay a few more days. If not, head for home!

SPECIAL EVENTS

First three weekends of February. Winterlude. Concerts, fireworks, snow and ice sculpture competitions, skating and sporting events throughout the region. In downtown Ottawa on Dows Lake and in Hull.

Mid–May. Canadian Tulip Festival. The world's largest tulip festival features more than three million blooms and a variety of cultural, floral, and horticultural-based activities.

Mid–May to mid–June. A Symphony of Sound and Light. Against the backdrop of the Parliament Buildings you can catch a half-hour sound and light show on Canada's history. Bleacher seating, shows are free. Check dates and times with Parliament Hill Infotent, (613) 239–5000.

Late May. A Canadian Sunset Ceremony. Evening outdoor equestrian performances by the Royal Canadian Mounted Police, including the world-famous Musical Ride at Canadian Police College.

First week of July. Bluesfest. The largest blues festival in Canada with fifteen acts in downtown Ottawa. Main site is Major's Hill Park.

Early July to Labor Day. A Symphony of Sound and Light.

Last half of July. Ottawa International Jazz Festival. A ten-day musical extravaganza with more than 125 performances at four official sites. Main site is Confederation Park.

End of July to first week of August. Ottawa Chamber Music Festival. One of the largest events of its kind in North America, featuring some of the world's finest musicians. Most performances are in downtown churches.

Mid-August. The Casino of Sound and Light, Hull. Teams from many countries compete in this international fireworks competition held at Leamy Lake.

End of August. Central Canada Exhibition, Ottawa. Entertainment, outdoor shows and attractions, large midway, themed pavilions, and agricultural displays. Landsdowne Park.

End of August. Ottawa Folk Festival. A lively celebration of traditional music held at Brittania Park. Dancing, storytelling, and crafts.

OTHER RECOMMENDED RESTAURANTS AND LODGINGS

Hy's Steak House, 170 Queen Street, Ottawa. (613) 234–4545. Steaks to die for. Expensive, but superb!

Kemp's Steakhouse and Pub, 5816 Hazeldean Road, Stittsville (exit onto Terry Fox Drive from the Queensway, and go south to Hazeldean Road, also known as Old Highway 7). (613) 836–1665. The three-story Gothic-style stone building was Kemp's Tavern in 1868; now owners Denise and José-Luis Perez serve lunch and dinner Monday–Friday and dinner only on Saturday.

FOR MORE INFORMATION

Ottawa Tourism and Convention Authority, 130 Albert Street, Suite 1800, Ottawa, ON K1P 5G4. (613) 237–5150 or (800) 363–4465.

Peterborough

EXPLORING THE KAWARTHA LAKES

2 NIGHTS

*Petroglyphs • Caves • Serpent mounds • Pioneer village
The world's highest lift locks • A gracious country resort*

Peterborough, a busy city of 68,000, makes a great base for exploring the Kawarthas, a series of large lakes riddling this hilly, picturesque section of the Canadian Shield. The city has some unique attractions and three noteworthy superlatives—the lift locks on the Trent-Severn Waterway, which are the world's highest; Centennial Fountain in Little Lake, which at 250 feet is the highest jet fountain in Canada; and the Hunter Street Bridge spanning the Otonabee River, which is the world's longest span without steel reinforcement.

The invention of the incandescent lamp by Thomas Edison led to formation of the Edison Electric Company, which located here in 1890. Two years later the name changed to General Electric Co., and the plant is Canada's largest electrical manufacturing unit. It specializes in heavy electric turbines and produced Canada's first atomic-powered generator.

Peterborough is also the name of a famous canoe and canoe manufacturing company. Jonathan Stephenson made the first basswood canoe here in 1870.

The city is on both banks of the Otonabee River, part of the Trent Canal System and, like most Ontario communities, started with a water-powered sawmill and gristmill. The mills here were built in 1821 by Adam Scott, and the settlement was first known as Scott's Plains. Two years later a wave of southern Irish immigrants arrived courtesy of an assisted emigration plan of the British Colonial Office. This was directed by the Hon. Peter Robinson, and the settlers honored him by naming the county and community after him.

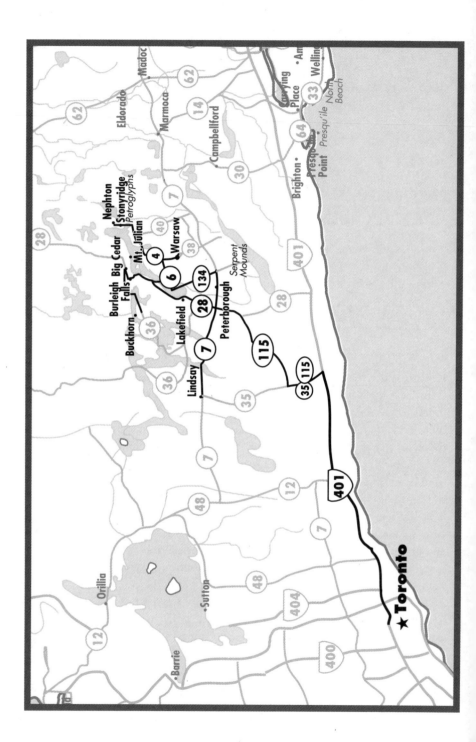

That's all history, but there's plenty for today's visitor to do. An ideal approach to the Kawarthas is to rent a houseboat and spend a week visiting the villages and towns at a leisurely pace, but the following two-night itinerary lets you cover the highlights.

DAY 1

Morning

Take Highway 7 or Highways 401 and 115 to Peterborough, a distance of 138 km (86 miles).

It may not sound like a big deal, but when you're underneath the huge **Peterborough Lift Lock** and a 40-foot houseboat and its passengers are on the way up, the marvel of it sinks in. The world's highest hydraulic lift lock, built in 1904, lifts boats—and the 1,700 tons of water they're floating in—65 feet straight up in less than ten minutes.

The lock and **Trent Canal** operate mid-May through mid-October and in winter there's public skating on the canal. Overlooking the lock is the **Lift Lock Visitor Centre** where slides and films explain the workings of the Trent Canal System and the Peterborough Lock. At Hunter Street East at Ashburnham Drive. Open daily from mid-May through mid-October; in winter open only Wednesday–Sunday. No admission fee, lots of free parking.

LUNCH: Stoney Lake Cruises operates two-hour lunch tours, with a hot buffet and salad bar, through the lift locks May through mid-October. From the end of May through June tours are given on Saturday and Sunday at 1:30 P.M.; from the end of June to Labor Day cruises are at 11:00 A.M. and 1:30 P.M. daily. The company also offers dinner cruises July through August. The two-hour tours cost $15 and the dinner-dance cruise costs $35. From the end of June through mid-August on Wednesday and Saturday, the *Island Princess* offers special dinner tours to the **Festival of Lights.** The festival features free concerts from 7:30 to 9:30 P.M. followed by an illuminated boat show wrapped up with a fireworks display. Reservations recommended for meal cruises. (705) 654–5253.

Afternoon

There's free admission to the **Art Gallery of Peterborough,** which overlooks Little Lake. Open Victoria Day to Thanksgiving, Tuesday–Sunday 1:00 to 5:00 P.M., until 9:00 P.M. on Wednesday. The rest of the year, Tuesday–

Sightseeing along the Trent Canal.

Friday noon to 4:00 P.M., Saturday 10:00 A.M. to 5:00 P.M., Sunday 1:00 P.M. to 5:00 P.M. (705) 743–9179.

Costumed guides show you through the **Hutchison House Museum,** a nineteenth-century doctor's home 2 km (1.5 miles) north of Lansdowne on Aylmer Street, then west on Brock Street. Admission $2.00. Open May through October, Tuesday–Sunday 1:00 to 5:00 P.M.; November through March, Monday–Friday 1:00 to 5:00 P.M. Closed in April. (705) 743–9710.

There's no admission fee to **Riverview Park and Zoo,** a fifty-acre park on the Otonabee River just north of the city. There are playgrounds with slides and rides, a spray pool, picnic facilities, a miniature railroad, and a zoo with more than 200 species.

DINNER AND LODGING: One of Ontario's oldest and most gracious country resorts is 40 km (25 miles) north on Stoney Lake. When **Viamede Resort**

opened in 1865, its guests were mostly Americans. It's now open year-round and draws more Canadians. There are thirty-three rooms in the main lodge; fourteen one-, two-, and three-bedroom lakeside cottages; and seven super-deluxe motel-style suites. The 175-seat Empress Dining Room overlooks Stoney Lake, and French doors open onto a licensed patio. A favorite item on the menu is chateaubriand with béarnaise sauce for two.

In summer there are all the usual activities of a lakeside resort. As for winter activities, Viamede is an hour's drive from the **Bethany** and **Devil's Elbow** alpine ski areas and in the middle of a network of 85 km (53 miles) of cross-country ski trail.

Room rates range from $105 to $195 per person, double occupancy, including breakfast and dinner. To get there, take Highway 28 north to Mount Julian and look for signs to the resort. (705) 654–3344.

DAY 2

Morning

BREAKFAST: At Viamede Resort.

Warsaw Caves Conservation Area is 8 km (5 miles) east of Lakefield, 2 km (1.2 miles) east of County Road 4, north of Warsaw. Here you can go underground and follow tunnels in limestone bedrock carved by prehistoric rivers. Bring a powerful flashlight. The conservation area has caves and potholes created by glacial meltwaters 10,000 years ago that can be seen along 13 km (8 miles) of hiking trails. Open daily June to Labor Day. Admission $6.00 per car, $7.00 on weekends. (705) 745–5791.

Buckhorn is a village of 250 on the Trent Canal between Buckhorn and Lovesick Lakes, 18 km (12 miles) north of Lakefield and 30 km (20 miles) north of Peterborough. The **Gallery On The Lake** is 3 km (2 miles) east, off Highway 36, on Gallery Road and open daily 9:00 A.M. to 5:00 P.M. This is Canada's largest privately owned art gallery and it has paintings, sculptures, art supplies, and the **Buckhorn School of Fine Arts.** Free admission. (705) 657–3296.

The **Whetung Craft Centre & Art Gallery** is on the **Curve Lake Reserve,** between Buckhorn and Chemong Lakes, 8 km (5 miles) west of Highway 507 on Curve Lake Road. The log and stone building is guarded at the entrance by large totems. Inside there's an impressive display of aboriginal crafts and fine art from across Canada. Open daily 9:00 A.M. to 9:00 P.M. July to Labor Day and 9:00 A.M. to 5:00 P.M. the rest of the year. Closed December 25 to January 4. (705) 657–3661.

LUNCH: Try the good, home-style food at **Smitty's Family Restaurant** in Peterborough at 139 George Street North. Reservations not needed. (705) 741–3604.

Afternoon

Keene is 10 km (6 miles) southeast of Peterborough, and **Serpent Mounds Provincial Park** is 3 km (2 miles) south of Keene on County Road 34, on Rice Lake. About 2,000 years ago, the Point Peninsulas, a nomadic Indian tribe, buried their dead in nine earth mounds, the largest of which is 200 feet long and shaped like a serpent. An interpretation center explains the site and displays artifacts recovered in archaeological digs. Open mid-May to Labor Day for regular provincial park fees; free off-season.

Six km (4 miles) north of Keene, **Lang Pioneer Village** has twenty fully restored pioneer buildings between the 1846 Lang Grist Mill and the 1870 Hope Sawmill. The site includes a store, church, inn, blacksmith shop, cider barn, shingle mill, homesteads, and displays and demonstrations of pioneer arts and crafts throughout the summer. Open late May to Labor Day, Monday–Saturday noon to 5:00 P.M., Sunday 1:00 to 4:00 P.M.; during the rest of the year open Monday–Friday 9:00 A.M. to 4:00 P.M. (705) 295–6694.

Canada's largest single concentration of Indian rock carvings was discovered in 1954. They're now protected in **Petroglyphs Provincial Park** at the east end of Stoney Lake outside the hamlet of Stonyridge. The site, 50 km (35 miles) northwest of Peterborough, offers well-preserved symbols and figures carved on a flat expanse of white marble 21 meters (17.5 yards) wide. There are more than 900 carvings believed to be of Algonkian spirit figures and made 500–1,000 years ago. The site, off Highway 28, 11 km (7 miles) east on Northey's Bay Road, is open daily mid-May to Thanksgiving, 10:00 A.M. to 6:00 P.M. Admission $6.00 per car. (705) 877–2552.

The 144-passenger *Chippewa II* offers 35-km (20-mile) day and evening cruises through Lower Stoney Lake and Upper Clear Lake from late May through mid-October. Departures are from a dock 7 km (4 miles) north of Burleigh Falls, off Highway 28 on the Mount Julian–Viamede Road. The boat cruises past some of the 1,128 islands of Stoney Lake and other points of interest. The day cruise costs $15; the dinner cruise is $30. For reservations call (705) 654–5253.

From Lindsay, 45 km (30 miles) west of Peterborough, cruises of varying length are offered on the Kawartha Lakes and along the Trent-Severn Waterway. The forty-four-passenger *Skylark VIII* offers five- and six-hour dinner cruises to Fenelon Falls or Bobcaygeon and shorter daytime sightseeing trips on the lakes and waterway. For reservations call (705) 324–8335.

DINNER: Locals dine at **Carousel Restaurant,** whose menu runs the gamut of steaks, seafood, pastas, salads, and a great buffet. At 119 Lansdowne Street East. (705) 745–0060.

LODGING: Viamede Resort.

DAY 3

Morning

BREAKFAST: At Viamede Resort.

See the places of interest you couldn't fit into yesterday's itinerary and then head for home—it's only a ninety-minute drive.

SPECIAL EVENTS

End of May. Victoria Day, Lakefield. Free horse and wagon rides and kiddie sports.

Late June to mid-August. Summer Festival of Lights, Peterborough. Canadian talent; musical, dance, and theatrical entertainment; illuminated boat show; fireworks. At Del Crary Park.

July 1. Multicultural Day, Peterborough. Foods from countries around the world and family entertainment. At Del Crary Park.

Early July. Peterborough Annual Exhibition, Morrow Park. Crafts, home baking, flower displays, and livestock shows.

Early August. Contest Day, Lang Pioneer Village. Pioneer games, such as nail driving, log sawing, and hay-bale tossing.

Early August. The Peach Tea, Peterborough. Celebrating the peach season, house tours, old-time fiddle music, tea, scones, peaches, cream, and blueberries. At Hutchison House Museum.

OTHER RECOMMENDED RESTAURANTS AND LODGINGS

Burnham House, 760 Lansdowne Street East. (705) 742–4299. Traditional North American menu with prime rib, lamb, poultry, fish, and great desserts. In an old yellow brick mansion. Open daily for lunch and dinner.

The Electric Clove, 25 George Street South. (705) 876–6721. Specializes in salads and pasta. Open daily.

Champs Bar, 203 Simcoe Street. (705) 742–3431. Offers pub grub—chip 'n' dip, basket-cut fries—and cheap draft beer.

Comfort Inn, 1209 Lansdowne Street West. (705) 740–7000 or (800) 221-2222. This modestly priced hostelry allows pets, an unusual privilege in hotels of this size: It has 104 rooms and 12 suites. There's also an indoor pool and whirlpool. Rates range from $85 to $160, which includes continental breakfast.

Holiday Inn Peterborough Waterfront, 150 George Street North. (705) 743–1144 or (800) 465–4329.

FOR MORE INFORMATION

Peterborough Kawartha Tourism and Convention Bureau, 175 George Street North, Peterborough ON K9J 3G6. (705) 742–2201 or (800) 461–6424.

Picton, Prince Edward County, and Belleville

QUINTE'S ISLE AND
THE NEARBY MAINLAND

2 OR 3 NIGHTS

A bucolic island • Canada's Plymouth Rock • Sand dunes
Superlative dining • A cozy mansion

New Englanders wandering **Quinte's Isle** could easily find themselves wondering whether they had left home. Not only is the scenery similar; the people are, too. So similar are the pages of history that brought both places into being that there's a village here locals call the Plymouth Rock of Ontario.

You won't find Quinte's Isle on your road map. It shows instead as Prince Edward County, a large island riddled with bays and inlets in the northern corner of Lake Ontario, west of Kingston and immediately south of Belleville.

Prince Edward County wasn't always an island. It was once a peninsula known to settlers as Little Spain, but the construction of the Murray Canal cut Prince Edward County from the mainland, creating Ontario's only island county. It's linked to the mainland by three bridges and a free ferry between Glenora and Adolphustown 9 km (6 miles) east of Picton on Highway 33.

The island has a coastline of more than 800 km (500 miles). There are neatly kept farms, many surviving from the pioneer era when barns and drive sheds were erected at the roadside to avoid building and plowing driveways. For mile after mile on quiet side roads the only sign of life is cattle grazing in rolling, shaded meadows. The county was first known as Presqu'ile de Quinté,

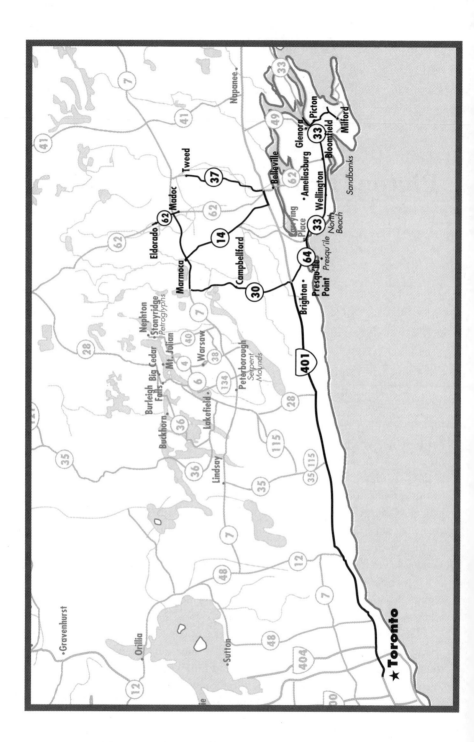

taking its name from Kenté, a mission to the Indians maintained by the Sulpicians from 1660 to 1680.

The district's earliest burial ground is here, and an 1822 Loyalist church is now a parish meeting hall. Picton is a serene little town of 4,000 with fine old buildings and strong associations with Sir John A. Macdonald, Canada's first prime minister. Sir John's father operated a flour mill there and young John practiced law at the Picton courthouse. The island draws thousands for its quiet bays and sandy beaches, geological oddities, and history, much of which is preserved in museums.

DAY 1

Morning

Take Highway 401 to exit 509, a distance of 157 km (98 miles), and follow signs to Brighton. Take County Road 64 to Carrying Place and then Highway 33 across the island to Picton.

LUNCH: Fine dining is offered at Isaiah Tubbs' **The Restaurant on the Knoll Overlooking the Sandbanks at West Lake.** (That's the correct name of the restaurant and that's what it overlooks.) The cuisine is North American. Lunch entrees run $6.00–$11.00, dinners $15.00–$22.00. On West Lake Road at West Lake. (613) 393–2090.

Afternoon

At the age of six, William Macaulay inherited 500 acres of land from his father, who died in 1800. While William was studying theology at Oxford, a village grew on his land, which as early as 1816 he called **Picton** after Gen. Sir Thomas Picton, a major-general in the Napoleonic wars. William built **St. Mary Magdalene Church** in 1825 and was its first rector. Nearby he built the Georgian-style **Macaulay House** and in 1864 added a new sanctuary, chancel, tower, and spire. In 1970 the church became the **Prince Edward County Museum.**

In 1974 the county bought Macaulay's former home, restored it, and furnished it to the 1850s era. The church and house comprise **Macaulay Heritage Park,** open Victoria Day to Labor Day, 10:00 A.M. to 4:30 P.M. Monday–Friday and 1:00 to 4:30 P.M. Saturday and Sunday. At Church and Union Streets, 1 block south of Highway 33.

In 1831 Prince Edward County was declared a separate administrative district, contingent on having a courthouse at Picton. The stone Greek Revival structure was completed in 1834 and **Picton Court House** is one of Ontario's oldest public buildings still in use. Tours are available by prior arrangement, and the attached jail may also be visited. A double gallows is kept handy, although it hasn't been used since 1884. It's at Church and Union Streets. To arrange a tour, call (613) 476–3833.

The **White Chapel,** also known as Conger Chapel or Old Chapel, is a wooden Methodist meetinghouse built in 1809. It was the first Methodist church in the county and has been maintained as a place of worship longer than any other church of Methodist origin in Ontario. Open Sunday in July and August. On Highway 49 go 3 km (2 miles) north of Picton. To arrange a visit call the church office at (613) 476–6050, Monday–Friday 9:00 A.M. to noon.

The **Lake on the Mountain** really shouldn't be there, perched 200 feet above Lake Ontario, so there have been many theories about it . . . and of course there's an Indian legend. The legend, however, is a love story and has nothing to do with how the lake was formed—only why you may hear anguished cries echoing across it at dawn.

The process by which the lake was formed remains unknown, but here's the most popular theory: Through glacial action a ravine was created, and approximately 96,000 years ago at the eastern end of the lake, a 35-foot-deep plug of glacial fill blocked the ravine. It is believed that the glacier stood still for a time, creating a plunge basin, or falls, deepening the bottom of the ravine to 96 feet. The lake provides a flow of sixty gallons per minute of beautifully clear, cold water for the fish tanks of the **Glenora Fisheries Research Station** below, adjacent to the Glenora Ferry Dock. But where that water keeps on coming from is a mystery because there's no visible inlet to the lake.

There are picnic tables around the lake and across the road there's a lookout across Picton Bay. To get there, follow County Road 7 to **Lake-on-the-Mountain Provincial Park,** just before you reach the Glenora Ferry Dock.

Interesting bits of history can be seen at **Ameliasburgh Historical Museum,** a collection of pioneer buildings and artifacts. Visitors enter through the First Methodist Church of Ameliasburgh, erected in 1868. In the churchyard are a log cabin, weaver's cottage, blacksmith shop, sap shanty, cobbler's shop, beekeeper's display, corn cribs, and an implement barn. A 1910 steam engine with 265,000-pound flywheel still works, and also of interest is a four-horse scoop used for excavations of the Murray Canal. Open daily

Sandbanks Provincial Park between Picton and Bloomfield.

10:00 A.M. to 4:30 P.M. June through August, and weekends in May and Labor Day to Thanksgiving. On County Road 19, about 6 km (4 miles) west of Highway 62. Admission $3.00. (613) 968–9678.

Sandbanks Provincial Park is 18 km (12 miles) from Picton and a beautiful place to visit, but it stands as a tacit warning about man meddling with nature. In their attempts to use the land, settlers felled the trees, tilled the land, and let their livestock overgraze the vegetation. The thin layer of topsoil eroded, increased the movement of the sand, and caused the dunes to form. They grew to a height of 80 feet and started traveling 40 feet a year. Sections of West Lake Road had to be replaced four times, many homes were abandoned, and a brick factory was eventually smothered by the sand.

Today a reforestation program has stabilized the dunes, and the park is a great place to tan, picnic, swim, camp, or sail. Exhibits at the visitors center explain the history, and staff answer questions and guide nature hikes. Reservations are recommended for the 411 campsites. (613) 393–3319.

The day-use **North Beach Provincial Park** is at the west end of the island 35 km (22 miles) from Picton. The park has no camping, but there's a beautiful beach 3 km (2 miles) long. It's open mid-June through September.

Mariners Park Museum is at the hamlet of South Bay on County Road 9, about 16 km (10 miles) south of Picton. Most of the collection is wreckage recovered from steamboats, schooners, and barges that have sunk or been wrecked on the coast. Open daily 9:00 A.M. to 5:00 P.M., July through August, and weekends 9:00 A.M. to 5:00 p.m., Victoria Day through July and Labor Day to Thanksgiving. Admission $2.00. (613) 476–8392.

Scott's Mill is run by **Milford Pond Conservation Area,** and you can see how logs were turned into timber and wheat was turned into flour. Joseph Clapp built the mill in 1808, but half a century later it was bought by William Scott, whose family operated it for three generations until the 1950s. At Milford, 12 km (9 miles) south of Picton. Open Saturday, Sunday, and holidays July through August. (613) 476–7408.

DINNER: The **Bloomfield Inn** has a comfortable feel. It isn't one of those pretentious mansions where guests feel as if conversations ought to be whispered, in awe of grand fixtures and fittings. Henry and Angeline Hubbs had the place built in 1869 and the new owners haven't messed around with the original floor plan or woodwork. **Angeline's Restaurant** uses three of the rooms, furnished with antiques and old oils. Open in summer for dinner daily except Tuesday, and in winter Wednesday–Sunday. The menu offers pheasant breast with glazed raisins, poached Atlantic salmon in a lemon cream sauce and golden caviar, and three variations of local lamb. There's a low-calorie menu and the exact opposite—a three-course belt-strainer. Entrees are $17–$27. Angeline's is on Loyalist Parkway at County Roads 62 and 33. Reservations recommended. (613) 393–3301.

LODGING: The **Merrill Inn** at 343 Main Street East was built in 1870 for barrister Edwards Merrill, a buddy of Sir John A. Macdonald. It's a short stroll from downtown and has been converted to a cozy twelve-room inn, where the visitor is made to feel like a guest in a friend's historic mansion. And the friend keeps a refrigerator stocked with juice and soft drinks and a sideboard with croissants, muffins, and tea and coffee ready twenty-four hours a day. There are fireplaces and sitting rooms and a staff member is always available. In the basement there's an English pub. Rooms are $95–$160. (613) 476–7451.

DAY 2

Morning

BREAKFAST: At the Merrill Inn because it's included in your room rate.

Off the island there are things to see in Belleville, Corbyville, Tweed, Eldorado, Madoc, Marmora, Campbellford, and Brighton. All the sights can be fitted into an easy day, making a loop in either direction.

Belleville, a city of 42,000, is 36 km (24 miles) north of Picton by Highways 33 and 62. It's situated at the mouth of the Moira River, which powered its first sawmill and gristmill in 1790. It has an impressive county courthouse, and the 1833 Italianate mansion **Glanworth** houses **Hastings County Museum,** a collection of antique furniture and art. The museum has a fine collection of antique lighting equipment and recalls the early days with a reproduction general store and pioneer kitchen. Victorian afternoon teas are offered in July and August. From June through August open 10:00 A.M. to 4:30 P.M. Tuesday–Friday, 1:00 to 4:30 P.M. Saturday and Sunday. From September though May open 1:00 to 4:30 P.M. Tuesday–Sunday. Admission $3.00. (613) 962–2329.

Just off Highway 37 north of Belleville, **J. P. Wiser Distillery** at **Corbyville** is in a bucolic setting on the Moira River. Henry Corby started making whiskey in 1859 as a sideline to his gristmill. Free tours are offered mid-May through August, 9:00 A.M. to 2:30 P.M. Monday–Friday, except on holiday Mondays. The tour is preceded by a fifteen-minute film. The half-hour tour ends at a reception center where a 150-year-old parquet bar glistens under Tiffany lamps. Visitors are usually offered a sample. (613) 962–4536.

The town of **Tweed** on Highway 37 (on your way to Madoc and Marmora) used to boast of having **North America's Smallest Jail**. It's a darling little limestone building on the main street, measuring 20 by 16 feet. But an even smaller jail was found in Port Dalhousie on Lake Ontario (now a part of St. Catharines). Tweed has another unique characteristic: Some imaginative soul has decorated all the hydrants with amusing animal faces well worth a look.

Eldorado was such a boomtown in 1866 that it had nineteen hotels. The excitement was over Ontario's first gold strike, but it was short lived. The population is now forty-nine and the only "gold" in town is at the only business, a creamery that makes Eldorado Gold Cheese.

Madoc, at Highways 7 and 62, was settled in 1820 and named after a legendary Welsh prince said to have discovered America in 1170. Five km

(3 miles) north of town on Highway 62 there's a pioneer museum. **O'Hara Mill Museum** includes the 1840 sawmill, an 1848 schoolhouse, a pioneer homestead, and antique vehicles and machinery. Open daily except Monday, May 24 to Labor Day.

Marmora was named after marble (from the Latin word *marmor*) because it had quarries, but the biggest mining operation was for iron. In the mid-1950s Bethlehem Steel Corp. stripped 20 million tons of limestone from above magnetite beds to allow open-pit mining. Docks were built in Picton to handle 1,500 tons of ore shipped daily to their refining plant at Lack-awanna, New York. The operation stopped years ago, and water has seeped into the pit. Even partially filled, the excavation is enormous and draws sightseers. It can be seen 0.5 km (0.3 miles) east of Marmora from a fenced viewing area just south of Highway 7.

Three locks on the Trent Canal system bypass **Healey Falls,** a series of cascades over which the Trent River drops 75 feet at **Campbellford.** Eighteen km (12 miles) south of town on Highway 30 is **Codrington Fish Culture Station** where brown trout are hatched and reared. At Codrington turn west on County Road 27 for 1.6 km (1 mile). Visitors are welcome daily year-round 9:00 A.M. to noon and 1:00 to 4:00 P.M.

Proctor House Museum is in a nineteenth-century mansion overlooking **Brighton** and Lake Ontario that was originally owned by a wealthy shipping magnate. It's furnished to period. Open daily 10:00 A.M. to 4:00 P.M. and Sunday 1:00 to 4:00 P.M. in July and August. At 96 Young Street, west of Highway 30 at Proctor Park Conservation Area. (613) 475–2144.

Just south of Brighton, a hook-shaped peninsula jutting into Lake Ontario has been turned into 2,000-acre **Presqu'ile Provincial Park.** (The translation from French is "almost an island.") The strange land formation used to be two limestone islands left by glaciers 10,000 years ago, but a series of sand and gravel spits formed, linking them to the mainland.

In 1802, a model town called Newcastle was to have been constructed there as capital of a new district comprising the present-day counties of Northumberland and Durham. In 1804 the courthouse was ready for use. It was to be inaugurated with the trial of an Ojibwa charged with murdering a fur trader. On October 7 the schooner *Speedy* departed York (Toronto) with the prisoner, lawyers, witnesses, judge, and other influential people. On October 9 *Speedy* rounded High Bluff Island during an unexpected storm, hit a rock, and sank without a trace. The entire party perished. The following spring the government of Upper Canada declared the town site of Newcastle an inconvenient location for a jail and courthouse. Two years later they chose the village of Amherst, later renamed Cobourg.

Head back to Toronto on Highway 401 west.

SPECIAL EVENTS

Mid-July. Kente Portage Festival, Carrying Place. Military reenactments, canoe races, children's programs, crafts, zoo, and concerts. At Fort Kente.

Last week and a half of July, first week of August. Quinte Summer Music Festival, Picton. Festival started in 1984 with the theme "in celebration of the oldest musical instrument—the human voice." For additional information about the festival or its artist-in-residence program, call (613) 393-2939.

Early August. Doll Show, Competition, and Sale, Marmora. Show and sale of dolls following a doll and toy making competition.

Mid-August. Cornfest, Athens. Sidewalk sales, arts and craft shows, entertainment, corn-on-the-cob, parade, antique steam engine.

Mid-September. Loyalist Parkway Amazing Country Adventure, Prince Edward County. Rural festival featuring crafts, concerts, attractions at local farms. Throughout Prince Edward and Addington Counties along Highway 33.

OTHER RECOMMENDED RESTAURANTS AND LODGINGS

Isaiah Tubbs Resort, 12 km (9 miles) west of Picton on Highway 33. (613) 393–2090 or (800) 267–0525. This super-posh resort offers rooms and suites with fireplaces, Jacuzzis, indoor and outdoor swimming pools, saunas, and a whirlpool. There are also twelve cottages and thirty-five housekeeping cottages. The resort offers a number of packages. Their rates range from $194 to $213. That gets you the best available room at time of booking, plus dinner and breakfast.

FOR MORE INFORMATION

Prince Edward County Chamber of Tourism and Commerce, Box 50, Picton ON K0K 2T0. (613) 476–2421.

NIAGARA
PENINSULA
ESCAPES

Hamilton

BIRMINGHAM OF CANADA

2 NIGHTS

Botanical gardens • Military history • Safari and game farm
Football hall of fame • Theater and opera

First impressions can be misleading, and this industrial city of almost half a million is a classic case. Hamilton isn't attractive when seen from the Burlington Bay Skyway. The Dofasco and Stelco mills, producing 60 percent of Canada's iron and steel, are on the waterfront facing the Skyway, and their stacks belch greasy smoke across the bay. It isn't the sort of place you'd expect to find 2,700 acres of gardens and exotic plants, a symphony orchestra, a modern and active theater, forty-five parks, a 100-voice choir, and an opera company. But they're all here, in Ontario's second-largest city and Canada's third-busiest port. So is the Hamilton Tiger-Cat Football Team, frequent winner of the Canadian Football League's Grey Cup.

The city's downtown is on a plain between the harbor and the base of "the mountain," a 250-foot-high section of the Niagara Escarpment. Downtown Hamilton is a potpourri of glass-walled high-rises, century-old mansions, boutiques, hotels, museums, and historic sites— all within walking distance of each other. The city is also a good base from which to explore nearby Buffalo and Niagara Falls.

ESCAPE ONE

NIAGARA PENINSULA

DAY 1

Morning

Take the Queen Elizabeth Way (QEW) west from Toronto and Highway 403 west. Watch for signs to **Royal Botanical Gardens** (RBG) at Highway 403, Plains Road, and Highway 6. RBG has 2,700 acres of natural areas, five major garden areas, and 48 km (30 miles) of trails that wind across marshes and ravines, past the world's largest collection of lilacs, two acres of roses, an acre of iris, 125,000 spring bulbs in the Rock Garden, and all kinds of shrubs, trees, plants, hedges, and flowers.

It's open all year except Christmas with a full calendar of special events: sugar shanty in the spring, bird feeding in the fall, plant sales, art exhibits, and festivals for specific blooms. The **Mediterranean Garden Greenhouse** is a welcome change from winter's snow. Two teahouses are open May 1 to Thanksgiving; one serves only teas and ice cream, while the other has hot meals. Adults $7.00. Outdoor garden areas open daily year-round 9:30 A.M. to 6:00 P.M., and the Mediterranean Garden is open daily year-round, 9:00 A.M. to 5:00 P.M. For information call (905) 527–1158.

LUNCH: At RBG.

Afternoon

There's free parking and admission at **Gage Park and Chrysanthemum Show,** a seventy-seven-acre park of perennials and rose gardens, summer annual bed displays, specimen trees, and a permanent tropical greenhouse. Nine growing houses produce annuals used in city parks as well as 240 varieties of mums. The mum is Hamilton's official flower, and since 1920 the public has been invited to a mum show with 75,000 blooms during the first three weeks of November. Open year-round. At Main Street East and Gage Avenue. (905) 546–2044.

One of Hamilton's early sobriquets was "Birmingham of Canada," and one of the men responsible for that industry was Dr. Calvin McQuesten, who bought his mansion, **Whitehern,** in 1852. He was a New England medical doctor who came to Hamilton to join his cousin John Fisher, who was manufacturing Ontario's first threshing machine. The business expanded to include steam locomotives, cooking ranges, and farm equipment and eventually became the giant Massey-Ferguson Company.

The Georgian-style limestone house at 41 Jackson Street West was built in 1840, and its design is so rigidly symmetrical that four "blind" windows are permanently shuttered to achieve perfect balance. The house is furnished to period and everything is original, since the house passed directly from the last surviving family member to the Hamilton Parks Board. The formal dining room on the ground floor steals the show. The table is set with crystal, china, pewter, and silver service, and the sideboards groan with solid silver tea and coffee services and crystal decanters twinkling under imitation gaslights. Admission $3.50. Open daily June to Labor Day 11:00 A.M. to 4:00 P.M. From Labor Day to May open 1:00 to 4:00 P.M.; closed Christmas and New Year's Days. (905) 546–2018.

Steam buffs have called it "a cathedral to steam," but for the casual visitor the **Hamilton Museum of Steam and Technology** at 900 Woodward Avenue is just the city's restored waterworks pumping station. It's the only one of its type in North America, and the two enormous 1859 steam-powered Beam engines were restored to mint condition after standing idle for seventy years. The museum has a picnic area and book and gift shop. Small admission fee. Open Monday–Friday 11:00 A.M. to 4:00 P.M. year-round; Sunday and holiday hours are 1:00 to 4:00 P.M. October through May and noon to 5:00 P.M. June through September. Closed Saturday, Christmas Day, and New Year's Day. On Sunday and holidays the engines run on steam power. Look for the tall Victorian-style chimney, which has been a landmark for sailors for well over a century. (905) 549–5225.

DINNER AND LODGING: Hamilton has a number of major downtown hotels, including the venerable 1914 **Royal Connaught** at 112 King Street East. The hotel's restaurant is **Fran's.** Meats are broiled over an open fire of mesquite in a room replete with hanging plants.

The hotel has 206 rooms, including twenty-one suites, and one of Canada's longest indoor water slides, which drops two stories into an indoor swimming pool. There's also a sauna and whirlpool, and the **Yuk Yuk Komedy Kabaret** provides evening entertainment. Rates $99–$209. For information contact The Royal Connaught Hotel, 112 King Street East, Hamilton ON L8N 1A8. (905) 546–8111, or toll free (800) 446–4666.

DAY 2

Morning

BREAKFAST: At the Royal Connaught.

Hamilton has **Canada's largest indoor farmers' market,** started in 1837. It consists of 176 stalls spread over more than 20,000 square feet. Its new home adjoins **Jackson Square** and the new **Eaton Centre.** In the market you can get fruits and vegetables, meats, poultry, and seafood, and some stalls have crafts, jams, jellies, preserves, fresh flowers, and baked goods. Open Tuesday, Thursday, and Saturday 7:00 A.M. to 6:00 P.M., Friday 9:00 A.M. to 6:00 P.M. At 55 York Boulevard. (905) 546–2096.

Each of the thirty-five military aircraft in the **Canadian Warplane Heritage Museum** is ready for takeoff. A gift shop is stocked with aviation clothing, books, videos, models, souvenirs, and toys. The museum also has a comprehensive library of aviation history. Admission $7.00. Wheelchair-accessible. Open daily 10:00 A.M. to 4:00 P.M. Located in Hangar 4, Hamilton Airport at Mount Hope. (905) 679–4183 or (800) 386–5888.

Sir Allan Napier MacNab, a War of 1812 hero and Upper Canada's pre-Confederation prime minister, had the thirty-five-room Italianate villa called **Dundurn Castle** built in 1832–35. It's furnished to reflect the opulence in which MacNab lived at the height of his political career. Admission $6.00. Open Tuesday–Sunday and holiday Mondays 10:00 A.M. to 4:00 P.M. June to Labor Day, noon to 4:00 P.M. during the rest of the year. Closed Christmas and New Year's Days. At Dundurn Park, York Boulevard. (905) 546–2872.

Hamilton Military Museum is on the grounds of Dundurn Castle and houses a collection of military equipment, uniforms, and memorabilia dating from 1790 through World War II. Displays include uniforms and weapons from the War of 1812, the Victorian era, and the Boer War. Admission $1.75. Open year-round, daily June to Labor Day 1:00 to 5:00 P.M.; during the rest of the year closed nonholiday Mondays. Closed Christmas and New Year's Days. (905) 546–4974.

LUNCH: Hess Village is a village within a city. It's a collection of refurbished turn-of-the-century buildings enjoying a second lifetime as boutiques and restaurants. It's 2 blocks from the city center and a fun place to wander, particularly in summer when many restaurants operate patios. Try **Gown and Gavel Restaurant and Pub** (905–523–8881) or **Ivory's** (905–529–9767), across the street from each other at numbers 24 and 25 Hess Street South.

Dundurn Castle.

Afternoon

In 1912 the family of Hamilton-born painter Blair Bruce donated thirty of his paintings to the city on condition that they be housed in a permanent gallery. Thus began the **Art Gallery of Hamilton,** which today has a collection of more than 7,400 paintings, graphics, and sculptures in a magnificent building. No admission fee; donations welcome. On King Street across Summer's Lane from the Convention Centre. Open all year, Wednesday–Sunday 10:00 A.M. to 5:00 P.M., until 9:00 P.M. on Thursday. Closed statutory holidays. At 123 King Street West. (905) 527–6610.

The answer to just about any question you may have about Canadian football can be found at the **Canadian Football Hall of Fame and Museum,** the national shrine to pigskin. Grey Cup highlights are shown continuously in a theater, and in the Hall of Fame great players and builders of the game are honored. Nine months of the year the museum is home to the Grey Cup, donated in 1909 by Lord Grey for the Amateur Rugby Football Championship of Canada. That award is presented to the winning team in late November each year, when a mania besets the normally stolid citizens of whatever Canadian city hosts the game. Admission $3.00. The museum is in Civic Square beside Whitehern and Hamilton City Hall. Open Monday–Saturday 9:30 A.M. to 4:30 P.M. year-round; from May through November also open Sunday and holidays noon to 4:30 P.M. Closed Good Friday. At 58 Jackson Street West. (905) 528–7566.

Visitors may tour the campus of **McMaster University,** founded in Toronto in 1887 and moved to Hamilton in 1930. Tours during the academic year, September through April, are normally available on Wednesday and Friday by advance notice. During late spring and summer, campus tours are usually available Wednesday and Friday at 10:00 A.M. and 2:00 P.M. or by appointment. To arrange a tour, contact the Division of Student Liaison, Gilmour Hall, Room 102, at (905) 525–9140 ext. 3659.

Admission to the 300-acre **African Lion Safari and Game Farm** theme park includes a safari trail through a large game reserve in your own vehicle or, for an additional charge, a guided tour in an air-conditioned bus. Also, you get a cruise aboard the *African Queen* and a journey on the Nature Boy Scenic Railway. There are birds-of-prey demonstrations, parrot shows, and elephant roundups, plus a petting area and jungle playground for children. West of Hamilton off Highway 8, south of Cambridge. Open daily mid-April through late October. Call for hours of operation. Admission $16.95 adults, $10.95 children. (519) 623–2620 or (800) 461–9453.

Wild Waterworks is an aquatic playground in Confederation Park open daily mid-June to Labor Day. There are two huge water slides, the **Action River,** a children's water play area, a wave pool, food concession, a children's playground, a souvenir shop, and a picnic area. You can rent go-carts, Windsurfers, or inflatable rafts. General admission $9.90. From the QEW, exit onto Centennial Parkway, Highway 20 North, and follow signs. (905) 561–2292.

Battlefield House Museum is in Stoney Creek, just west of Hamilton. The furnished 1795 home of U.S. emigrant Mary Gage and her two children is surrounded by thirty-four acres of park. Open mid-May through June, Sunday–Friday 1:00 to 4:00 P.M.; July through August, daily 11:00 A.M. to 5:00 P.M.; Labor Day to Thanksgiving, Sunday–Friday 1:00 to 4:00 P.M.; and December, Sunday 1:00 to 4:00 P.M. Battlefield House Museum is at 77 King Street West at Highway 20. (905) 643–1261.

The **Women's Institute,** whose worldwide membership now numbers 7 million, had its origins in an 1873 Gothic home, now the **Erland Lee Museum Home.** James Lee and his family came from Maryland in 1792 and some of their possessions are on display. In 1896, descendant Erland Lee attended a meeting of the Farmers' Experimental Union at Guelph's Ontario Agricultural College. Adelaide Hoodless of Hamilton was the speaker, and she so inspired Lee that he had her invited to Ladies' Night of the Saltfleet Farmers' Institute. The world's first Women's Institute was formed at that meeting. On its seventy-fifth anniversary, the WI bought the Lee home to turn it into a museum. Open 10:00 A.M. to 4:00 P.M. Tuesday–Saturday, closed in February. At 552 Ridge Road. (905) 662–2691.

Displays at the **Dundas Historical Society Museum** include costumes, glass, china, a pioneer store, a Victorian bedroom, and a children's corner with toys, dolls, and dollhouses. The first paper produced in Upper Canada was made at Crooks Hollow near Dundas in 1826 by Scottish immigrant James Crooks. A working model of his mill shows how he made paper. Open Monday–Friday 10:00 A.M. to 5:00 P.M. and Sunday May 1 to October 31, 2:00 to 5:00 P.M. At 139 Park Street West. (905) 627–7412.

From **Big Creek Boat Farm** near Caledonia, 20 km (14 miles) south of Hamilton, a variety of cruises, including lunch and dinner cruises, are offered on the Grand River from mid-May through September. Cruises are available only by reservation and rates vary from $25 to $30. Before or after your cruise, browse the farm's bake and craft shops. Big Creek Boat Farm is on Highway 54 between Brantford and Caledonia, 17 km (12 miles) east of Brantford. (905) 765–4107.

Flamboro Downs harness-racing track just west of Hamilton has matinée and evening races year-round, though not on a daily basis. Two dining areas overlook the track. The **Confederation Room** offers buffet food, and there's full service at **Top O' The Turn Dining Room.** From Hamilton take Highway 6 to Clappison's Corners; turn left on Highway 5. Drive through the lights at Brock Road and watch for the racetrack on your right. For schedule call (905) 627–3561.

The **Joseph Brant Museum** across the west end of Lake Ontario, in Burlington, is a reconstruction of Chief Joseph Brant's last home. Galleries exhibit Woodland Indian culture, Brant memorabilia, Burlington history, and Canadian costumes. Open daily year-round. At 1240 Northshore Boulevard East, Burlington. (905) 634–3556.

DINNER: More than fine food awaits guests of the **Ancaster Old Mill.** For those interested, there's history—lots of it. The building in which you'll dine is the fourth mill on the site since 1792 and was built in 1863 on the foundations of the other three, which burned. During the War of 1812 the mill was the scene of what became known as the Bloody Assizes.

Many recent arrivals from the United States had been attracted by the offer of inexpensive farmland. They felt no loyalty to either side during the War of 1812 and refused to take up arms against American invaders. This created hard feelings among Loyalist settlers in the area, and eventually nineteen men were arrested and charged with treason and with aiding U.S. soldiers. There was no jail, so prisoners were kept in the basement of the mill while awaiting trial.

Eleven prisoners were banished to the British penal colony in what is now Tasmania, Australia, and eight were ordered hanged, drawn, and quartered. If that ambience doesn't put you off your dinner, try to get a table overlooking the stream, which still powers the gristmill that makes flour for the restaurant's bread. Before or after dining tour the·mill and browse a shop featuring Canadian-made gift items. At 548 Old Dundas Road in Ancaster. (905) 648–1827.

LODGING: The Royal Connaught.

Evening

The **Theatre Aquarius** group presents plays September through May at the 750-seat Theatre Aquarius. For box office information contact Theatre Aquarius, 190 King Street West, Hamilton ON L9H 1V5. (905) 522–7529.

Opera Hamilton performances are held September through April in the **Great Hall of Hamilton Place** (on Summers Lane, opposite the Art Gallery of Hamilton). For information contact: Opera Hamilton, 2 King Street West., Plaza Level, Hamilton ON L8P 1A1. (905) 527–7627.

DAY 3

Morning

BREAKFAST: For a breakfast that will carry you home without letting you even wonder about lunch, try the Hungry Man's Breakfast at **Steve's Open Kitchen,** 149 James Street South. They're open weekdays at 7:00 A.M., Saturday at 8:00 A.M., and Sunday at 9:00 A.M. The Hungry Man's Breakfast costs

$5.95 and includes three eggs, bacon, ham, sausage, home fries, and toast and jam. (905) 529–9913.

After your second—or third—cup of Steve's coffee, return to Toronto on Highway 403 and the Queen Elizabeth Way.

THERE'S MORE

There are eleven **factory outlet stores** in the Hamilton area, offering everything from Arrow shirts to Kodiak boots, paints to negligées. The Greater Hamilton Visitors Convention Services has a free pamphlet listing them, the hours they're open, the products they sell, and where they're located. Write to Greater Hamilton Visitors Convention Services, City Hall, 71 Main Street West, Hamilton ON L8N 3T4, or call (905) 526–4222.

SPECIAL EVENTS

First week of May. Rhododendron Society of Canada Annual Sale, Hamilton. At the Royal Botanical Garden.

Second week of May. Show of African violets and other Gesneriads, Dutch auction, information, and plants for sale at RBG, Hamilton.

Mid-May. Cherry Blossom Festival, Hamilton. At RBG.

Last half of May. Lilac Festival, Hamilton. At the world's largest lilac collection, music, dance and theater performed among the fragrance of thousands of lilacs. At RBG.

Early June. Greater Hamilton Tattoo, Hamilton. Military bands, choirs, musicians, dancers, and military display teams. At Copps Coliseum.

Mid-June. Hamilton International Air Show. Vintage, modern, and military aircraft exhibits at Mount Hope–Hamilton Airport.

End of June, first week of July. Rose Festival, Hamilton. Two acres of roses, music, food, kids' crafts, and games. At RBG.

Mid-July. Greater Hamilton Aquafest. Waterfront activities, stage shows, midway, 1812 military reenactment camp, hydroplane races, tall-ship cruises, car show, sailing parade of lights. At Hamilton Harbourfront.

End of July. Annual Antique Steam and Gas Engine Show, Hamilton. Models and full-size engines, steam trains operating on a 1,200-foot track, model boats. At Hamilton Museum of Steam and Technology.

Second week of August. Festival of Friends, Hamilton. Canadian festival of art and music with concerts, workshops, crafts. Free. In Gage Park, Main Street East and Gage Avenue South.

Early September. Herb & Harvest Festival, Hamilton. Old-fashioned country atmosphere, herbal plants, homemade condiments, gourmet cooking, music, games, giant pumpkin and squash contest, scarecrow picnic. At RBG.

Mid-October. Burlington Antique Show and Sale. Ontario antiques dealers at the RBG.

OTHER RECOMMENDED RESTAURANTS AND LODGINGS

Erie Beach Restaurant, 77 King Street. (905) 577–1130. Great fresh fish dinners along with steaks and other nonseafood dishes.

Chester's Restaurant, 60 King Street East. (905) 529–9568. If you remember a favorite imported beer, lager, or ale, chances are you can get a mug, stein, glass, or bottle of it here. They stock more than 200 brands and also serve inexpensive lunches and dinners.

Sheraton Hamilton Hotel, 116 King Street West. (905) 529–5515 or toll free (800) 325–3535. New 305-room tower hotel with all the trimmings, from indoor pool, sauna, and whirlpool to twenty-four-hour room service and a variety of dining options. Connected by skywalk to Hamilton Convention Centre, Hamilton Place Theatre Auditorium, and the Art Gallery of Hamilton. The hotel's shopping concourse, Jackson Square, has more than 250 shops, boutiques, and cinemas, and it adjoins the indoor Farmers' Market.

FOR MORE INFORMATION

Greater Hamilton Tourism, 1 James Street South, 3rd Floor, Hamilton ON L8P 4R5. (905) 546–4222 or (800) 263–8590.

Thorold and Welland

NO PLACE FOR A GOOD NIGHT'S SLEEP

1 OR 2 NIGHTS

Ships • More ships • Even more ships • And a shrinking mill

Guests at Thorold's Inn at Lock Seven don't come for a good night's sleep—at least not from April through November. Most of the guests are ship-watchers, a peculiar breed who get a kick out of watching ships. They come from far and wide, many on the same week year after year, to this nondescript town in the Niagara Peninsula, just to watch ships.

The twenty-four motel units in three stories overlook the seventh and final lift over the Niagara Escarpment for ships heading to Lake Erie. Ship-watching is somewhat akin to bird-watching; you shouldn't write it off as a foolish pursuit until you've tried it. But if ship-watching isn't for you, then neither is Thorold. There is little else to see or do in this paper-mill town of 17,500. If you do come to ship-watch and want a change of scene, there are some attractions in nearby Welland and Port Colborne.

DAY 1

Morning

It's an easy two-hour drive to Thorold from Toronto. Take the Queen Elizabeth Way (QEW) to exit 49, Highway 406. Take Highway 406 to Highway 58 and turn left on Pine Street in Thorold. Follow Pine Street to the first four-way stop. Turn right on Clairmont Street, and drive to the dead-end where the Inn at Lock Seven is located. For information contact the Inn at Lock Seven, 24 Chapel Street South, Thorold ON L2V 2C6; (905) 227–6177.

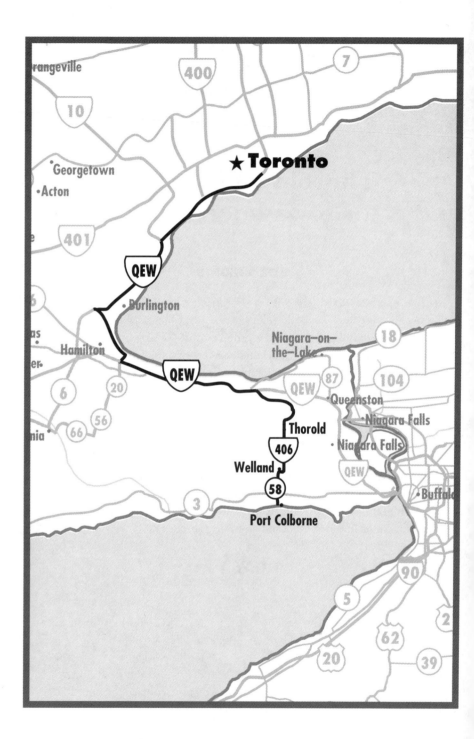

LUNCH: Keystone Kelley's at 338 Merritt Street, about a mile away, is popular with all age groups. The restaurant is in a renovated house and the walls
are laden with Canadiana and antiques. Service is fast and friendly and there's
something on the imaginative menu for every palate.

Afternoon

The St. Lawrence–Great Lakes Waterway stretches 3,680 km (2,300 miles) and
lifts vessels a total of 602 feet between the St. Lawrence River and the final lift
into Lake Superior at Sault Ste. Marie. There have been canals through this part
of the Niagara Peninsula since 1829, but the present system, with a depth of 27
feet, was completed in 1932. The entire length of the canal system is lighted.

The 42-km (26-mile) **Welland Canal System** lifts ships 26½ feet
between Lakes Ontario and Erie, a height about double that of Niagara Falls.
An eighth lock at Port Colborne on Lake Erie, called a regulating lock and
the world's longest at 1,380 feet, makes the final adjustment to the level of
Lake Erie.

It takes a ship about twelve hours to pass through the locks. Ships ease into
a lock, the gates are closed, and when valves open to admit water from a
higher level, the ship rises. It takes about ten minutes for 24 million gallons of
water to fill each lock. When water levels in the two locks are the same, the
gates are opened, the ship is untied, and it sails into the next lock.

Each procedure is noted by whistle blasts, and the ships—which can be up
to 730 feet long—have whistles that can be heard for several kilometers. In an
average year the system accommodates 1,200 oceangoing vessels and 3,000
lake freighters. The ships, in turn, carry 44 million tons of goods, mostly
wheat, iron ore, and coal. A single lake freighter can carry a million bushels of
grain, the harvest from 50,000 acres.

Locks 4, 5, and 6 are the most impressive on the Welland Canal. They're
called twin flight locks and allow simultaneous locking of ships in both directions. At Lock 3 near St. Catharines, there's a large elevated platform to provide an optimum view of the locking procedure. There are free parking, a
picnic area, a snack bar, tourist information, and rest rooms. (Take the Glendale Avenue exit from the QEW and follow signs.)

Serious ship-watchers usually settle into the **Inn at Lock Seven** for a
week. They have shipping guides to identify each vessel and know its tonnage,
size, home port, cargo, and probable destination. Some bring electronic scan-
ners to monitor conversations between the lock master and captain. And they
all have binoculars.

Welland Canal

The Welland Canal System has a free telephone service for boat-watchers. Dial (905) 688–6462 for a recording advising what ships are en route to which lock and their estimated time of arrival. Three traffic tunnels pass under the Welland Canal and eleven railway and highway bridges cross it. Three of the highway bridges rise 120 feet to provide clearance for passing ships. Those bridges are at Glendale Avenue in St. Catharines, Highway 20 in the hamlet of Allanburg, and Clarence Street in Port Colborne.

DINNER: Fong's is 3 blocks along Clairmont Street and serves Chinese and Canadian cuisine. Your other choice in Thorold is **Pine Centre Restaurant and Sports Bar,** offering Canadian and Greek cuisine. For variety, you're close to Niagara Falls and Niagara-on-the-Lake; see Niagara Peninsula Escape Three for recommended dining spots.

LODGING: The Inn at Lock Seven . . . but don't bother complaining when you can't sleep through the ships' bells and whistles. Rooms on the second and third floors have balconies overlooking the lock and those on the ground floor have patios.

DAY 2

Morning

BREAKFAST: Enjoy the home-style cuisine at the Inn at Lock Seven dining room.

For a break from ship-watching, visit **Welland.** This industrial city of 45,000 is bisected by the canal and calls itself "Rose City of Ontario." Welland has improved considerably since 1829 when a *New York Spectator* reporter wrote that it resembled "a swamp with a ditch running through it." The newspaper account is in the **Welland Museum,** at 65 Hooker Street, which chronicles the history of the four canals. Open Tuesday–Saturday year-round and Sunday afternoon mid-May through Labor Day. (416) 732–2215.

Welland has climbed on the giant mural bandwagon of Chemainus, B.C., but they've done it with a vengeance. There are twenty-nine **giant murals** on downtown buildings, the longest of which is 130 feet, and the tallest, three stories high. The Welland program was a bid to snag some of the 14–16 million tourists visiting nearby Niagara Falls each year. Visitors can pick up a mural tour map and in summer watch artists at work. (416) 735–8696.

The two-week **Welland Rose Festival** in early June celebrates the flower that gave Welland its sobriquet. There are shows to judge the finest bloom, a Rose Queen contest, parades, boat races, an aquatic show, and a Coronation Ball.

Farther down the canal at Port Colborne, there's no admission charge to the **Port Colborne Historical and Marine Museum,** a six-building complex on parklike grounds where afternoon tea is served (at a price) at **Arabella's Tea Room,** a 1925 cottage. The anchor of the museum is an 1853 Georgian-style home, but the eye-catcher is the red and white wheelhouse of a lakes freighter. A carriage house cum blacksmith shop contains a display of early agricultural implements; an 1818 log schoolhouse and a restored log home furnished with 1850s artifacts are also on the grounds. Exhibits trace the history of the Welland Canal and the businesses that grew up along it. Open noon to 5:00 P.M. May through December. (905) 834–7604.

DINNER: It's a twenty-minute drive to Niagara Falls or forty minutes to Niagara-on-the-Lake, both of which are major tourist centers and have numerous excellent restaurants. Check Niagara Peninsula Escape Three for some appetizing ideas.

LODGING: The Inn at Lock Seven.

THERE'S MORE

Like magnetic hills, reversing falls, and other strange phenomena, you have to see the **Shrinking Mill** to believe it. Drive west from Port Colborne on Highway 3 and turn left at Cement Plant Road. Continue south (toward the lake) and at the stop sign at Lakeshore Road make another left. Follow Lakeshore Road east toward Gravelly Bay. As you look ahead down the straight, tree-lined Lakeshore Road, the grain elevator of Maple Leaf Mills is in full view. As you get closer, the structure appears to shrink.

SPECIAL EVENTS

Early May. Welland Native Cultural Festival. Aboriginal dances and drum demonstrations, storytelling, crafts, food. At Welland Arena, 501 King Street.

Mid-May to early June. St. Catharines Folk Arts Festival. Ethnic food, arts and crafts, dancing, singing, and music at Montebello Park and throughout St. Catharines.

Second and third weeks of June. Welland Rose Festival. Numerous special events, including a parade, Day in the Park, and Coronation Ball. At various locations.

Late June. Festival St. Jean, Welland. Celebration of Welland's French heritage, entertainment, family day, games, music, pancake breakfast. At Club Richelieu, 565 River Road.

Mid-July. Ethnic Day in the Park, Port Colborne. Celebrating the city's multicultural heritage with ethnic food booths, ethnic folk dancing. At Knoll Lakeview Park, Sugarloaf Street.

Early August. Canal Days Festival, Port Colborne. Nautical and marine celebration of the city's maritime heritage, live entertainment, fine arts and crafts show, marine demonstration. At Port Colborne Museum, 280 King Street.

Late August. Heritage Folklore Festival, Welland. Celebrating ethnic diversity with open houses at city's cultural centers, arts and crafts, demonstrations, dance, food.

Late September. Niagara Grape and Wine Festival, St. Catharines. Celebrating Niagara Ontario's grape and wine industry, featuring tastings, vineyard tours, gourmet dinners, concerts, parades, artisan shows.

Early October. Niagara Food Festival, Welland. Thirty restaurants and wineries serving their specialties, demonstrations, live stage entertainment, buskers, ice carving. At Merritt Island.

Mid-October. St. Catharines Oktoberfest. Featuring a band from Bavaria, downtown farmers' market, dancing, food, entertainment.

FOR MORE INFORMATION

Thorold Chamber of Commerce, 3 Front Street North, Thorold ON L2V 2G1. (905) 680–4233.

Niagara Falls and Niagara-on-the-Lake

A PLACE TO HOLD SOMEBODY'S HAND

2 NIGHTS

Breathtaking natural wonders • Quirky museums
Wine tastings • Gardens • A revolving restaurant

The accent was New Jersey; the tone universal. Dad and the two kids were wiped out and melting in the July steambath. "Jeez, Bernice! We've been *under* the falls; we've been *over* the falls; we've been *behind* the falls; we've been *around* the falls. What on Earth do you want to do now?"

Bernice, like many visitors to one of North America's premier tourist attractions, wanted to do it all. And that now meant a trip *across* the Great Whirlpool Gorge on the Spanish Aero Car.

There is probably no major tourist attraction exploited as thoroughly as Niagara Falls. As the New Jersey family had done, you can go over the falls in a helicopter; you can get almost directly underneath them on a *Maid of the Mist* cruise boat; you can go around them on a variety of bridges across the Niagara River and Gorge; and you can go behind them in a tunnel.

And to be certain you have missed nothing to do with the spectacle of Niagara, you can hang in there like Bernice and ride the Spanish Aero Car across the Great Whirlpool Gorge.

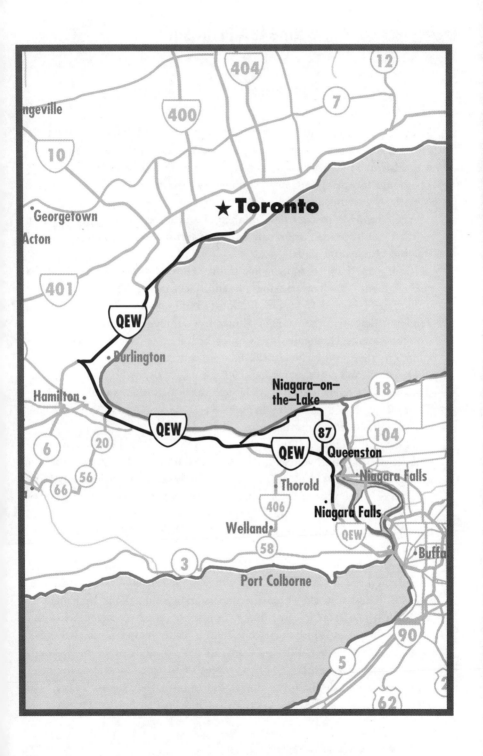

NIAGARA PENINSULA

DAY 1

Morning

Follow the Queen Elizabeth Way (QEW) to Niagara Falls. Take exit 30 (Highway 420) for Rainbow Bridge and go right on Victoria Avenue, which intersects **Clifton Hill,** heart of downtown Niagara Falls. The 130-km (81-mile) trip should take less than ninety minutes on the four-lane QEW, which is always busy and usually under construction.

At Clifton Hill turn left, descend the hill, and at the bottom turn right. On your left you'll see the **American Falls** and **Bridal Veil Falls** and, moments later, the **Horseshoe Falls.**

More than 300 years ago, the first travel writer to visit Niagara Falls waxed a tad eloquent: "The universe does not afford its parallel," he wrote. "The roar of them can be heard 15 leagues [72 km (45 miles)] away." And Father Louis Hennepin described their height as 600 feet, although they're actually only 176 feet. Despite Hennepin's gross exaggerations, few have ever been disappointed by their visit to Niagara Falls.

Daredevils and death, scares and the bizarre have always been a part of Niagara, and the daredevils keep coming despite all sorts of laws to prevent people from tempting fate. The exploits of those legendary characters are enshrined in Niagara Falls museums.

The best thrill is free. But it is dangerous. Do not do it alone. If you do try it alone, you may find yourself, if you're lucky, on a quick trip back to your hotel in a city police cruiser. The thrill is simply standing at **Suicide Point** and staring at the very edge of Horseshoe Falls where a blue-green sheet of water glides smoothly over the edge in a translucent sheet. If you stand and stare at that curve long enough, it beckons you. It hypnotizes you and coaxes you to join its plunge.

Repeat: Do not do this alone. This is a place to hold somebody's hand. Nobody in the tourism infrastructure will talk officially about that fatal allure. If they'll discuss it at all, it's on the understanding they won't be named or quoted. It is a fact that at least a dozen human bodies are recovered below the falls or in the Giant Whirlpool each year. Some who jump considerably stick a note in their pocket. But for many, there's no explanation or apparent motive. Some years ago the guardrail was moved farther back from the edge of the point. Still, although no official will admit it, the Niagara Falls Police Department keeps an eye on people who stand alone at Suicide Point.

Looking at the falls is free, photographing them is free, nearby public washrooms are free, and walking around the beautiful flower beds is free, claims that can be made at few of the world's major tourist attractions.

LUNCH: At **Queenston Heights Restaurant** a few miles north (downriver) of the falls you can have a relaxed meal away from the frenzy of the falls traffic while overlooking a golf course and Niagara Gorge. At Niagara River Parkway North, Queenston. (905) 262–4274.

Afternoon

There's a lot more that's free in Niagara Falls if you know where to look for it, thanks to the Niagara Parks Commission (NPC). The NPC was formed in 1885 to preserve the area around the falls for the benefit of visitors. Its mandate was to operate at no cost to taxpayers and to provide free access.

The NPC raises funds from its attractions, restaurants, gift shops, golf courses, campgrounds, and parking lots. It operates under the direction of twelve appointed commissioners and continues acquiring land to improve the park system. And thank God for the NPC! Its outlets pay fair exchange rates, stand behind their goods and services, and have established a level of retail integrity that forces others to give good value.

From a small block of land around the falls, the NPC has gradually acquired most of the land fronting the Niagara River between Niagara-on-the-Lake at the mouth of the river and Fort Erie at its head, a 56-km (35-mile), 3,000-acre ribbon of park. There are parking areas adjacent to pavilions, picnic tables, and barbecues and the public is welcome at no charge.

One of the NPC's newest attractions, the **Butterfly Conservatory,** is in the **Niagara Parks Botanical Gardens,** 9 km (5.6 miles) north of the falls. Two thousand butterflies from fifty species from around the world flutter around the 11,000-square-foot building. Open daily 9:00 A.M. to 5:00 P.M. except Christmas. Admission $7.00. (905) 356–8119.

If it's a hot day and you want a dip before lunch, lifeguards are on duty daily at **Dufferin Islands** in **King's Bridge Park,** well marked a half-kilometer (0.3 mile) above the falls on your right. Just south (upriver) of the Horseshoe Falls there's no charge to visit the NPC's **Greenhouse and Fragrance Garden,** open year-round. This showplace of exotic plants and flowers will delight horticulturalists and gardeners. A retail outlet sells seeds, bulbs, and gardening tools. Open daily. You're also welcome to wander the grounds of the **NPC School of Horticulture,** several miles north (downriver) of the falls on the Niagara Parkway.

The school has been graduating professional gardeners since 1936, and students display their expertise with flowers and shrubbery on the school grounds. From the school it's just a short distance to one of the world's largest floral clocks, 8 km (5 miles) downriver. The clock's 40-foot-wide "living" face is planted in a different design each year, created with 25,000 plants.

Heading back upriver, you might want to experience the **Great Gorge Adventure.** It's at 4330 River Road. You descend by elevator and follow a tunnel to the edge of the cascading waters of the Whirlpool Rapids. Open May through October. In May, open Monday–Friday 9:00 A.M. to 5:00 P.M., Saturday and Sunday 9:00 A.M. to 6:00 P.M. June through August, open daily until 8:00 P.M. September through October, open daily 9:00 A.M. to 5:00 P.M. Admission $4.75 adults, $2.40 children six to twelve. (905) 374–1221.

Or, bring along your bicycles. A **bicycle trail** parallels Niagara Parkway from Fort Erie to Niagara-on-the-Lake. The terrain is flat and the paved pathway winds between beautiful homes in landscaped settings on one side and the Niagara River with its abundant birdlife on the other. (On the northern section there are small wineries that offer samples of their products.)

There are **free band concerts** on summer Sundays at **Queenston Heights Park, Queen Victoria Park,** and **Old Fort Erie.** Other free things to do include **Rainbow Bridge Carillon recitals, Brock's Monument,** and the **Queenston Heights Battlefield Walking Tour.** Information kits available free, of course, from Niagara Parks Commission, P.O. Box 150, Niagara Falls ON L2E 6T2 (905–356–2241), or from booths along the Niagara Parkway. And don't forget to catch the **Illumination of the Falls.** That's every night of the year, and the best way to enjoy it is while strolling through **Queen Victoria Park,** which has indirect landscape lighting of the manicured grounds. There's no admission charge.

The Honeymoon City and its American neighbor light up each winter from the end of November through the third week of February. The **Festival of Lights** started in Niagara Falls, Ontario, in 1981 and now stretches the length of the Niagara Parkway between Fort Erie and Niagara-on-the-Lake, and across the border to Niagara Falls, New York. The city claims a lot of superlatives during this period: the world's largest Christmas tree (the Skylon Tower), the world's largest gift (Your Host Motor Inn decorated to look like a giant gift-wrapped box), the world's largest candle (the Minolta Tower), and the world's largest bells (the four 54-foot-high bells atop pen stock gates at the Ontario Hydro plant, sequentially wired so the clappers appear to move).

Both cities are the focal points of the Festival of Lights, with massive corporate displays using millions of colored bulbs, but smaller businesses and private citizens keep adding to the act. There are now so many displays to see in and around the falls that tours can take as long as three and a half hours.

The falls area is beautiful after a long cold snap. Spray freezes on everything and there are lovely ice formations on trees, railings, lamp posts—and your car, if you happen to leave it where spray is landing. During a cold winter, a bridge of ice usually forms across the Niagara Gorge below the Horseshoe Falls. Crossing the ice bridge was popular until one suddenly collapsed, dashing three adventurers to their deaths.

DINNER: The **Revolving Dining Room** in the Skylon Tower was Canada's first. The room makes a full circle every hour and the sight of the illuminated falls—at any time of the year—is one long remembered. The Skylon's **Summit Suite Restaurant** serves buffet breakfasts, lunches, and dinner, but does not revolve. Reservations recommended. (905) 356–2651.

LODGING: It's generally true in Niagara Falls that the closer you are to the falls, the higher your room rate. Many of the motels and hotels have sites overlooking the falls, and since you've come here to see them, why not consider a room with one of the best views? The best views are from the 216-room **Skyline Brock Hotel,** the 399-room **Skyline Foxhead Hotel,** or the 208-room **Skyline Village Inn,** all at 5685 Falls Avenue. Room rates $69–$329. Information or reservations: Skyline Foxhead Hotel, Maple Leaf Village, 5685 Falls Avenue, Niagara Falls ON L2E 6W7. (905) 374–4444 or (800) 263–7135.

DAY 2

Morning

BREAKFAST: At your hotel.

To follow Bernice and her family under, behind, and around the falls will cost you a lot, but if you're going to "do" the falls, you might as well "do" them completely. If you arrive in Niagara Falls by train or bus, you can catch the **Niagara Falls Shuttle** from those depots. The shuttle links you with the **People Mover System.** If you drove and are staying at a hotel or motel, leave your car and take the shuttle to the People Mover System.

One of the Maid of the Mist *boats.*

You can buy an all-day pass for the People Mover System (double buses)—the easiest way to get to and from all the major attractions between the Niagara Greenhouse (above the falls) and the Spanish Aero Car, 8 km (5 miles) downriver. The buses operate continuously and you can get on and off as many times as you wish.

Under the Falls. You make this trip on one of the three *Maid of the Mist* boats, a cruise started in 1846. Passengers are issued hooded rain slickers for the thirty-minute trip because the boats get so close to both the American and Horseshoe Falls the spray soaks everything.

The statistic of 155 million liters of water per minute thundering over the falls is meaningless; most of us couldn't begin to picture one million liter bottles lined up in a row (a liter is equal to 1.1 quarts). But from river level where the waters crash onto the rocks and ricochet in a fury of white spray, the energy of the falls can be appreciated—all five million potential horsepower of it. The *Maid of the Mist* boats sail daily from both sides of the river from May through late autumn. Additional information: (905) 358–5781.

Behind the Falls. From Table Rock House you can descend in an elevator. The price of your admission also includes use of rubber boots and a hooded rain slicker. From there you walk to an observation plaza under the lip of Horseshoe Falls. A tunnel takes you almost to the middle of the 2,160-foot-wide falls behind the wall of crashing water. Open year-round.

Over the Falls. Niagara Helicopters Ltd. operates four choppers on tours over the falls. The ten-minute trips at 1,400 feet take you across the Giant Whirlpool, the Lower Rapids, Whirlpool Rapids Bridge, Rainbow Bridge, and the American and Bridal Veil Falls. Then the pilot banks sharply and follows the curve of Horseshoe Falls. Those few seconds when your eyes can follow the fall of the water into the churning maelstrom below are worth the price of the flight. Niagara Helicopters operates in good weather year-round from 3731 Victoria Avenue. (905) 357–5672.

Above the Falls. Three towers offer views over the falls. The view of the Horseshoe Falls is best from either the **Skylon** or **Minolta** Towers, but the **Casino Niagara Tower** has the best view over the American Falls, the Gorge, and the rapids above the falls. Acrophobes should know the Skylon is 775 feet high, the Minolta is 665 feet high, and the Casino Niagara is 359 feet high.

The **Niagara Spanish Aero Car** crosses the Whirlpool Basin down the gorge from the falls. The cable car has been operating since 1918, and from it you get a bird's-eye view of the whirlpool and lower rapids. This trip is not for the faint-hearted because when you're swinging and swaying high above the roiling whirlpool, those cables look awfully long . . . and very thin. Open March through November; times vary with the seasons. In summer, open daily 9:00 A.M. to 9:00 P.M. On the Niagara Parkway 3.25 km (2 miles) downriver from the falls. Admission $5.00 adults, $2.25 children six to twelve.

LUNCH: The **Secret Garden Restaurant,** 5827 River Road (across from the *Maid of the Mist* office) has a full American/Canadian-style menu, fast service, and daily specials. Lunch will cost you $5.00–$9.00. (905) 358–4588.

Afternoon

For those who enjoy this sort of thing, there's every imaginable museum or exhibit in Niagara Falls.

The **Niagara Falls Museum** claims to be North America's oldest museum and is chock-a-block with items of interest, from stuffed birds and fish to mineral and Egyptology exhibitions considered among the best in the world. It is also home of the **Daredevil Hall of Fame,** an area devoted to barrels and other contraptions in which people have drifted over Niagara Falls. The museum was founded in 1827. There are twenty-six galleries on four floors. The museum claims to have 700,000 exhibits, so gauge your time accordingly. Open daily April through October and weekends November through May. At 5651 River Road, at the end of the Rainbow Bridge. Admission $6.75 adults, $6.25 seniors, $4.95 students eleven to eighteen, $3.95 children five to ten. (905) 356–2151.

Three major chain museums have branches on "museum alley," Clifton Hill, almost immediately opposite the American Falls, and others are as close to the area as they could find property. All are open year-round.

The **Guinness World of Records Museum,** 4943 Clifton Hill, is worth the time and money—if you're into the weird and often amazing exploits of people in their efforts to achieve recognition. Documented here are all sorts of biggests and smallests and tallests and most expensives. Admission $6.50 adults, $4.25 children six to twelve. (905) 356–2299.

Ripley's Believe It Or Not Museum, 4960 Clifton Hill, is every bit as interesting as the Guinness Museum and anyone interested in the unusual will have difficulty dragging himself or herself out of this museum in less than two hours. Admission $7.00 adults, $3.99 children six to twelve. (905) 356–2238.

Louis Tussaud's Waxworks Museum, 4915 Clifton Hill, has galleries of wax figures of famous people—such interesting contrasts as Queen Victoria; actor George Burns; Canada's first prime minister, Sir John A. Macdonald; and Mother Teresa. Some likenesses fall disappointingly short; others are startlingly lifelike. Admission $6.49 adults, $3.50 children six to twelve. (905) 374–6601.

Lundy's Lane Historical Museum at 5810 Ferry Street has exhibits of pioneer artifacts and military displays about the War of 1812. Open daily 9:00 A.M. to 4:00 P.M. May 1 to November 30, and weekdays noon to 4:00 P.M. December 1 to April 30. Admission $1.60 adults, 50 cents children six to twelve. (905) 358–5082.

Niagara Falls Art Gallery is a five-level complex housing a series of 160 panels on the Passion of Christ by Canadian artist William Kurelek. Paintings and sculptures by other artists are also in the gallery at 8058 Oakwood Drive, 3 km (2 miles) from the Horseshoe Falls at QEW and McLeod Road. Open Monday and Wednesday–Saturday 10:00 A.M. to 5:00 P.M., Sunday 1:00 to 5:00 P.M. (905) 356–1514. Donations requested.

Niagara Falls Imax Theatre at 6170 Buchanan Avenue, adjacent to the Skylon Tower, offers a forty-five-minute film on Niagara Falls shown on Canada's largest movie screen, over six stories high—ten times larger than the screen at your local theater. Open daily year-round. Tickets $7.50 adults, $7.00 students twelve to eighteen, $5.50 children six to eleven. For schedule call (905) 358–3611.

Marineland, 1.5 km (1 mile) from Horseshoe Falls, is a year-round marine park, game farm, and theme park that has the **world's largest steel roller coaster.** The daily marine show claims the world's largest troupe of performing dolphins and there are killer whales, clowns, and trained seals. Children can pet and feed 500 deer, get nose-to-nose with exotic fish, and meet cartoon characters. During July and August, open 9:00 A.M. to 6:00 P.M.; off-season hours are 10:00 A.M. to 4:30 P.M. The rides are open mid-May through early October. Attractions vary according to season but admission rates are also adjusted. Adults $9.50–$24.95. (905) 356–9565.

At **Niagara Go-Karts Inc.,** you can race on the ten-turn course daily March 1 to November 15, weather permitting. At 7104 Kinsmen Crescent (QEW at McLeod Road exit). (905) 356–9030.

Niagara Falls Brewing Company, 6863 Lundy's Lane, is a popular microbrewery that offers free tours and tastings. Open year-round, but call in advance. (905) 374–1166 or (800) 267–3392.

DININER: It's unlikely there is a single North American fast-food franchise not represented in, or very close by, Niagara Falls. There are also outlets for every known form of junk food from cotton candy to fudge, from every known flavor of ice cream to donuts and caramel popcorn. There are no gourmet restaurants on the Canadian side, but a number of places come close.

When locals want an especially good meal they go to one of two Italian restaurants: the **Capri** at 5438 Ferry Street, which has soft chairs and a softly tinkling piano, or **Casa D'Oro Dining Lounge** at 5348 Victoria Avenue, where dinner can stretch through the evening in the adjacent disco.

LODGING: Skyline Village Inn.

Evening

Casino Niagara is the Honeymoon City's newest attraction, located at the end of the Rainbow Bridge, 5705 Falls Avenue. Built around the former Maple Leaf Village Tower are 96,000 square feet of gaming space with such eye-catchers as three-story-high waterfalls. The 2,700 slot machines take tokens from a quarter to $100, and the 144 gaming tables offer all the popular games. There are restaurants and stores, and the casino never closes. (905) 374–3598 or (888) 946–3255.

DAY 3

Morning

BREAKFAST: Order room service and enjoy it overlooking the falls.

Take Niagara Parkway north (downriver) 10 km (6 miles) to **Queenston,** a pretty village of 500. From the early to mid-1800s Queenston was a trans-shipment point on the Great Lakes system and a booming river town—there were thirteen inns. Now it's a sleepy place with well-kept estates and bungalows and one remaining inn. There are three historic structures worth a visit, each recalling a Canadian hero.

Brock's Monument. Just above the village on a shoulder of the Niagara Escarpment, a 185-foot-high shaft marks the grave of Gen. Sir Isaac Brock. In 1810 Brock was sent to assume command of Fort George and in 1811 was promoted to major-general and appointed provisional lieutenant-governor of the Province of Upper Canada. When the War of 1812 broke out, he was the heart and soul of the defense of Upper Canada.

With brilliant audacity he attacked Detroit and captured Gen. William Hull and his entire army. Brock was knighted for this, but the news did not reach Canada until Brock had died on the battlefield at Queenston Heights, a battle in which the British defeated the American invaders. The massive monument, with interior stone stairs to a lookout, was erected in 1854.

Laura Secord Home. In June of 1813 Laura Secord hiked 32 km (20 miles) to warn British soldiers of a surprise attack planned by the Americans. Two days later the British and their Native allies intercepted the American attack and forced their surrender at the Battle of Beaver Dams. Laura received 100 gold sovereigns from England's grateful Prince of Wales and in 1910 the Canadian government erected a monument to her on Queenston Heights.

In 1969 Laura Secord Candy Shops acquired the Laura Secord homestead and restored it to the 1812 period. Only the fireplace and foundation are original. The rest was assembled with wood, pegs, handmade nails, and hand-wrought hardware. So faithful is the reproduction that red paint for some of the furniture and the moldings was made from ox blood and buttermilk, and blue paint was made from blueberries and buttermilk. The home has one of Canada's finest collections of period furnishings. Open Victoria Day to Labor Day daily 10:00 A.M. to 6:00 P.M.

The Mackenzie Home. Some Canadians would claim it hasn't happened yet, but William Lyon Mackenzie, who lived in Queenston in 1823–24, is credited with having brought responsible government to Canada. The NPC opened Mackenzie House in 1990. A stone marker, placed by the Niagara Historical Society at the turn of the century, notes: OF WILLIAM LYON MACKENZIE. THE BIRTHPLACE OF RESPONSIBLE GOVERNMENT, 1823–1824.

Continue north on the Niagara Parkway to **Niagara-on-the-Lake.** This historic town of 12,000 is one of Ontario's showplaces. Stately homes sit back from tree-shaded streets, well separated from their neighbors. Most are at least a century old and their owners keep the rose trellises painted and the brass door knockers gleaming. There are a dozen lovely inns, most built for that purpose a century and a half ago.

Niagara-on-the-Lake's 1800s appearance is taken seriously; any proposed new business is screened by council to ensure that no chrome, glass, or neon-bedecked atrocity mars the Victorian character. Even the Liquor Control Board of Ontario had to erect Victorianesque signs advertising the sale of "wine and spirits." The best way to experience Niagara-on-the-Lake at any time of year is to stroll. If knowing precisely what you're seeing is important, get a copy of the free historic guide from the chamber of commerce at 153 King Street.

Don't miss **Niagara Apothecary.** It's on Queen Street across from the 1848 Court House and replicates a pharmacy that opened there in 1866. The counters are solid planks of walnut and the crystal chandeliers are reproductions of original gasoliers. No admission charge. Open daily mid-May to Labor Day, noon to 6:00 P.M.

After your stroll you can drive to **Shaw Festival Theatre** or **Fort George,** both just outside the downtown. A stagestruck Toronto lawyer's dream in 1961 now has an impressive track record and world-class reputation. Lawyer Brian Doherty started the festival with a few Shaw plays produced on weekends in the old courthouse.

Within a decade the 356-seat Court House Theatre couldn't supply enough seats for an ever-lengthening season. Government kicked in most of the $3 million to build the 863-seat Shaw Festival Theatre, which opened in 1973. Shaw Festival is the only theater group in the world specializing in the works of George Bernard Shaw and his contemporaries. The festival runs from the end of April through mid-November. (905) 468–2172 or (800) 511–7429.

Fort George National Historic Park is a British fort that was fully restored in 1939. Today's visitor can explore every area from the powder magazine to the elegantly furnished officers' mess. Soldiers in period dress perform drills and musical programs on the parade square. Open daily mid-May through October, other times by appointment.

LUNCH: The **Prince of Wales Hotel** spreads along an entire block of Picton, the main street, between King and Davy Streets. The original portion was built in 1864 as Long's Hotel, but the Weins family has been adding on both sides since 1975 with such architectural integrity that you can't tell where the original stops and the additions begin. Inside there's a lot of polished woodwork and brass and hanging plants, and wood-burning fireplaces snap and crackle autumn through spring. The hotel has three dining rooms; try their glass-walled **Patio Restaurant** overlooking the main street, a park, and the Niagara River.

Afternoon

On your way from Niagara-on-the-Lake to the Queen Elizabeth Way (QEW) returning to Toronto, you'll pass **Harvest Barn Country Market** on Lincoln County Road 55. The Niagara Peninsula is Ontario's fruit basket and from midsummer to late fall, fruit and vegetable stands proliferate. One of the best is Harvest Barn Country Market. It's painted hydrant red with a red-and-white striped awning across its front. Inside are local fruits and vegetables and exotic offerings from around the world. There is a bakery with crisp sausage rolls, tiny loaves of bread, and fruit pies. There's a salad bar, and you can buy apple juice, apple cider, or grape juice. There are picnic tables and that's where, on sunny days, knowledgeable locals enjoy a fun lunch.

THERE'S MORE

There are a number of museums on Clifton Hill in Niagara Falls. The **Haunted House** and the **Funhouse** are at 4743 Clifton Hill. Admission to each: $6.25 adults, $4.25 children six to twelve. (905) 357–4330. **Movieland Wax Museum** is at 4950 Clifton Hill. Admission $6.75 adults, $4.50 children six to twelve. (905) 358–3061. **Criminals Hall of Fame Wax Museum** is at 5751 Victoria Avenue at the top of Clifton Hill. Admission varies depending on season from $6.25 to $6.75. (905) 374–3011.

SPECIAL EVENTS

Mid-June. Strawberry Festival, Niagara-on-the-Lake. Jam-making, sampling of foods made with strawberries, entertainment, flea market. At St. Andrews Church.

First week of July. Niagara Doll and Bear Artisan Show, Niagara-on-the-Lake. Antique dolls and bears at Queen's Landing.

First weekend of July. Artistry by the Lake, Niagara-on-the-Lake. Free outdoor art exhibit with works by eighty artists in Queen's Royal Park.

End of July. War of 1812, Niagara-on-the-Lake. Reenactment from the War of 1812 at Fort George.

Early August. Niagara Peach Celebration, Niagara-on-the-Lake. Parade, peach farmers and vendors, street entertainment, antique farm machinery and steam equipment. On Queen Street.

Third weekend of September. Art by the Falls, Niagara Falls. More than 100 juried exhibitors, jewelry, paintings, home fashions, glass, pottery. At Rapidsview Park, opposite Marineland.

OTHER RECOMMENDED RESTAURANTS AND LODGINGS

Niagara Falls

Michael's Inn, 5599 River Road. (905) 354–2727. Has themed rooms, all commanding great views of the American Falls and the Niagara Gorge. Midnight at the Oasis, for example, contains a Jacuzzi for two surrounded by mirrors, a ½-foot-high stuffed tiger, palm-leaf wallpaper, and bamboo trees. The 130-room property has an indoor pool with water slide, sauna, whirlpool, gift shop, lounge, and The Embers, a dining room with glass-enclosed kitchen so you can watch your steak char-broiling on an open-hearth spit. Room rates range from $49 to $228. Dinner rates range from the daily $9.95 special up to $30.

Niagara-on-the-Lake

The Buttery, 19 Queen Street. (905) 468–2564. Has a popular patio for lunches and also indoor dining space. You'll need reservations for their popular Henry VIII feasts on Friday and Saturday nights.

Oban Inn, 160 Front Street. (905) 468–2165. One of the region's most popular inns. Great for lunches, dinners, or a tall, cool one around the piano bar.

The Pillar and Post, 48 John Street. (905) 468–2123 or (800) 361–6788. Country-style decor and full menus for lunch and dinner. During recent renovations a spa was added.

FOR MORE INFORMATION

Niagara Parks Commission, P.O. Box 150, Niagara Falls ON L2E 6T2. (905) 356–2241.

Niagara Falls, Canada Visitor and Convention Bureau, 5433 Victoria Avenue, Niagara Falls ON L2G 3L1. (905) 356–6061 or (800) 563–2557.

Chamber of Commerce and Visitor and Convention Bureau, 153 King Street, Box 1043, Niagara-on-the-Lake ON L0S 1J0. (905) 468–4263.

NEAR NORTH
ESCAPES

Bracebridge, Gravenhurst, Huntsville, and Dorset

MUSKOKA AND THE NEAR NORTH

3 NIGHTS

Santa's home • Luxury in the wilderness
Cruising in history • Pioneer Village

The District of Muskoka is the start of Ontario's Near North and the name of a huge, lake-and-river-riddled area of great natural beauty. *Muskoka* is synonymous with summer cottages, deluxe resorts, and riots of autumn color, attractions shared by neighboring Haliburton County to the east. Both are get-away-from-the-concrete playgrounds for those from the heavily populated south. A four-lane highway from Toronto bisects Muskoka, putting its central town, Huntsville, two hours away.

The district got its name from an Ojibwa chief named Mesqua-Ukee, or Yellowhead, who aided the British in the defense of Little York (Toronto) against the Americans. The chief and his people then settled near Lake Couchiching.

Muskoka has been a playground for the well-to-do since the late 1800s. A. P. Cockburn saw the possibilities first and convinced the government to install a lock at Port Carling connecting Lakes Muskoka and Rosseau and to dig a channel at Port Sandfield connecting Lakes Rosseau and Joseph. He promptly put a fleet of steamers on the lakes and then worked to get the railroad to the lakehead in Gravenhurst.

There followed an era of grand hotels in this pristine wilderness setting. The resorts, typically, were massive three- or four-story wooden buildings with turrets, cupolas, gables, and wide, sweeping verandas where guests sipped

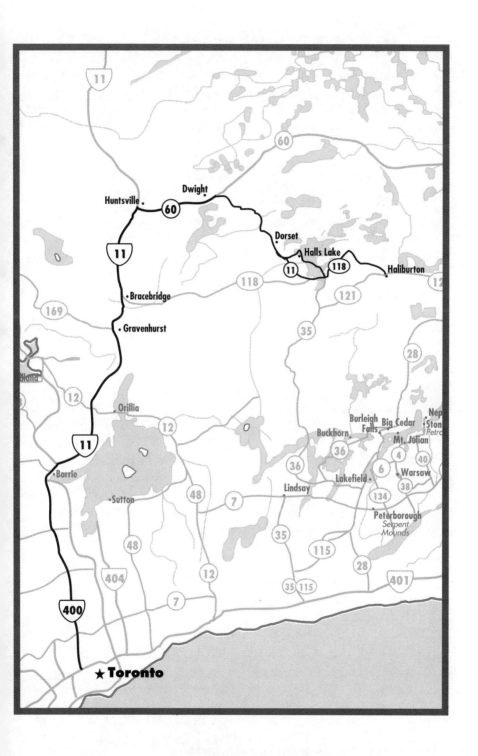

refreshments while lounging in wicker furniture. By day there were fishing, boating, croquet, hiking, and golf, and at night, ballroom dancing. Many guests so enjoyed themselves they built summer mansions in the area, some of which survive to this day, along with a handful of the great old hotels.

DAY 1

Morning

Take Highway 400 north to Highway 11 and drive north to the Bracebridge turnoff. **Severn Bridge** is where you enter the District of Muskoka. As you cross the Severn River you'll notice an immediate difference. Coniferous trees now predominate and you'll see patches of bald granite and sandy soil.

LUNCH: Old Station Restaurant at the Top of the Hill is at 88 Manitoba Street. Their Caesar salad draws many locals for lunch, but the menu includes everything from steaks, seafood, and pastas to finger foods. Open daily 11:00 A.M. to 9:00 P.M. Lunch costs $5.00–$8.00. (705) 645–9776.

Afternoon

Santa's Village is well marked from Bracebridge. This is the jolly man's summer home, and before or after letting him know what they'd like to find under the Christmas tree, youngsters can have a heck of a time on all sorts of rides: the *Kris Kringle* paddle wheeler cruises the Muskoka River, and the **Candy Cane Express Train** takes visitors through the **Enchanted Forest.** There are minibikes, bumper boats, paddleboats, pony rides, shows at **Humpty Dumpty Theatre,** and **Rudolph's Roller Coaster Sleigh Ride.** Open 10:00 A.M. to 6:00 P.M. seven days a week mid-June through Labor Day, weather permitting. (705) 645–2512.

    Woodchester Villa and Museum is one of Ontario's few remaining octagonal houses. It became a museum in 1982, a century after it was built for Henry James Bird, owner of the town's woolen mill. The core of the museum's artifacts is the private collection of W. Alvin Kaye of Cobourg, who gathered "old and interesting things." Open weekends May 24 through mid-June and Labor Day to Thanksgiving, and daily mid-June through Labor Day. (705) 645–8111.

    In July and August the 200-passenger *Lady Muskoka* takes two cruises daily from Bracebridge along the Muskoka River and Lake Muskoka. The cruises each last two and a half hours and depart at 11:00 A.M. and 2:15 P.M.

Inn at the Falls at Bracebridge.

Saturday evening there's a dinner cruise that lasts from 7:00 to 10:00 P.M. and a Sunday brunch cruise is from 11:00 A.M. to 1:30 P.M. In May and June and from Labor Day through October, cruises are by reservation only. The *Lady Muskoka* departs from Muskoka Riverside Inn on Beaumont Drive in Bracebridge. Weekday cruises cost $14 for adults. (705) 646–BOAT or (800) 263–LADY (Ontario only).

DINNER AND LODGING: Inn at the Falls has one of the prettiest settings of any hotel in the province. Jan and Peter Rickard bought the 1863-vintage turret-topped mansion in 1988 to offer the upscale market a very special getaway retreat as well as provide the community and passersby in the know with a classy country pub and a venue for those special lunches or dinners.

For dinner there are two choices. The inn's **Fox & Hounds Pub** serves pub fare around a fireplace in winter or outside on the patio. **Victoria's** is an elegant dining room offering superb food with a European flair. All dining areas overlook English gardens, the pool, and the Muskoka River.

There are five guest rooms and two suites in the original mansion, all furnished with antiques. The suite in one room was owned in the 1880s by the governor-general of Bermuda. A sleigh bed in another once belonged to Sir William Mulock, appointed Canada's postmaster-general in 1896 by Sir Wilfred Laurier. Rooms in the Mews, in a two-story motel-type annex, command the best view of the falls.

The Rickards have gradually acquired all the properties along the dead-end block of Dominion Street, at the end of which the original inn is located. There's a conference center. Room rates range from $80 to $225. (705) 645–2245.

DAY 2

Morning

BREAKFAST: At the Inn at the Falls.

Return to Highway 11 and drive the 15 km (10 miles) to Gravenhurst.

The initials RMS stand for Royal Mail Ship, and the 128-foot **RMS *Segwun*** is the sole survivor of a fleet of steamships that once provided the most common form of transportation through the Muskoka Lakes. The *Segwun*, which carries ninety-nine passengers and a crew of twelve, was prefabricated in Scotland's Clyde shipyards and reassembled in Gravenhurst in 1887. Cruises from one to eight hours long depart from a dock on Muskoka Bay from early June through mid-October. The *Segwun* is very popular and reservations are strongly recommended. Contact Muskoka Lakes Navigation and Hotel Company Ltd., 820 Bay Street, Sagamo Park, Gravenhurst ON P1P 1G7. (705) 687–7820.

During the last three weeks of June and from September through mid-October, the *Segwun* offers a daily lunch cruise from 11:30 A.M. to 2:00 P.M. From July through September there are breakfast cruises Wednesday and Sunday 9:15 to 11:00 A.M., one-hour cruises Tuesday and Thursday–Saturday at 10:00 A.M., and afternoon cruises Wednesday, Friday, and Saturday 2:15 to 4:15 P.M. Fares: one-hour cruise, $10.25; two- or two-and-a-half-hour cruise, $18.75; dinner cruise, $49.50; four-hour Millionaires Row cruise, $32.90; eight-hour, three-lake cruise on Sunday, $50.

LUNCH: Mr. J's at 415 Bethune Drive is open daily for lunch and dinner. Offerings include soups, salads, steaks, seafood, and specials. (705) 687–8846.

Afternoon

Dr. Norman Bethune is probably Canada's least-known hero—that is, in Canada. In China, however, his name is as widely known as is Wayne Gretzky's in Canada. Bethune was born in the 1880 frame home now called **Bethune Memorial House** when it was the manse of Knox Presbyterian Church, where his father Malcolm was minister for four years.

The modest house is a shrine of sorts for Chinese diplomats visiting North America, and so many have come bearing gifts since it opened in 1976 that a museum has been built to showcase some of the more spectacular and exotic ones. Bethune is remembered for heroic work in China as a field surgeon and medical educator. During his short but remarkable career he gained an international reputation for innovative surgical techniques and the invention of many surgical instruments.

Bethune was a socialist, which made him a misfit in Canada in those days. He spent only two years in China before his untimely death by blood poisoning in 1939 at the age of forty-nine. He is buried in a mausoleum at Wu Tai-Shan in Shansi Province, near the Bethune International Peace Hospital and the Bethune Medical School. China has honored him with a statue and commemorative postage stamp.

The house has been restored and furnished to re-create its probable appearance around 1890. Exhibits and artifacts trace Bethune's life and accomplishments. No admission charge. Open 10:00 A.M. to 5:00 P.M. daily June 1 to Labor Day and Monday–Friday the rest of the year; closed on winter statutory holidays. (705) 687–4261.

Return to Highway 11 and drive 30 km (20 miles) toward Huntsville. Watch for signs to the 1873 Wesleyan Methodist **Madill Church,** one of the few remaining square-timbered churches in Ontario, just west of Highway 11. Capt. George Hunt, an English army officer who arrived in 1868, is buried in the cemetery. Hunt, after whom Huntsville is named, was a road builder, merchant, and rabid teetotaler. He was the first settler here, and he divided his land and sold lots to abstainers, with a "no drinking" clause written into the deeds, effective through his lifetime. (This, it is said, explains the development of Huntsville on the *west* side of the Muskoka River, where there are steep hills, rather than on the flat east side where Hunt's restrictions applied.)

Continue on to Huntsville, several kilometers east of the Highway 11 funnel from the south. (This is likely what has spared the town from provincial government planners who would normally have converted the attractive and twisting main street to a four-lane thruway.) The visitor may get off Highway 11 on a summer weekend and join a traffic jam into Huntsville, but the stop-and-go permits enjoyment of the pretty town of 12,000 on the Muskoka River between Fairy Lake and Hunters Bay.

On a pleasant day the view from **Lions Lookout Park** is lovely. Follow signs from downtown, which direct you up a winding road to a rocky, pine-clad knoll. There's a picnic shelter from which you can overlook the townsite and Fairy Lake.

You pass the road into **Muskoka Pioneer Village** on your way to Lions Lookout Park. The park board fortunately doesn't view its role as a mandate to make the museum the biggest or most comprehensive in the world and, refreshingly, doesn't seem to feel it has to amortize the project with each season's receipts. The result is a small, complete village of fourteen historic buildings on a thirty-three-acre site. A friendly staff makes you feel comfortable. If cash is burning a hole in your pocket, you can buy jams, jellies, fudge, lemonade, muffins, or bread from the old bake oven. The village has an 1896 schoolhouse, the **Wesley Methodist Church,** and a blacksmith shop. There's a two-story log barn containing pioneer farm machinery and a two-story village inn. (Don't get any ideas about slipping in for a cool one; it's a temperance inn that used to be on the Colonization Road between Nipissing and Rosseau.)

There's a sawmill, a modern museum building, and a stable for the horses, which pull visitors around the site at no extra cost. Of particular interest is the **Darling House.** It measures 16 by 20 feet, and within that tiny space Hannah and James Darling raised nine children. The main museum is open all year, but the village is open daily July 1 to Thanksgiving, 10:00 A.M. to 5:00 P.M. in summer, 11:00 A.M. to 4:00 P.M. in fall. Admission $6.00. (705) 789-7576.

DINNER AND LODGING: From modest beginnings as a small family resort on Fairy Lake in 1896, three generations of the Waterhouse family have expanded the **Deerhurst Inn and Country Club.** This premier Muskoka resort is now owned by Newcastle Hotels, who continue the five-star service and special touches. It's all here: indoor and outdoor pools, sauna, whirlpool, tennis, golf (eighteen holes), squash, exercise room, racquetball, water-sports facilities, a variety of dining and drinking venues, and even a Las Vegas–style nightclub show. For dinner, you can sample one of the original three dining rooms overlooking Fairy Lake.

To get to Deerhurst, take Highway 60 east of town for 7 km (4 miles) and turn right on Canal Road. For reservations write Deerhurst Resort, R.R. 4, Huntsville ON P0A 1K0, or call (800) 461–4393.

DAY 3

Morning and Afternoon

Spend the day enjoying the facilities of Deerhurst, with meals at any of their dining rooms. In summer, facilities are available for any sports activity you care to pursue; in winter you can drive a dog team or snowmobile, or ski alpine or cross-country. Or rekindle a romance while sipping iced champage in front of a crackling fire in a luxurious suite overlooking a lake ringed by evergreens and white birch. The resort is deep in the heart of Muskoka's deer, moose, and bear country, but you can spend an evening watching big-city cabaret and enjoy cuisine normally found only in the better restaurants of major cities.

LODGING: Deerhurst Inn.

DAY 4

Morning

BREAKFAST: At Deerhurst Inn.

Continue east on Highway 60 and, just past the village of Dwight, turn right on Highway 35 to **Dorset.** Just before you reach Dorset, at the east end of Lake of Bays, there's a 100-foot observation tower that overlooks the south end of Algonquin Park, Lake of Bays, the Village of Dorset, and Lake Kawagama.

Dorset is a pretty village on a narrows between two bays of the Lake of Bays that bisects the village and is crossed by a one-lane bridge. On the north side of the village is **Robinson's General Store.** It opened in 1921 as a general store to provide basic goods required by people in the area: axes, sugar, coal oil, rope, and more. As the population grew, customers demanded different goods and to meet the demand . . . the inventory grew. That required more floor space, and additions sprouted off the little general store in all directions; then additions grew off the additions. With the exception of the World War II

NEAR NORTH

years, the store has been continuously open and operated by a Robinson. The present owner, Brad, is the fifth generation to run the store.

During the tourism boom of the 1970s, the store was "discovered" by city folk who now make the pilgrimage to this shopping mecca, where most items retail at lower prices than in the south. The store is more or less departmentalized but is a stocktaker's nightmare. "The place just grew in all directions," an employee explains. "That section used to be the local hotel," she adds, pointing vaguely to the hardware section where Brad Robinson and another man were wrestling a stove through the door.

LUNCH: In downtown Dorset, Canadian and Louisiana cuisine is served at **The Fiery Grill.** In winter, get a table near the fire; in summer, on the deck overlooking Cedar Narrows. (705) 766–2344.

To return to Toronto from Dorset, take Highway 117 west 43 km (27 miles) to rejoin Highway 11 just north of Bracebridge. Take Highway 11 south to Highway 400 on Toronto's western edge.

THERE'S MORE

If you're not in a hurry to get home, continue on Highway 35 from Dorset for 34 km (21 miles) to Carnarvon. There, turn left on Highway 118 and drive 25 km (15 miles) to Haliburton.

Haliburton Highlands Museum is 1 km (0.6 mile) up Bayshore Acres Road just north of the town of Haliburton. The museum complex includes an 1867 barn full of early agricultural implements, a settler's square-timbered house, and a turn-of-the-century frame home. In a modern building, exhibits chronicle the region's history. There's also a superb collection of 100 species of stuffed birds including the now-extinct passenger pigeon. Open daily in summer 10:00 A.M. to 5:00 P.M. and in winter the same hours, Tuesday–Saturday. (705) 457–2760.

In the former railway station, now called **Rails' End Gallery,** there are changing displays of arts and crafts. Open year-round, daily July to Labor Day and Tuesday–Saturday the rest of the year.

From Haliburton, backtrack 25 km (15 miles) to Carnarvon and take Highway 118 a distance of 53 km (33 miles) to Muskoka Falls and Highway 11. Take Highway 11 south to Highway 400 on Toronto's western edge.

SPECIAL EVENTS

Late May. Muskoka International Air Show, Bracebridge. Exhibitions, sight-seeing rides in modern and vintage aircraft, displays. Muskoka Airport, Highway 11, between Gravenhurst and Bracebridge.

Early July. Bracebridge Antique Show and Sale.

Mid-July. Muskoka Pioneer Power Show, Bracebridge. Antique tractors and automobiles, parade, steam demonstrations, log cabin, hay press, music, crafts.

Late July. Pioneer Logging Games and Steam Show, Huntsville. Muskoka Pioneer Village.

Late July. Garden Tour organized by the Horticultural Society, Huntsville. Maps available at Huntsville Chamber of Commerce Office.

End of August. Horse-pulling demonstration and pig-calling contest to celebrate the harvest. Muskoka Pioneer Village.

Mid-September. Shades of Autumn, Huntsville. The annual charity scarecrow contest, Muskoka's biggest nonprofit bake sale. Huntsville Town Centre.

OTHER RECOMMENDED RESTAURANTS AND LODGINGS

Bracebridge

Muskoka Riverside Inn, 300 Ecclestone Drive. (705) 645–8775, (800) 461–4474. The inn serves reasonable breakfasts, lunches, and dinners from a comprehensive menu.

Gravenhurst

Ascona Restaurant, 110 Old Ferguson Road, corner Bethune Drive. (705) 687–5906. Owners Merv and Inge Dunlop offer reasonably priced European-style dishes.

FOR MORE INFORMATION

Bracebridge Chamber of Commerce, 1-1 Manitoba Street, Bracebridge ON P1L 1S4. (705) 645–8121.

Gravenhurst Chamber of Commerce, 685-2 Muskoka Road North, Graven-hurst ON P1P 1M8. (705) 687–4432.

Huntsville-Lake of Bays Chamber of Commerce, 8 West Street North, Unit 1, Huntsville ON P1H 2B6. (705) 789–4771 or (888) 696–4255.

Muskoka Tourism, R.R.2, Kilworth ON P0E 1G0. (705) 689–0660 or (800) 267–9700.

Manitoulin Island
GITCHI-MANITOU'S IDYLL

2 NIGHTS

A cliffside resort • Rural beauty • A hiking adventure
An 1870 lighthouse

The largest freshwater island in the world sits at the top of Lake Huron, plugging the mouth of Georgian Bay. Shaped like a giant doorstop with the sharp end pointing northwest, Manitoulin Island is almost exactly half the size of Prince Edward Island, at 1,068 square miles, and contains more than 100 lakes.

The island is 160 km (100 miles) long and its width varies from 3 to 64 km (2 to 38 miles). The shoreline, riddled with inlets and bays, is a cartographer's nightmare. Stubby points poke into Georgian Bay in all directions and dozens of smaller islands form an archipelago to confuse the most seasoned mariner. Manitoulin is pretty and rugged; there are granite outcrops, forests, meadows, rivers, and rolling countryside. Only 20 percent of the land is arable and much of the rest is used for grazing sheep and cattle.

A popular Indian legend says that when Gitchi-Manitou, the Great Spirit, was creating the world, he selected the finest of each component of creation. From the waters he took the most blue and sparkling lake; from the skies he chose the fleeciest cloud and the brightest stars; from the land he selected the most fertile fields and the greenest forest.

He set all these things aside, and when he had completed his task of creation, he took the choicest pieces and fashioned them into an island. He placed it on the waters of the Great Northern Inland Sea, Lake Huron, and it drifted north and came to rest beside the rocky coastline of the north shore. Manitou reserved this special place for himself, and it was named the Island of

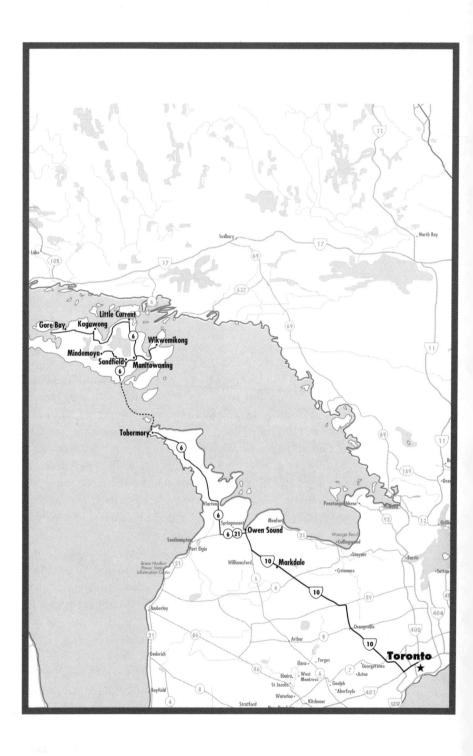

Manitou. Indians believe the island is the dwelling place of both the good spirit Gitchi-Manitou and the evil spirit Matchi-Manitou.

When people first came to the island isn't known, but archaeological digs at Sheguindah have produced evidence of humans living there more than 30,000 years ago, the oldest trace of mankind on the continent. Who those people were, where they came from, or where they disappeared to remains a mystery; there is no interim record of human habitation on the island until Samuel de Champlain encountered some island residents in 1650.

Although separated from the tip of the Bruce Peninsula by about 30 km (19 miles) of water, Manitoulin Island is a continuation of the Niagara Escarpment. It is linked to the northern mainland by a swing bridge and to the tip of the Bruce Peninsula by a seasonal ferry service from Tobermory. Yachting aficionados rate the waters among the best in the world, and hunters and fishermen have been beating the area's bushes and waters for generations.

DAY 1

Morning

Stow your loaded picnic hamper and cooler in the car. Between mid-June and early September, plan on catching the 3:40 P.M. ferry from Tobermory to South Baymouth. Take Highway 10 through Brampton and Orangeville to Primrose on Highway 89. Turn west on Highway 10/89 to Shelburne and take Highway 10 north through Dundalk to Flesherton. At Flesherton, turn east on Highway 4 and look for signs for a left turn to **Eugenia Falls Conservation Area** on Grey County Road 13. Just before you reach the conservation area there's a general store where you can get an ice-cream cone for dessert.

LUNCH: In the conservation area there are picnic tables near a pretty waterfall that drops from Lake Eugenia.

Afternoon

Return to Highway 4 to Flesherton, take Highway 10 north through Markdale to Chatsworth and then Highways 6 and 10 to Owen Sound. In Owen Sound turn left on Highways 6 and 21 and go 6 km (4 miles) to Springmount and then take Highway 70 north through Hepworth to pick up Highway 6 north again. Continue to Tobermory. The way to the ferry dock is well marked.

In summer, reservations are not available on either the 11:20 A.M. or 3:30 P.M. ferry; it's first come, first served. Ontario Northland operates two large ferryboats, the 143-car **Chi-Cheemaun** and the 130-car **Nindawayma,** from the end of April through October. In July and August the ships make a total of six daily return trips. (*Chi-Cheemaun* is an Ojibwa word for "Big Canoe"; *Nindawayma* translates as "Little Sister.") Each ship has a snack bar and cafeteria.

From South Baymouth, take Highway 6 to secondary road 542 through Mindemoya to the fifth side road and follow signs.

DINNER AND LODGING: Rockgarden Terrace Resort perches atop a limestone cliff overlooking Lake Mindemoya. For guests who don't favor hiking down to the lake, a heated outdoor pool also overlooks the lake. So do the dining room, health spa, chalets, and all of the eighteen motel units on three levels.

The property has been developed by the Oswald Argmann family and is very much a family affair. Mother Angela applies her expertise in the kitchen, father Oswald manages the operation, and daughters Ossie, Heidi, and Carmen all pitch in. Guests can remain aloof if they wish or get involved and become honorary members of the friendly family for the duration of their stay.

The resort also has four large chalets and a fully equipped honeymoon cottage some distance from the main buildings, with two bedrooms, a fireplace, and a deck. The chalets, ideal for two couples and several children, each have a Franklin fireplace, a small refrigerator, a four-piece bathroom on the first floor, and a three-piece bathroom upstairs.

The resort invites lazy days beside the pool or on a motel unit veranda, or you can be up at dawn chasing pickerel, whitefish, and perch in the lake, or salmon and trout in spring and fall in the **Mindemoya River.** In winter, cross-country ski and snowmobile trails start at the front door.

The property even contains one of Manitoulin's tourist attractions. In the cliff on which the resort stands, there's a **limestone cave** discovered in 1888 by three Mennonite preachers who were hunting. In the cave they found the skeletons of seven Indians, believed to have been Ottawa Indians hiding from Iroquois who overran the island in 1652. (The skeletons were removed to a Toronto museum that was subsequently destroyed by fire.) En route to the cave are several depictions of classic children's stories beautifully showcased in tiny log cabins.

The resort's dining room serves outstanding continental and Canadian cuisine with an Austrian accent. The menu offers three treatments of veal cutlets, Hungarian goulash, shrimp, chicken, fish, and several steaks. Don't miss out on the Rockgarden Terrace Viennese Veal Cutlets.

Rates are $75–$86 per person. For more information contact Rockgarden Terrace Resort, R.R. 1, Spring Bay ON P0P 2B0. (705) 377–4652.

DAY 2

Morning

BREAKFAST: At the Rockgarden Terrace Resort.

Manitoulin Island is one of those places best explored at your own pace and following your own whims. The photographer or nature lover will want to slowly wander the backroads, soaking up its quiet rural beauty or surprising deer grazing by the roadside. There are pretty bays, empty beaches, and sleepy villages. It's not the sort of place you can "do" in a day; a week of dedicated sightseeing gives you a good feel for the place, but you'll have only scratched the surface. The major tourist sights are listed here, but the best places will be those nooks and crannies you discover on your own.

Little Current, with 1,500 people, is the largest community and Manitoulin's gateway from the north. The swing bridge is the only way on or off the island by car in winter, and during summer it opens every hour on the hour for fifteen minutes to allow boats through the North Channel.

The **Little Current–Howland Centennial Museum** is 18 km (12 miles) south of Little Current in Sheguiandah on Highway 6. Seven buildings in a wooded park contain Native and pioneer artifacts. Open daily mid-May through mid-September, 10:00 A.M. to 4:30 P.M. (705) 368–2367.

Thirty-three km (22 miles) farther south on Highway 6 in Manitowaning is another museum complex of pioneer log homes, a cut stone building, and a fully equipped blacksmith shop. **Assiginack Museum** is on Arthur Street, in an 1850s jailhouse, and is open daily June through September. Also in Manitowaning, in **Heritage Park,** is an 1883 gristmill and a former Great Lakes ferry, the **SS *Norisle.*** From June through September, visitors can tour the museum and the *Norisle* daily.

Nineteen km (13 miles) west of Little Current, at the junction of Highway 540 and Bidwell Road, is the start of **Cup and Saucer Hiking Trail.** It's so named because of the little hill—the cup—that sits atop the bigger hill, the saucer. Budget three hours for this trek. Add more time to take the **Adventure Trail** from that point, up ladders through a natural rock chimney and across a narrow ledge.

At the entrance to **Kagawong** on Highway 540 is the trail that leads to **Bridal Veil Falls,** a delicate, lacy cascade that drops over a limestone ledge.

There are a picnic area and stairs so you can go below the falls and walk behind them, a treat on a hot day. The front street of Kagawong has a turn-of-the-century mood; drop into the **Anglican Church** to see the pulpit made from the planks of a wrecked ship.

Eleven km (7 miles) west of **Meldrum Bay** at the west end of Manitoulin Island, you can climb an **1870 lighthouse** that overlooks the treacherous Mississagi Strait. Historians believe this is where the *Griffon* came to grief in 1679. The ship was built at Niagara for René-Robert Cavelier Sieur de La Salle. The *Griffon* was 60 feet long and weighed sixty tons. La Salle sailed on her maiden voyage in August 1679 to Green Bay on Lake Michigan, where he left her. Days later, laden with furs, she sailed for Niagara and was never seen again. Stories of a wreck and the discovery of several sailors' bodies in nearby caves still bring divers hoping to end the speculation. Iron and wood samples from a wreck indicate the appropriate antiquity, but authentication has not yet been possible. The Mississagi lighthouse is open daily 9:00 A.M. to 9:00 P.M. May 24 through September. Admission is $1.00 per person for parking and $1.00 per person for the museum. (705) 368–3021.

Remnants of the ship believed to have been the *Griffon* are housed in the **Gore Bay Museum,** a stone jail built in 1890 and in use as a jail until 1930. It used to be the jailhouse and home of the jailer. The former cells display relics from shipwrecks, pioneer furniture, and curios gathered by settlers. Open to the general public May to Canadian Thanksgiving (second Monday in October), Monday–Saturday 10:00 A.M. to 4:00 P.M., Sunday 2:00 to 4:00 P.M. Admission $1.00 for children, $2.00 for adults, and $1.50 for senior citizens; special events $3.00. Open March to May and Thanksgiving to November by appointment only. In Gore Bay at the west end of Dawson Street. (705) 282–2040.

The extreme eastern end of Manitoulin Island is **Wikwemikong,** believed to be North America's only unceded Indian Reserve and therefore, in theory at least, not part of Canada. After the War of 1812, the government of Upper Canada wanted to control the land on the southern shore of Georgian Bay. There was pressure to remove the Indians from their valuable land and make it available to white settlers. The government also realized tribes that had been living near whites had been ravaged by disease and alcohol. Sir Peregrine Maitland, lieutenant-governor of Upper Canada, proposed that the solution to both problems was to segregate the Indians on Manitoulin Island.

Wikwemikong Pow Wow on Manitoulin Island.

This was accomplished by a treaty in 1836. The government sponsored the founding of an "Establishment" for the 268 displaced Indians, which became the village of **Manitowaning.** By 1842 there were 700 white settlers. The government supported the Establishment for twenty years before concluding that the attempt to segregate the Indians was a failure. Government commissioners then suggested that the 1836 treaty be voided and in 1861 negotiations were started to persuade the Indians to cede their land to the government and permit it to be sold to white settlers. The commissioner of Crown Lands got signatures from groups living west of Heywood Sound and Manitoulin Gulf, but the treaty was rejected by the Wikwemikong Indians. Missionaries protested the treaty, claiming signatures were obtained by unethical methods. The government finally agreed to create a reserve for the Wikwemikong residents, an area of 105,000 acres (300 square miles).

One of the island's most colorful annual events is the **Wikwemikong Pow Wow** held each August on the civic holiday weekend. Native dancers accompanied by drummers and singers come from across North America to compete for prizes while performing the legendary steps of their ancestors.

DINNER: Twin Bluffs Bar and Grill at 6 Eleanor Street specializes in local organic food, and anyone wondering about the origin of the meat is invited to tour the local farm where it's raised. The decor is funky—leopard skin chairs, huge collages of *Time* and *Life* magazine pages, and a movie poster collage on the ceiling as well as original artwork and pottery displays, some of which are for sale. There are daily specials and the menu is a hodgepodge ranging from burgers to gourmet fare. Fish lovers come here for whitefish. Dinner costs $8.00–$16.00. Open daily. (705) 282–2000.

LODGING: Rockgarden Terrace Resort.

DAY 3

Morning

BREAKFAST: At the Rockgarden Terrace Resort.

From mid-June through September there's a 9:10 A.M. ferry from South Baymouth to Tobermory; in spring and fall there's an 11:10 A.M. departure. You can extend your Manitoulin Island escape by returning via Sudbury and Parry Sound. See Near North Escape Three for attractions, dining, and accommodations in that area.

SPECIAL EVENTS

Mid-June. Chi-Cheemaun Festival. Parade, fireworks, pancake breakfast, children's entertainment, water events, street dance, band concert, minigolf tournament. At the Community Centre and harbor area.

Mid-July. Fly-In and Community Fair, Gore Bay/Manitoulin Airport. Fly-in breakfast, trade fair, airplane rides, skydiving, paragliding, aerobatics, children's activities, live entertainment. Highway 540 West.

Mid-July. Summer Fest, Manitowaning. Parade, drag races, talent show, demolition derby. At Assignack Community Centre, Vankoughnet Street.

Early August. Lions Haweater Festival, Little Current. Antique show, horse show, water sports, fun games, parade, fireworks, dances, go-cart races. At Howland Recreation Centre, Highway 6.

Early August. Annual Competition Pow Wow, Wikwemikong. Ojibwa dance and drum competition. At Thunder Bird Park.

Mid-August. Marine Heritage Weekend, Tobermory. Nighttime Spirit Walk, historic diving exhibits, marine displays, street theater, demonstrations, music, *Tecumseh* schooner tours. At the harbor area and Community Centre.

OTHER RECOMMENDED RESTAURANTS AND LODGINGS

Red Roof, 24 Water Street. (705) 282–2618. A gorgeous octagonal building overlooking the busy harbor. Cuisine is buffet style with a wide range of choices. Open only June through August daily for breakfast, lunch, and dinner.

FOR MORE INFORMATION

Manitoulin Tourism Association, Box 119, Little Current ON P0P 1K0. (705) 368–3021.

Sault Ste. Marie and Sudbury

THE AGAWA CANYON SNOW TRAIN

4 NIGHTS

A ruined fort • Wilderness adventure • Pioneer buildings
The Soo Locks • A trip through a mine

The first thing you have to learn about Sault Ste. Marie is that nobody ever calls it that. It's "the Sault." The smaller town of Sault Ste. Marie across the St. Marys River in Michigan is called "the Soo." Same spelling of both, but different pronunciations.

The next thing to learn about the Sault is that despite its population of 81,000 and status as a city, it's an overgrown small town. The town site is compact because it's on the inside of a sharp bend in the St. Marys River and hemmed in by 270 degrees of water. The city overlooks a rapids in the river (30 km) 20 miles downstream from the southeast corner of Lake Superior. When winter arrives—and it comes early and leaves late—there aren't many tourists. The community closes in on itself and folks display great originality in conceiving ways to entertain themselves when the nights are long, the mercury is low, but the spirits are high.

Sault residents get to know the faces they see frequently so you'll notice people chatting on the streets and exchanging greetings. That isn't to the exclusion of visitors, who will find a genuinely warm welcome and all sorts of help when they get lost downtown, which can be a maze for the uninitiated.

The Sault rivals Hamilton with its one-way street system that sometimes appears as though all streets go in only one direction. But, unlike Hamilton, there's no mountain to help you get your bearings, only a curving river that compounds your confusion.

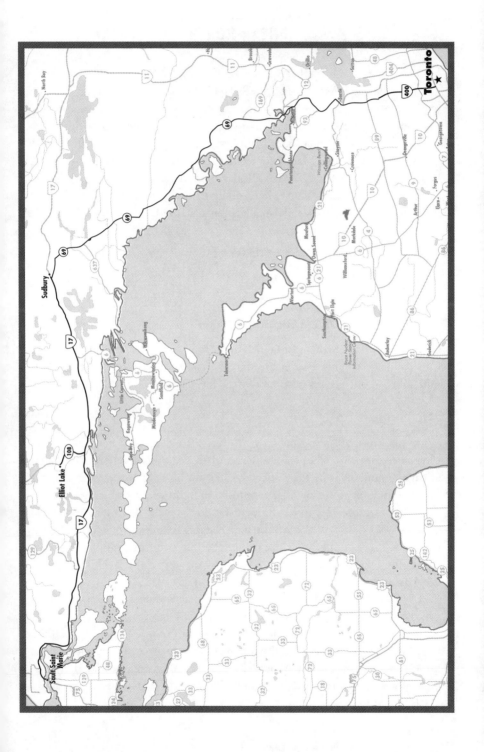

The Sault has always been a natural meeting place and cultural melting pot. Long before Etienne Brulé "discovered" the rapids in 1622, Ojibwa tribes of the Algonkian Indians gathered there. Whitefish, their staple food, could easily be caught at the rapids year-round, and during the winter the rapids often were the only open water for miles around.

When Père Jacques Marquette established a mission at the rapids in 1668, he named it Sainte Marie de Sault. Today more than half the city's population has cultural roots from somewhere other than the British Isles, with large numbers from Italy, France, Poland, Scandinavia, the Ukraine, and Germany.

DAY 1

Morning

From Toronto, it's a 690-km (431-mile) drive to the Sault. Take Highway 401 west to Highway 400, and Highway 400 north.

LUNCH: Try **Bay Street Cafe** in Parry Sound. It's near the dock where Canada's largest sightseeing cruise ship, the *Island Queen,* offers 64-km (40-mile), three-hour cruises of some of the Thirty Thousand Islands.

Afternoon

With 465 km (290 miles) still to go to reach the Sault, you may decide you can't spare three hours for the cruise, but there's another interesting diversion at Parry Sound. In 1927 the district forester got his department to erect a 90-foot fire lookout tower on a hill overlooking the town. It had an observation deck and became the town's trademark, so when it was declared unsafe another was requested. The Ministry of Natural Resources obliged and, after driving to the parking lot at the top of the hill, you can climb the **98-foot tower** for a superb view over Parry Sound and some of the **Thirty Thousand Islands.**

Continue northwest on Highway 400 and at Sudbury go west on Highway 17, the southern route of the Trans-Canada Highway.

If you can spare the time, consider the 84-km (52-mile) round-trip off the highway to **Elliot Lake, Uranium Capital of the World.** The sobriquet is no longer true because the mines have closed, but in their heyday they produced 74 percent of Canada's uranium. The town first appeared on a map in 1901 and rapidly grew to a population of 20,000.

Elliot Lakers also call their town "Jewel in the Wilderness," and the place has some interesting claims to fame. In 1942, 500-year-old pine trees from Elliot Lake provided veneer for the all-wood Mosquito fighter bombers used by the Royal Canadian Air Force in World War II. In 1946, the first jet aircraft to crash in Canada did so 29 km (18 miles) north of town. The first uranium claims were staked in 1952 and that's when the town boomed. By 1959 the population was 24,000. Today there's another "boom." Entrepreneurs bought the empty mining company homes for a song and woo retirees by offering houses at 20–30 percent of their value farther south.

The town's short history is chronicled, and the story of uranium told, in the **Nuclear and Mining Museum,** a tidy, well-organized display in the Municipal Office at 45 Hillside Drive. There are mineral samples, wildlife displays, and artifacts from logging days. (If you take your time browsing you'll be able to drop such nuggets as this at your next gathering: The heat produced from one pound of uranium is equal to that produced by 3 million pounds of coal.) Open June through September 8:00 A.M. to 8:00 P.M. weekdays, 9:00 A.M. to 5:00 P.M. on weekends. Open September through May 9:00 A.M. to 4:30 P.M. weekdays, weekends by appointment. (705) 848–2084.

Return to Highway 17 and head west. At **Blind River,** 140 km (87 miles) east of the Sault, **Timber Village Museum** displays pioneer lumbering and agricultural artifacts and scale replicas of a logging camp, riverboats, and a blacksmith's shop carved in wood. Outside are working models of logging techniques and unique snowmobile prototypes. On Highway 17 just east of town. Open June 1 to Labor Day.

Three km (2 miles) north of Thessalon on Highway 129 is **Thessalon Township Heritage Park and Museum.** Three log buildings illustrate different types of pioneer construction. Displays include stone tools and weapons from the Archaic Period and lumbering and farming artifacts from the late 1800s. Open daily 9:00 A.M. to 5:00 P.M. July through August, other times by appointment. (705) 842–3800.

In Bruce Mines, also on Highway 17, about 65 km (40 miles) southeast of the Sault, the **Bruce Mines Museum** is in the 1894 Presbyterian church. The most highly prized artifact is one of two music box/slot machines manufactured in Chicago in 1876, which found its way to a hotel in nearby Rydal Bank. Bruce Mines is the oldest copper-mining town in Canada. Production began in 1847, and declining profits closed the operations in 1876. The museum also has a doll's house once owned by the Marquess of Queensbury, formulator of the rules of boxing. His son, also Marquess of Queensbury, ran the mines in their declining years. He lived in a mansion a few blocks from the museum. The lower floor now houses a tavern, and the ornate shingling and woodwork of the upper floors and four-story circular tower are badly in need of repair. Bruce Mines Museum is open daily mid-May through mid-October.

DINNER AND LODGING: Since you'll be taking the Agawa Canyon Snow Train, try to get a room at **Bay Front Quality Inn** at 180 Bay Street. **Gran Festa** at the inn has good prices and friendly service. There's an indoor pool, sauna, whirlpool, and exercise room. Most important—since the train leaves at 8:00 A.M. and you should be at the station by 7:30 A.M.—the hotel is directly across the street from **Algoma Central Railroad Station.** That means you can enjoy the hotel's breakfast, stroll across the street, and leave your car parked at the hotel. When you return at night, exhausted, you just have to cross the street to your hotel room. Reservations suggested: (705) 945–9264 or (800) 228–5151.

DAY 2

Morning and Afternoon

BREAKFAST: In your room or at Gran Festa.

Be in the station no later than 7:40 A.M. (8:00 A.M. in winter). The **Agawa Canyon Train** or the **Snow Train**—the name varies with the seasons—runs from the Sault to kilometer 182 (mile 114) in summer, and to kilometer 192 (mile 120) in winter. Tour trains operate daily June 5 to October 15, and only on Saturday and Sunday January through March. There are no tours during the other times of the the the year.

LUNCH: Dining-car service is continuous 7:00 A.M. to 3:45 P.M. and includes full breakfast, hot and cold lunches or picnic box lunches, sandwiches, and cold drinks.

In summer the train stops for two hours in **Agawa Canyon,** a rugged chunk of wilderness 19 km (12 miles) long with cliff walls up to 800 feet high through which the Agawa River meanders. During the stopover passengers can lunch in a pretty park, hike to their choice of three waterfalls, or climb 372 steps to a point 250 feet above the train and overlook the canyon.

The Agawa Canyon Snow Train trip is spectacularly beautiful, but the summer trip is just too many hours of looking at trees and rocks occasionally relieved by lakes, rivers, and a couple of trestles. The curved trestle that stretches 1,550 feet across the Montréal River and 130 feet above it is spectacular—if you're not afflicted with acrophobia! What saves the trip is the enthusiasm of the pleasant young crew and getting to know fellow passengers.

As the train pulls out of the Sault, you'll receive a souvenir guide that describes everything you'll see along the way and everything you ever wanted to know about Agawa Canyon and **Algoma Central Railway.**

Summer rates (June 3 to September 8) are $52 adults, $16 children five to eighteen, $10 children under five. **Fall color tours** (September 9 to October 14) are $62 adults, $36 children. The snow train is $53 adults, $27 children five to eighteen, $10 children under five. Write: Agawa Canyon Tour, Passenger Sales, Algoma Central Railway, 129 Bay Street, Sault Ste. Marie ON P6A 6Y2 (705) 946–7300 or (800) 242–9287.

DINNER: For a memorable dining experience try **A Thymely Manner** at 531 Albert Street East. The restaurant is in an old house and dining rooms are small and cosy. They are open for lunch and dinner Tuesday–Sunday and offer dishes created from old family recipes brought from Italy. There are lots of fresh pasta and seafood dishes, and the desserts are unusual and delightful. Dinner will cost $15–$30 per person; reservations are recommended. (705) 759–3262.

LODGING: Bay Front Quality Inn.

DAY 3

Morning

BREAKFAST: In your room or at Gran Festa.

Hiawathaland Sightseeing Tours operates three tours in and around the Sault by double-decker bus and three wilderness tours outside the city. From June 15 to Labor Day there are three city tours daily, and Labor Day to October 15, two tours. The two-hour tour covers 35 km (22 miles) and takes you past just about every point of interest. From June through October there's a seventy-five-minute evening tour that lets you look down from the international bridge onto the world's busiest lock system. A third tour shows you both cities in the daytime in two hours. The three other tours are all-day trips by minivan to **Wawa, Aubrey Falls,** or **St. Joseph Island.** Contact Hiawathaland Sightseeing Tours, Box 185, Sault Ste. Marie ON P6A 5L6. (705) 759–6200.

One of the Sault's most-touted attractions is a boat tour through the **Soo Locks,** the sixteenth and final lift for ships bound for Lake Superior from the St. Lawrence River. The locks raise ships to about 600 feet above sea level— a vertical rise of 600 feet from the mouth of the St. Lawrence River 3,200 km (2,000 miles) downstream.

There are five locks through the rapids. The oldest is the Canadian lock, built in 1895 and now out of commission. Your boat will be lifted only about 21 feet through one of the four operating locks on the American side, but if you haven't been through a lock before it's an interesting experience. Two-hour tours aboard the 200-passenger **MV** *Chief Shingwauk* or the 156-passenger **MV** *Bon Soo* leave from **Norgoma Dock** downriver from Holiday Inn, May 15 to October 15. The tour takes you to both ends of the Canadian locks, past Soo, Michigan, and the massive Algoma Steel Mill, the Sault's biggest industry and major employer. For information contact Lock Tours Canada, Box 325, Sault Ste. Marie ON P6A 5L8. (705) 253–9850.

LUNCH: One of Ontario's best-value restaurants for good food with no frills is **Mike's,** a tiny place at 518 Queen Street East. Mike's has been serving huge early breakfasts for sport fishermen, as well as lunches and dinners, since 1932. There are two tables for two and about twenty stools like those at the dime-store lunch counters of the 1950s. You won't believe the prices or the size of the servings; they'll help you understand why most patrons and staff are on a first-name basis.

Afternoon

You may want to tour the **MS** *Norgoma,* a 188-foot 1950 ship that was the last overnight passenger cruiser on the Great Lakes. She's berthed near Holiday Inn, and during June through October students take you on a twenty-minute tour for a modest fee. There isn't much to see other than the way the ship used to look to its passengers, but the young guides are enthusiastic and make the tour fun. (705) 942–7447.

Charles Oakes Ermatinger was a first-generation Canadian born in Montréal to Swiss parents. He was an independent fur trader and he married Mananowe (Charlotte), daughter of influential Chief Katawebeda, a move that didn't hurt his business dealings with the Indians.

He had an elegant home built in 1814 of local red fieldstone that's the oldest building in Canada west of Toronto and is now known as the **Ermatinger Old Stone House.** Charles and Charlotte lived there in style with their thirteen children, seven of whom survived to adulthood. Their home was "the" social center for the communities on both sides of the river, and invitations to their annual caribou dinner were eagerly sought.

The two-story Georgian-style home was beautifully finished. Charles augmented his fur-trade wealth by building a flour mill and encouraging others to grow wheat and oats, which he processed for a percentage. The home is fully furnished and costumed guides show you through and demonstrate cooking, baking, and crafts in the summer kitchen.

The museum's prized possession is an original map of the Great Lakes drawn by French mapmaker M. Bellin from notes supplied by early explorers and fur traders. Considering the vast areas covered by the map, the outline of the five Great Lakes is surprisingly accurate. Distances were measured in that era by the length of time it took a man to smoke a pipe of tobacco as his canoe was paddled along. Each explorer's canoe contained one official pipe smoker so the distances covered by his pipe-smoking were consistent.

Admission by donation. Open April 1 to May 31, Monday–Friday 10:00 A.M. to 5:00 P.M.; June 1 to September 30, daily 10:00 A.M. to 5:00 P.M.; and October 1 to November 30, daily 1:00 to 5:00 P.M. At 831 Queen Street East. (705) 759–5443.

The **Sault Ste. Marie Museum** is nearby in the striking former post office building, a 1902 monument to federal government spending, at the corner of Queen and East Streets. The cut stone walls have Romanesque arched windows on the first three stories, and there's an Italianate four-story clock tower. The building has a spacious oak staircase, a skylight three stories above the main foyer floor, and a plate-glass floor.

Exhibits and artifacts trace the history of the Sault back 10,000 years, including a re-creation of the city's Queen Street as it would have appeared in 1910. There are a hands-on area for children and a section on natural history. The one-of-a-kind homemade 1948-vintage motorized toboggan is particularly interesting. Admission by donation. Open year-round, Monday–Saturday 10:00 A.M. to 5:00 P.M.; Sunday 1:00 to 5:00 P.M. At 690 Queen Street East. (705) 759–7278.

DINNER: Try **Cesira's Italian Cuisine** at 133 Spring Street. This is one restaurant that's properly named, so don't go looking for roast beef and Yorkshire pudding or barbecued ribs. There are some steaks—poivre, Diane, tartare, New York, filet mignon, sirloin, and Chateaubriand—but it's the traditional Italian food that keeps the regulars coming back for heaped, steaming plates of Cesira's family dishes.

Cesira makes her own pasta for the fettucine, lasagna, ravioli, cannelloni, and tortellini dishes. Other dishes feature giant tiger shrimp, lobster tail, king crab, and veal. And there are French dishes like shrimp flamed in Pernod and lobster tails flamed in brandy at your table.

The five-room restaurant is in two turn-of-the-century homes ingeniously combined into one building. Reservations recommended: (705) 949–0600.

LODGING: Bay Front Quality Inn.

DAY 4

Morning

BREAKFAST: At Gran Festa or Mike's.

Check out of the hotel and take the ninety-minute tour of Canada's largest forest research complex, the **Great Lakes Forestry Centre.** It's at 1219 Queen Street East. There are audiovisual presentations and you can visit the laboratories and greenhouses. Open late June through end of August, Monday–Friday, 10:00 A.M. to 2:00 P.M.

Start back toward Toronto on Highway 17 east. Forty km (25 miles) south of the Sault follow signs to **St. Joseph Island.** Once on the island, have a light foot on the gas. You never know when moose or deer may amble across the road. Another good reason to drive slowly on the 24-by-30-km (16-by-20-mile) island is to enjoy its beauty, particularly in the spring. That's when wild lilac trees bloom and the countryside is redolent with their scent. The island is the most westerly of the Manitoulin chain, an extension of the Niagara Escarpment. It's in the mouth of the St. Marys River and connected by a causeway and bridge to the mainland.

Back in fur-trade days a British fort at the southeast tip of the island safeguarded the trade route from Montréal to the upper Great Lakes. British forces established a base camp in 1796 and two years later started building Fort St. Joseph, the most westerly outpost in all of British North America, now **Fort St. Joseph National Historic Site.** (From the point at which you turn south off Highway 17 onto Highway 548, it's 51 km [31 miles] to the fort site.)

By 1803 the blockhouse, guardhouse, stockade, and powder magazine were completed and Montréal fur traders moved to the island, building huts, stores, and wharves. The Indian Department at the fort strengthened relations with the Ojibwa, who came regularly for the ceremonial exchange of gifts.

The friendship stood the British in good stead. When the War of 1812 broke out, the fort's garrison, strengthened by Indians and fur traders, was first off the mark. The expedition recaptured nearby Fort Michilimackinac, on what is now Mackinac Island, from the new republic of the United States without bloodshed. The Americans sought revenge in 1814, when they raided Fort St. Joseph and burned it to the ground. It was never rebuilt, but in the mid-1960s University of Toronto archaeologists conducted preliminary research at the site. In the mid-1970s a three-year program by Canada Parks archaeologists unearthed details about the size and layout of the military and commercial communities at the site and stabilized the ruins.

Today you can wander on the rounded peninsula on which the fort and commercial buildings once stood and see the outlines and a few above-ground stone ruins of the forty-two building sites that have been identified. Your best bet is to start at the **Interpretation Centre,** where you can see artifacts and a layout of the fort and get a free walking-tour booklet to tell you where to go and what you're looking at when you get there.

While you're exploring the site and imagining what a bleak, desolate, and lonely outpost it must have been, you're likely to see ships from anywhere in the world passing close to land on their way up or down the Great Lakes. The visitor center is open daily late May through Thanksgiving weekend. (705) 246–2664.

There's also a museum on the island at the corner of Twentieth Sideroad and I Line, 6 km (4 miles) south of the bridge. **St. Joseph Island Museum** has six pioneer buildings—a church, store, barn, and log cabins—containing more than 3,000 artifacts. There are such oddities as a handmade wooden bicycle and a winter hearse. Open in June on Saturday and Sunday 2:00 to 5:00 P.M., and daily July and August 10:00 A.M. to 5:00 P.M. Closed Labor Day. (705) 246–2672.

An unusual stone is found on the island and makes a popular souvenir. The proper name for **puddingstone** is Jasper Conglomerate. It was formed more than a billion years ago when bits of bright red and brown jasper and pebbles of white quartz, mixed with sand and other minerals, were fused together with white quartzite by volcanic action. Glacial movement deposited the conglomerate in a narrow band 80 km (50 miles) long, running north and west of Bruce Mines. The stone was named by pioneers, to whom it resembled suet pudding with plums, currants, cherries, and raisins. The conglomerate is a hard stone that can be cut and polished, and gift shops sell items made from the stone—everything from bookends to paper weights, earrings to doorstops.

Return to Highway 17 east and head for Sudbury. At Massey, 95 km (59 miles) west of Sudbury on Highway 17 and the junction of the Sauble and Spanish Rivers, the **Massey Museum** has a surprisingly extensive collection of interesting displays.

As you'll learn at the museum, the game of broomball was invented here and the fact is noted in the town crest, which features two crossed brooms and a ball. The game was first played in, May 1912 after members of a men's soccer team noticed a child swatting a ball with a broom. The men borrowed brooms, set up rules, and played a frenzied and historic game that resulted in numerous injuries.

There are also beautifully crafted wooden miniatures of logging equipment and sleighs, and artifacts from the banks of the Sauble and Spanish Rivers dated at 4,000 B.C. The museum is at 160 Sauble Street (Highway 17). Open daily mid-June to Labor Day and on weekdays in October and March through mid-June.

The city of Sudbury used to bear the brunt of a lot of unkind jokes; after all, didn't the U.S. astronauts go there to train in the type of terrain they were likely to encounter on the moon? The city might be **Nickel Capital of the World,** but wasn't it a fact there was nothing green for miles around it? And, really, the city core thirty years ago was a warren of ramshackle, grit-stained, crumbling buildings. Residential areas close to downtown were boxlike houses jammed together with front and back yards that were just patches of gravel, cinders, and weeds.

But you should see Sudbury now! It's a modern, vibrant, clean city of 162,000 people with imaginative and boldly designed architecture. The streets are well lit, and the downtown is anchored by a spiffy **Civic Square Provincial Tower.** There are band concerts in the park, art centers, and a cruise on **Lake Ramsey,** one of a number of lakes within the city limits.

And everything around the city is turning green. What killed the vegetation was a smelting method used in the 1920s known as heap roasting. This involved piling ore with a high sulphur content on beds of timber and then igniting the wood. The piles burned for months, sending off dense clouds of sulphurous fumes in the constant exposure of which no vegetation could survive.

In 1970 the Greening of Sudbury program was launched. Hundreds of students, financed by various employment incentive grants, spread tons of lime on all the soil in and around the city. Now, where there was nothing but blackened rock and leached soil, the earth among the rocks has recovered and supports the growth of special varieties of coarse grass and a young forest of poplar and other deciduous trees.

The residential areas of the city now have well-maintained homes with lush lawns and flower beds. The people of Sudbury have a justifiable pride in their city.

Northern Ontario's biggest tourism magnet, **Science North,** opened in 1984 and has been an unqualified success. This hands-on science museum is housed in two snowflake-shaped buildings that cling to a rocky ledge on the shores of Lake Ramsey. The buildings are startling; they resemble stainless-steel-sheathed science-fiction spacecraft. (The museum also administers the **Big Nickel Mine** and the **Path of Discovery Bus Tour.** Tickets are sold for one, two, or three of the attractions, with discounts on combination tickets. Only Science North is open in winter.)

The buildings sit atop a giant cavern blasted out of the rock, which symbolizes the Sudbury Basin, and the buildings represent the glaciers and climate that shaped the Sudbury landscape. The smaller of the two buildings houses administration offices and a licensed restaurant that serves excellent lunches and dinners.

The showpiece of the main display building is the **Creighton Fault,** an ancient geological fracture named after the town of Creighton, where it begins. The unmapped fault was discovered during construction of Science North by a backhoe operator. The debris was cleaned out and architects rejigged the building so the 13-foot-deep crack could be viewed.

The entrance is up a ramp blasted through solid rock. First stop is in a massive, rock-walled cavern with seating for 250 people where a 3-D film is shown. It's a patriotic award-winner called *A Place to Stand* about Ontario's people, geology, flora, and fauna. This is not your average museum with static displays. It's a place where everybody can get right into it—from lying on a bed of nails (be sure to try it!) to fashioning a soapstone carving to creating your own hurricane or snowstorm. Young and eager staff answer questions and encourage participation in the dozens of laboratories.

One feature popular with youngsters is the **Trading Post.** All sorts of bugs, fossils, shells, feathers, rock samples, and shells are displayed and "for sale," but no money changes hands. Each item has a price, in points. Children earn points by working at the museum or bringing in specimens they have collected. Their treasures are identified and given point values. The treasures then can be swapped for items of similar point value.

Open daily year-round. Spring and fall hours are 9:00 A.M. to 5:00 P.M.; winter hours are 10:00 A.M. to 4:00 P.M.; and summer hours (late June to Labor Day) are 9:00 A.M. to 7:00 P.M. At 100 Ramsey Lake Road. (705) 522–3701 or (800) 468–4898.

LUNCH: Try the **Snowflake Room Restaurant** at Science North. There are daily lunch and dinner specials and a Sunday brunch. Reservations recommended: (705) 522–0376.

Afternoon

The **Big Nickel,** a 30-foot replica of the Canadian 1951 commemorative coin, has been synonymous with Sudbury for three decades. It is the largest coin in the world and stands on a barren hillside west of the city overlooking the smokestacks of the International Nickel Company (INCO). (That very tall stack, by the way, is no longer the world's tallest free-standing structure, a dubious distinction it earned when it was built in 1972. It's only 1,250 feet high. Toronto's CN Tower, opened in 1976, is 1,815 feet, 5 inches high.)

The Big Nickel is near the entrance to **Big Nickel Mine.** At 73 feet it is one of the shallowest mines in the area, but all the standard features of other mines have been incorporated in it so visitors and mining students can see the old and new techniques of getting ore to the surface.

Visitors are outfitted in hard hats, coats, and boots and lowered into the shaft in a "cage" elevator. In the "drifts," or tunnels, miners demonstrate drilling, loading drill holes with explosives, and the processes of blasting, scaling, mucking, and bolting. In one of the drifts, vegetables are grown under artificial light in an insect-free environment. There are a refuge station, a powder magazine, and a mailbox where you can send a friend a card from the world's only underground "post office."

The Big Nickel is at Highway 17 and Big Nickel Mine Road. The tour is given daily May 1 to June 25, 9:00 A.M. to 5:00 P.M.; June 26 to Labor Day, 9:00 A.M. to 7:00 P.M.; and Labor Day to October 9, from 9:00 A.M. to 5:00 P.M. (705) 522–3701.

The two-and-a-half-hour **Path of Discovery Bus Tour** leaves from the Big Nickel and Science North several times daily. Visitors are taken to the spot where Canadian Pacific Railroad worker Thomas Flannagan discovered copper and nickel ores about 4 km (2.5 miles) west of the town site in 1884. That discovery touched off a mining boom and for a time Sudbury was producing 80 percent of the world's nickel as well as significant quantities of copper, iron

Sudbury's Big Nickel, a 30-foot replica of the 1951 commemorative coin.

ore, cobalt, silver, gold, sulphur, platinum, osmium, iridium, rhodium, ruthenium, selenium, and tellurium.

The tour also goes to the edge of the **Sudbury Basin,** a massive indentation created two billion years ago by either a meteorite 4 km (2.5 miles) wide, a huge volcanic eruption, or a combination of the two. The event created an elliptically shaped depression 59 km (37 miles) long and 27 km (19 miles) wide. The tour visits Sudbury's oldest mine, historic sites in Copper Cliff, and the smelter and super stack at INCO, the world's largest integrated nickel mining, smelting, and refining complex.

There's also a stop at **Clarabelle Railway Station.** The tiny wooden building enjoyed its moment of glory in *Ripley's Believe-It-Or-Not* as Canada's smallest and busiest railroad station—it serviced both ore trains and the Canadian Pacific Railroad transcontinental line. (705) 522–3701.

There is no admission charge to **Copper Cliff Museum,** a collection of antiques housed in an 1890 log cabin on Balsam Street. Open Monday–Friday, June to Labor Day. (705) 674–3141 ext. 2460.

DINNER AND LODGING: The **Four Points Hotel** has an indoor pool with adjacent sauna and whirlpool, and a licensed dining room and coffee shop. At 1696 Regent Street South. (705) 522–3000 or (800) 325–3535.

Evening

The 297-seat **Sudbury Theatre Centre** offers a regular season of eight performances of classic and modern comedies, dramas, mysteries, and musicals September through June and also has a summer season. To find out what's on when you're in town, call (705) 674–8381.

DAY 5

Morning

BREAKFAST: At the Four Points Hotel.

Head for home. Take Highway 400 south to Highway 401 and then go east to Toronto.

THERE'S MORE

The free **Flour Mill Heritage Museum** houses a collection of antique furniture, weapons, early hand tools, and farm implements at St. Charles and Notre Dame Streets in Sudbury. Open mid-June to Labor Day, Monday–Friday 10:00 A.M. to 4:30 P.M., Saturday 1:00 to 3:00 P.M. (705) 674–2391.

It doesn't sound spectacular, but seen by night, **slag-dumping** *is.* Rail cars of molten slag are shunted out on a dump high above your observation point, and one by one, in sequence, the cars are dumped by remote control, tipping loads of molten rock to cascade down the side of the dumps like lava from a volcano. There used to be a telephone number visitors could call to get a recording that would tell them where, and at approximately what time, loads of slag would be dumped. INCO no longer provides this service and the switchboard operator at the main switchboard doesn't have that information. If you can't get the inside scoop from someone working at INCO, your best bet is to scout a nighttime dumpsite from up at the Big Nickel, get closer to it—if company security people don't have the roads blocked—and hope there will be another dump. Remember what you're getting close to . . . and don't get too close! The challenge of the search is worth the fantastic spectacle.

The art and museum exhibits at **Laurentian University Museum and Arts Centre** change frequently in this center housed in the former mansion and coach house of W. J. Bell, an early lumber magnate. In the attic there are local arts and crafts for sale. No admission charge. Open Tuesday–Sunday noon to 5:00 P.M., or by appointment. (705) 674–3271.

By advance notice, tours are available of **Laurentian University,** which overlooks Lake Ramsey. The tour includes the **Doran Planetarium,** the strikingly designed **Thorneloe Chapel,** and the **Arboretum.** Visitors may buy a day pass to the Olympic-size pool, sauna, weight room, and gym. (705) 675–1151.

During summer, the seventy-passenger *Cortina* makes up to five daily one-hour cruises around Lake Ramsey from her dock in front of Science North. The lake is the largest freshwater lake in North America inside a city's limits. Cruises run mid-May to Labor Day. (705) 522–3701.

SPECIAL EVENTS

Mid-July. Summer Rendez-Vous, Sault Ste. Marie. A celebration of the annual gathering of the *voyageurs* (employees of the fur companies who were hired to carry men and goods by canoe through the forests), fur traders, and indigenous peoples, with displays of native crafts, traditional foods, fur-trade goods, traditional music. At the Old Stone House, 831 Queen Street East.

Early August. Bushplane Days, Sault Ste. Marie. Aircraft rides, flying and stationary aircraft. In the downtown waterfront area.

Mid-August. Blueberry Festival, Sault Ste. Marie. A celebration of Algoma's favorite fruit, Ermatinger Old Stone House, 831 Queen Street East.

Late September. Annual Algoma Fall Festival, Sault Ste. Marie. Performing and visual arts, national and international artists, at Community Theatre Centre.

OTHER RECOMMENDED RESTAURANTS AND LODGINGS

Sault Ste. Marie

Alpen Hof, 674 Great Northern Road. (705) 949–6454. Bavarian-themed restaurant with fine German cuisine and also steaks, chicken, and seafood. Has Canada's largest free-hanging cuckoo clock.

Adolfo's, 920 Great Northern Road. (705) 254–4578. Serves reasonable lunches, afternoon teas, and dinners. Popular with locals.

Sudbury

Cassio's, 1145 Lorne Street. (705) 674–4205. Serving Italian and Canadian cuisine since 1937. They're big on seafood and offer a luncheon buffet Monday–Friday and a dinner buffet Saturday and Sunday. Brunch is served on Sunday.

Mr. Prime Rib, 777 Barrydowne Road. (705) 566–5353. This restaurant serves tender and delicious prime ribs, among other items. Reservations recommended.

Holiday Inn, 50 Brady Street. (705) 675–5602. Has 77 rooms, bar/lounge, and dining room.

Days Inn, 117 Elm Street. (705) 674–7517. Has 66 rooms, indoor pool, sauna, and dining room.

Howard Johnson Hotel, 390 Elgin Street South. (705) 675–1273. Has 88 rooms, indoor pool, whirlpool, bar/lounge, and dining room.

Comfort Inn by Journey's End Motels, 2171 Regent Street South. (705) 522–1101.

FOR MORE INFORMATION

Sault Ste. Marie Economic Development Corp., Civic Centre, 99 Foster Drive, Sault Ste. Marie ON P6A 5N1. (705) 759–5432 or (800) 461–6020.

Moosonee and Moose Factory

THE POLAR BEAR EXPRESS

ADVENTURE

3 NIGHTS

Bookworm's nirvana • Wilderness excursions • Bannock
Tundra • Water taxis • Gold mines

Once may be enough, but you'll never regret visiting Moosonee and Moose Factory. That isn't intended to sound negative; some people delight in returning to Ontario's end of steel every chance they get, but odds are they grew up in the North or spent a major chunk of their lives there.

Southerners respond to the North in one of two ways: They love it and don't ever want to leave, or they hate it and try never to return. Moosonee and Moose Factory may be considered Far North by southern Ontarians, but the two communities are only the southern gateway to the North. They're not even one-third of the way from Toronto to places like Pangnirtung or Iqaluit in the Northwest Territories. But they *are* more than 1,000 km (625 miles) north of Toronto.

North Bay calls itself Gateway of the North, and a sign at the railway station proclaims Moosonee to be Gateway to the Arctic. You can fly to Moosonee or take the **Polar Bear Express**, Ontario Northland's railway train. The Polar Bear makes a round-trip from Cochrane, 300 km (190 miles) south, daily except Friday, late June to early September. You can make a round-trip from Toronto, North Bay, or other points along the line, with an overnight in Iroquois Falls.

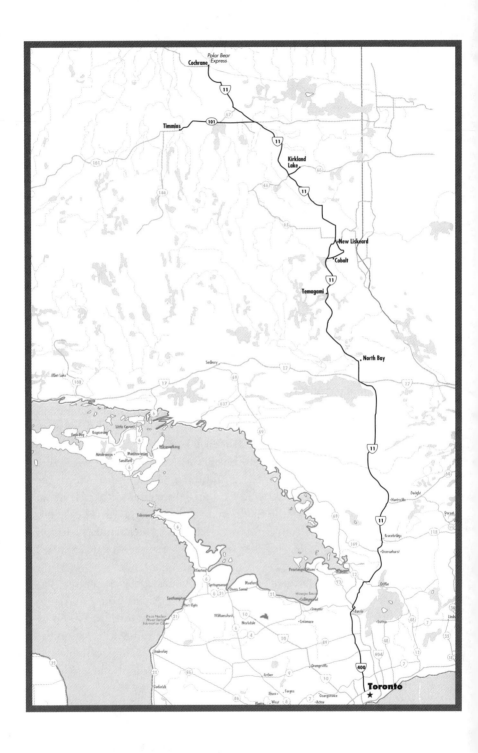

Reservations are advised. If you plan to overnight in Moosonee or Cochrane be sure to confirm reservations. There are lots of motels in and around Cochrane, but it only takes one motor coach to fill the largest.

DAY 1

Morning

Get an early start because it will be a long day! Take Highway 400 to Barrie, and then Highway 11 toward North Bay.

LUNCH: If you're getting hungry after 300 km (188 miles), have lunch at **Glen Roberts.** Look for the sign for Glen Roberts Road after you pass South River. Tom and Peggy Ludlow have been serving home-style lunches, teas, and dinners in their 1898 schoolhouse since 1975. Open daily, fixed lunch at $13 served noon to 3:00 P.M. If you're traveling with children, adjacent **Storybook Village** will brighten their trip ($4.00 admission). Puppet shows are at 11:00 A.M., 1:00 P.M., and 3:00 P.M. (705) 723–5327.

Afternoon

Stay on Highway 11, and 54 km (34 miles) north of North Bay watch for **Marten River Provincial Park** just before you reach Marten River. Within the park is a **reconstructed logging camp.** There's an excellent film about life in a 1920s camp at the **Interpretation Centre,** and there are guided tours at set hours on weekends, or you can wander on your own. The staff will answer questions. Open June 1 to Labor Day, admission $7.00 per person. (705) 892–2200.

Temagami, 36 km (23 miles) north, started as a rest stop on the long portage from Snake Lake into Lake Temagami and was the last stop on a six-day journey up the "birchbark highway" from the end of the rail in Mattawa on the Ottawa River. Temagami is 48 km (30 miles) long and contains more than 1,200 islands. You can get an idea of the region by hiking to the top of **Caribou Mountain,** which overlooks the town. Drive almost to the top on O'Connor Drive, which gets you to a ski chalet at the base of the "mountain." From there it's a fifteen-minute hike to the base of a derelict fire lookout tower.

At Latchford, about 36 km (23 miles) north of Temagami, you may want to look at the **Latchford Covered Bridge.** Full marks to the locals for this gimmick! The bridge is a large culvert over Latchford Creek and the town covered it with a wooden structure to earn a world superlative: **World's Shortest Covered Bridge.** (There's no sign telling you how short the bridge is, but it measures 11 feet, 3 inches.) It's a block west of Highway 11 and it's surprising to see how many tourists dutifully turn off the highway, drive slowly through the bridge, stop for a photograph, turn around, and resume their travel—probably wondering why they bothered.

Cobalt is a fascinating town of 1,500 with a mother lode of unique attractions. And let's get this straight right off the bat: Fred LaRose, credited with discovering the vein of silver that set off one of the greatest mining stampedes of all time, did not, repeat not, accidentally find the vein by throwing his pick at a curious fox. LaRose didn't even discover the first vein, but it makes a great legend!

In 1903, railway workers J. H. McKinley and Ernest Darragh spotted something glittering in Long Lake, a metal so soft they could make marks on it with their teeth. It was a "float" of silver, and they staked what became the McKinley-Darragh Mine, which in five years shipped 1,600 tons of ores, averaging 150 ounces of silver to the ton. LaRose, also a railway lineman, found a float "as big as my hand" and chased down the vein. He sold his claim to the Timmins brothers and Dave Dunlap for $30,000. That consortium went on to buy out the biggest gold strike in Timmins a few years later. These are some of the stories told, and illustrated with artifacts, at **Cobalt Mining Museum.**

The exhibits sprawl through seven large rooms. There are displays of claim-staking, mining drills, and scale models demonstrating mining techniques. The walls are papered with photos of Cobalt's heyday, when a streetcar line linked it with New Liskeard and the town had such a hot-shot hockey team that it played against the world-champion Montréal Canadiens in the latter team's first professional game.

This is not a museum for a quick browse. Every corner is crammed with items of interest even to the visitor without a mining background. When did you last see a device for warming twenty-five sticks of dynamite with hot water without getting them wet? Or slip into a darkened booth and see what black light does to revolving fluorescent mineral samples—chunks of hackmanite, norbergite, willemite, wernerite, and hyalite—considered the world's finest collection of fluorescent rock?

The museum also traces Cobalt's incredible history. When it wasn't making headlines with silver strikes it made them for other things: In 1906 a dynamite cache exploded, starting a fire that destroyed most of the town; a smallpox epidemic the following year took many lives; and in 1909 another fire left 3,000 residents homeless. There was an outbreak of influenza in 1918 that killed many people and a local depression from 1935 to 1946 when none of the more than 100 mines was working.

In the **Prospectors' Hall of Fame** are photographs and biographies of people who spawned legends with their bizarre behavior, strange eccentricities, courageous acts, or wild philanthropy after acquiring massive fortunes from ore discoveries. And there are offbeat exhibits like a tiny steam engine that was one of Henry Ford's childhood toys—nobody knows how it got there. Admission $3.25 adults, $2.75 seniors, $2.25 students. Open daily 9:00 A.M. to 5:00 P.M. July and August, 1:00 to 5:00 P.M. June and September, and at other times by special arrangement. (705) 679–8301.

At the museum you can get a free brochure for a self-guided tour of **Heritage Silver Trail.** The 6-km (4-mile) route takes you to five mine sites that illustrate the many mining techniques at the turn of the century. The route is marked by billboards, and there are explanatory signs at each site. **Little Silver Vein Mine,** known locally as the **Air-Conditioned Mine,** has an excellent view of an open *stope*, the cut remaining after a vein has been mined out. A trail leads to a tunnel, or *adit*, which you can enter to experience the sensation of being underground. No matter how hot the weather, you're greeted by a blast of icy air and can get even cooler by looking down the 200-foot rock cut whose bottom is permanently filled with ice.

One of the last things the visitor would expect to find on a highway in the middle of nowhere is a bookstore with an inventory of more than 500,000 titles. And, if the title you want isn't at **Highway Book Shop,** chances are good owners Lois or Douglas Pollard can locate a copy and mail it to you. Pollard started a small printing plant in 1957 and sold his first book that year after a customer paid his bill with books. As the inventory has grown, so have the rooms in which the books are stored. The shop is a warren of aisles through books stacked floor to ceiling. They're sorted more or less into categories and if there's something you can't find, clerks rummage through file cards and usually come up with what you're after. Open seven days a week. On Highway 11 just north of the turnoff to Cobalt. (705) 679–8375.

There's an astonishingly comprehensive collection of memorabilia from World Wars I and II in the **Bunker Military Museum** in the 1910 Ontario Northland Railway Station. There's a modest admission charge to see rooms of weaponry, uniforms, photos, newspaper and magazine articles, and other military artifacts. Open daily 9:00 A.M. to 5:00 P.M. June 1 to September 1.

DINNER AND LODGING: The forty-room **Waterfront Inn** at New Liskeard overlooks a sand beach on Lake Temiskaming. The bar/lounge is where the area's movers meet at the cocktail hour, and the town's best dining is in adjacent **Casey's Restaurant,** which has an outdoor patio and entrees from $8.00 to $16.00. The inn is connected to the municipal indoor pool and sauna, squash and tennis courts, exercise rooms, and a licensed sunroom lounge. Rooms are $70–$80. (705) 647–8711.

DAY 2

Morning

BREAKFAST: At the Waterfront Inn.

Take Highway 11 north and after 32 km (20 miles) watch for signs to **Kap-Kig-Iwan Provincial Park** just south of Englehart. The small park surrounds the Englehart River at a point where it is forced into a deep ravine and over a 70-foot drop. There are pathways down both sides of the river and you can hike to the falls and back in less than a half-hour. (Admission is $7.00 per vehicle, but if you just want to see the falls you can get a free half-hour pass.)

If you decide to visit **Sir Harry Oakes' Chateau** in **Kirkland Lake,** get off Highway 11 on Highway 112 and follow signs to Swastika and Kirkland Lake. (Swastika was named for the cross supposed to denote good fortune. Since it was also the Nazi emblem, during World War II the government tried to change the town's name to Winston, honoring Britain's Prime Minister Churchill. But the people of Swastika refused to relinquish a name that for them was a symbol of good faith, good luck, and good will.)

Kirkland Lake is sometimes referred to as the **Town with Streets Paved with Gold.** That's true. A road crew, instructed to take rock from a waste pile, took gold ore from another pile in error. The gold ore is sealed into the road under layers of pavement.

American Harry Oakes had prospected around the world before he staked the Tough Oakes and Lake Shore properties at Kirkland Lake in 1912. He was the only prospector to stake a property, finance it, and then bring it to the dividend stage—and dividend it was! Lakeshore Mine produced 8.5 million ounces of gold between 1918 and 1968. Lakeshore also became the deepest mine shaft at 8,178 feet and the tailings filled Kirkland Lake, all 4 square miles of it. (The lake now is being emptied of those tailings, which are being profitably reworked by Macassa Mine.)

Oakes's first house at Kirkland Lake was a small log cabin built in 1919. When it partially burned in 1929, he built a three-story log chateau overlooking his mine. He later built a magnificent stone mansion on the most prime real estate at Niagara Falls. In 1935 he moved to the Bahamas, was made a baronet of the U.K., and four years later was the victim of a sensational murder that has never been solved. The chateau has been restored and furnished with a hodgepodge of bits and pieces from community attics.

There is a hockey room to honor the fifty-one Kirkland Lake players who made it to the National Hockey League, an astonishing record for a town of fewer than 12,000 people. Open Monday–Saturday 10:00 A.M. to 4:00 P.M., Sunday noon to 4:00 P.M. Admission $3.00. (705) 568–8800.

LUNCH: It's a few kilometers out of your way, but **Antonio's Restaurant** in Kirkland Lake boasts their food is "the way it should be" and the claim is well founded. They have a weekday lunch buffet, burgers, pasta dishes, shrimp and crab mixes, salads, and sandwiches. All dishes are priced at $6.95. The restaurant is in the Don-Lou Motel at 8 Oakes Avenue, a former housing facility for married mine workers that was converted to a thirty-five unit motel in 1968. To save a few kilometers, cut off Highway 11 on Highway 112, about 19 km (12 miles) north of Englehart. At Highway 66 turn right, and Antonio's and the Don-Lou are on your right as you enter the town of Kirkland Lake. After lunch, turn left out of the motel and follow Highway 66 west to Highway 11, turn right and head for Cochrane. (705) 567–3283.

Afternoon

Continue on Highway 11 to your motel at **Cochrane.**

DINNER AND LODGING: Cochrane has eight motels ranging from seven to forty-two units, all of which provide early wake-up calls and late check-ins for returning Polar Bear Express trippers. Only two have restaurants: **Northern Lites** has forty-one units and a family-style restaurant. (705) 272–4281. **Chimo Motel** has thirty-eight units, a bar, and two restaurants. Room rates $67–$75. Entrees in the family restaurant are $8.00–$12.00, and in the **Fine Dining Restaurant,** $12.00–$35.00. (705) 272–6555.

DAY 3

Morning and Afternoon

BREAKFAST: Early—and at your motel. They're used to getting sleepy people fed before the train leaves.

Ontario Northland advises tourists that temperature and weather conditions in Moosonee and Moose Factory may change rapidly, and you should bring a warm sweater or jacket and a wind-repellent outer garment for wear in the canoes. The weather may be very hot and bright, however, so you might also want to pack sunscreen and sunglasses. Insect repellent is important to bring since mosquitoes and blackflies are a problem. And be sure to wear comfortable, sturdy footwear for walking.

The Polar Bear Express rail fare is $48 round-trip for adults, $24 for children ages five to eleven, $37 for adults over sixty. The three-day, two-night package from June 26 to September 6 is $281 per person single or $211 per person double. That gets you two nights in a Cochrane motel, the Moosonee/Moose Factory bus tour, two breakfasts, and dinner on the Polar Bear Express. Their four-day, three-night package offered from June 26 to September 6 adds a night in Moosonee and a lunch during the Wilderness Excursion. Rates are $397 single, $290 per person double. For information or reservations call (416) 314–3750 or (800) 268–9281, or send a fax to (416) 314–3729.

The train leaves Cochrane at 8:30 A.M. and arrives at Moosonee by 1:00 P.M. It departs Moosonee at 6:00 P.M. and returns to Cochrane at 10:05 P.M. Meals, light lunches, and snacks are available on both legs of the trip. On the return trip, beer and liquor are served in a club car with amplified piano and entertainer. Passengers sit on benches along both sides of the car requesting songs for the singer to belt out, or old-time favorites in which everyone joins.

Otherwise, both legs of the trip are fairly boring unless you meet interesting passengers. On both sides for mile after mile there is little to see but black spruce, white birch, aspen, poplar, and tamarack trees whose growth becomes more stunted as you travel north. Vast sections have been stripped bare by pulp loggers and other parts are ravaged by fire.

The track crosses a number of mighty rivers—the Abitibi, Otakwahegan, Kwataboahegan, and Moose—the latter traversed by an 1,800-foot-long trestle. Four of the bridges are **"upside-down" bridges.** Supporting girders normally are beneath bridges, but here they are on top to allow ice to pass underneath.

The four-and-a-quarter-hour layover gives the visitor ample time to see all the major attractions of **Moosonee** and **Moose Factory** since both are villages of less than 2,000. But to take in all the sights and excursions available requires staying over at least one night. The basic tour of Moosonee and Moose Factory is packaged, and the visitor should book one instead of trying to work it out for him- or herself. (Some tours must be booked at Cochrane.)

If you want to stay over in Moosonee, accommodation is limited to the thirty-room **Polar Bear Lodge** (705–336–2345) or the twenty-one-room **Moosonee Lodge** (705–336–2351), both on Enterprise Road overlooking the Moose River. Rates are high for the caliber of accommodation. (Alcohol is served at both hotels only during the dinner hour, 6:00 to 8:00 P.M.)

Moose Factory is on an island that can be reached only by taxi . . . and taxi here means a 20- to 24-foot-long NorWest freighter canoe powered by a 25- to 40-horsepower outboard motor. If you opt for your own tour, you'll have ample time to stroll through both communities. The organized tours, listed below, have a guide who provides amusing tales and the answers to your questions. See For More Information at the end of this chapter for details on how to book a tour.

Moose Factory Island Bus Tour. The island, one of many in the delta of the Moose River, is 8 km (5 miles) long and 1 km (.75 mile) wide at its widest point. It's a twenty-minute canoe ride on a route that winds along a channel between **Charles Island (Tidewater Provincial Park)** and **Sawpit Island.** Passengers transfer to a bus for a guided tour of the sights. Moose Factory was the second Hudson's Bay Company trading post, established in 1672 on what was then called Hayes Island, 24 km (15 miles) upriver from James Bay. It was captured by the French in 1686 and renamed Fort St. Louis. It was not reestablished by the Hudson's Bay Company until 1730 but has been in continuous operation since.

Wilderness Excursion. This six-hour tour is aboard the 100-passenger *Polar Princess.* Depending on tides, passengers may view the wreckage of the **MV** *Eskimo,* a supply vessel crushed by ice during an early freeze-up in 1957. The tour goes into James Bay and past **Ships and Island Waterfowl Sanctuary,** summer home of many water and shore bird species and a resting and feeding area in spring and fall for immense flocks of migrating geese and ducks. (The southern end of James Bay is the spout of the giant funnel of Hudson and James Bays, where sightings of beluga whale are not unusual.) A box lunch is served on board, and then the *Polar Princess* stops at **Moose Factory Island** where passengers transfer to a bus for an island tour.

Fossil Island Tour. This three-hour trip is made in freighter canoes upriver to Fossil Island. While passengers hunt for fossils, the guide builds a fire and serves a traditional snack of bannock and tea. (Bannock is unleavened bread, usually perked up with raisins, toasted over a fire on a stick.) The fossils in the loose limestone are from the Devonian Period, about 375 million years ago, when this region was the bottom of a shallow, semitropical ocean.

St. Thomas Anglican Church has holes drilled in the wooden floor, filled with plugs to let water *in*. The church floated off its foundations in one spring flood; allowing the water in prevents the church from floating away. The church was built in 1860 and has interesting plaques, memorials, and stained glass. The altar cloths and lectern hangings are of moose hide decorated with colored beads.

The **Hudson's Bay Post** is a modern building now named **Northern Stores.** Beside it is the staff house built in 1850. On sale are animal pelts, carvings, snowshoes, gloves, slippers, beadwork, and raw materials from which souvenirs and clothing are made. Nearby is an ancient press where furs were baled for shipment to England.

Some guidebooks will tell you the **Blacksmith's Shop in Centennial Park** on Moose Factory Island is the oldest wooden building in Ontario. It isn't, but the stone forge inside it may be the oldest stone structure. The original shop was built in the late 1600s, but it and the stones were moved farther from the river in 1820. During tourist season an apprentice blacksmith runs the forge. Adjacent to the Blacksmith Shop is a former **powder magazine,** the settlement's only stone building.

There are two cemeteries on the island. One is behind St. Thomas Anglican Church and the other is near the Blacksmith Shop. It is a neglected plot where Hudson's Bay Company servants and members of their families were buried. Many of the headstones sent from England make interesting and often poignant reading. They tell of infants dying in epidemics and youngsters lost in accidents.

At several points along the "tourist trail" the visitor will see a tepee with smoke curling from its vent and a sign advertising BANNOCK for a couple of dollars. This is the Native equivalent of a hot dog for a snack. If you're between meals, one bannock—they're about a foot long—makes tasty, filling nibbling.

Moosonee is Ontario's only tidewater port. Even though it is 24 km (15 miles) from James Bay, summer tides average 5 feet. The community came into existence in 1903 when the Revillon Frères Trading Company of France established a post to compete with the Hudson's Bay Company. The trip from Cochrane by canoe or snowshoe then took eight to ten days.

As you leave the Moosonee railway station on First Street, you face the Moose River. On your right is the **Railway Car Museum,** which houses displays of the region's natural and cultural history, explained by a guide. Admission is free.

The **Moosonee Visitors' Centre** is a small office building on your right farther down First Street. A guide will give you brochures and directions and answer questions. Next door is a small theater in which free videos on wildlife and natural and cultural history are shown.

Revillon Frères Museum is opposite the dock on Revillon Road that parallels the river. Displays and artifacts recall the heyday of the fur trade. (Note the tricolor flag of France flying from the flagpole.)

The **Ministry of Natural Resources Interpretive Centre** is farther down Revillon Road. It's a large room in the ministry building that houses exhibits explaining the area's geological and geographical history. The enormous polar bear hide isn't from the immediate area; the closest polar bear sighting to town was one shot 60 km (38 miles) north.

There are usually **Native handcraft stalls** on Revillon Road. Offerings range from moccasins and buckskin vests to trinkets, beadwork, and wood and stone carvings. This area is noted for **Tamarack geese,** now a recognized Canadian Native art form. These are an excellent investment as were Inuit soapstone carvings a few decades ago. The geese originally were used as decoys and meticulously crafted from very fine branch tips of tamarack. The birds traditionally were life-size, but smaller birds are available for tourists—at smaller prices.

DINNER: On the Polar Bear Express or upon your return to Cochrane.

LODGING: At your motel in Cochrane.

DAY 4

Morning

BREAKFAST: At your motel.

Take Highway 11 south to Porquis Junction and then Highway 67 to **Timmins.** "The City with the Heart of Gold" is the largest city in Canada. The city's population is only 47,000, but in 1973 it amalgamated and took in a number of towns and villages, an area of 1,200 square miles. Timmins is on the Mattagami River and named after Noah and Henry Timmins who formed one of the early mining syndicates and developed a gold mine staked in 1911 by Benny Hollinger.

Hollinger and his partner, Alex Gillies, both barbers from Haileybury, were an unlikely pair of prospectors when they hit town in 1909 with $145 between them. They discovered the Dome Camp was fully staked and were told to try their luck about 6 km (4 miles) to the west on open ground. By the toss of a coin, Hollinger staked his claims first and Gillies staked around him. They returned to Haileybury with their samples and the rest is mining history. The Hollinger mine, with an annual production of $10 million, delivered 20 million ounces of gold and was for years second in world production only to South Africa's Rand Mine.

The Timmins brothers were operating a general store in Mattawa on the Québec border when silver deposits were discovered at nearby Cobalt. They abandoned storekeeping, formed an association with local lawyer D. A. Dunlap, and bought a silver mine that proved very profitable. They parlayed those profits into buying out the Hollinger claim. Mine headframes bristle around Timmins—some still being worked and others, like the Hollinger Mine, closed.

Visitors to the **92 ramp of the Hollinger Gold Mine** are outfitted in coveralls, rubber boots, safety belts, lamps, and hardhats. There's an eight-minute orientation film on the history of mining and then a guide leads you down the ramp, eventually to the 200-foot level past displays of equipment, a simulated rock blast, and a simulated ore shoot. Back at the surface the **Costain Mineral Gallery** is on display and ore samples are for sale. Tours take ninety minutes and are offered daily June through September. Regular admission is $17; students and seniors pay $15. At James Reid Road off Moneta Avenue. (705) 360–8500.

LUNCH: Complete hot dinners and the usual snack food are available at the mine site.

Afternoon

The **Timmins Museum** is 6 km (4 miles) east of downtown Timmins in what used to be the town of South Porcupine. It's just south of Highway 101 on Legion Drive. The museum traces the history of Timmins and its mining industry. An extensive collection of mining films may be viewed and pieces of pre-1940s mining equipment are displayed on the grounds. Admission is $2.00

Hollinger Gold Mine at Timmins.

for adults, $1.00 for seniors, students, and children. From May 24 to Labor Day, open 9:00 A.M. to 5:00 P.M. Monday, Tuesday, and Friday; 9:00 A.M. to 8:00 P.M. Wednesday and Thursday; and 1:00 to 5:00 P.M. Saturday and Sunday. Winter hours are 9:00 A.M. to 5:00 P.M. Tuesday–Friday, 1:00 to 5:00 P.M. Saturday and Sunday.

Return to Highway 11 and head for North Bay. The **Homestead of the Dionne Quintuplets** is on the North Bay Bypass at Seymour Street beside the North Bay Regional Tourism Information Centre. A small admission is charged. The log cabin in which the quints were born on May 28, 1934, houses Dionne family artifacts, including the bed in which the quints were born, some baby clothes, and the frilly white dresses the girls wore in 1939 to meet King George VI.

Back on Highway 11 . . . and home.

SPECIAL EVENTS

Early May. Perennial Favourites Art & Craft Show, North Bay. Juried art and craft sale, with artisans from across Ontario.

Early June. Multicultural Festival, Timmins. Displays, parade, food, dancing, music. At MacIntyre Community Centre.

Last week of June. Summerfest, Cochrane. Games for adults and kids, bed races, sidewalk sales, outdoor concerts, truck drag races.

Last weekend of June. Summerfest, New Liskeard.

Mid-July. Kiwanis Club Beauce Carnival, Timmins.

Late July. Spirit Hikes, Cochrane. Corn roasts and woodsmen competitions at Greenwater Provincial Park.

First week of August. Summerworks Art and Craft Sale, North Bay. A selection of the finest work by local and regional artisans, at the Kennedy Gallery, 150 Main Street East.

Early August. Cobalt Miners' Festival, Cobalt. Mining competition, slow-pitch tournament, concerts, parade.

Early August. North Bay Heritage Festival and Airshow, North Bay. Fireworks, midway, interactive play area, arts and crafts, concessions, exhibits, performances, and singing contest. At Lee Park.

Early August. Claybelt Pioneer Days, Cochrane. Antique show and display, hay rides and games. At Hunta Museum, Highway 668 to 10 and 11.

Mid-August. Annual Fall Fair, New Liskeard.

OTHER RECOMMENDED RESTAURANTS AND LODGINGS

Cochrane

Westway Motor Motel. (705) 272–4285. Cochrane's largest motel.

New Liskeard

Breault's Quality Inn, on Highway 11 just north of New Liskeard. (705) 647–7357. Seventy-two units, indoor pool, sauna and whirlpool, games room, and attached licensed Golden Griddle Restaurant. $65–$125.

FOR MORE INFORMATION

Two Bay Tours, 16 Ferguson Avenue, Moosenee ON P0L 1Y0, offer a number of package tours and trips. The Moose Factory Island Bus Tour costs $19.75 (adults and children); The Wilderness Excursion is priced at $46 for adults and $23 for children (it includes a boxed lunch); and the Fossil Island Tour is $17 for adults and $8.50 for children. Call (705) 336–2944 to book the tours.

Cochrane Tourism Association, Box 2240, Cochrane ON P0L 1C0. (800) 354–9948.

INDEX

A

Aberfoyle Mill, 53, 54
Abraham Groves Grist Mill and
    Electric Light Company, 28
Action River, 212
Acton, 26
Adelaide Hunter-Hoodless Homestead
    Museum, 17
Admiral Bayfield's Bakery and Deli, 38
Adventure Passport, 140
Adventure Trail (Manitoulin
    Island), 255
African Lion Safari and Game
    Farm, 212
Agawa Canyon, 264
Agawa Canyon Train, 264
Agnes Etherington Art Centre, 170
Air Canada Centre, 152
Air-Conditioned Mine, 281
Airplane excursions,129, 231
Albion Hotel, 39
Al Dente, 20
Ale Trail, 56
Alexander Henry, 170
Algoma Central Railway, 265
Algoma Central Railroad Station, 264
Allan Gardens, 131
Allan Macpherson House, 173
Ambassador Bridge, 4
Ameliasburgh Historical Museum, 198
American Falls, 226
Amherstburg, 2
Ancaster Old Mill, 214
André's Swiss Country Dining, 90

Angeline's Restaurant, 200
Anglican Church, 256
Anna Mae's Bakery and Restaurant, 97
Anthony's, 179
Antonio's Restaurant, 283
Arabella's Tea Room, 221
Arboretum (Sudbury), 275
Armagh S. Price Park, 158
Art galleries,4, 18, 48, 54, 65, 66, 89,
    97, 109, 131, 132, 134, 138, 170,
    182, 189, 191, 211, 233, 248, 275
Art Gallery of Hamilton, 211
Art Gallery of Peterborough, 189
Art Gallery of Toronto, 131
Art Gallery of Windsor, 4
Art in the Park, 97
Assiginack Museum, 255
Athens, 156, 164
A Thymely Manner, 265
Aubrey Falls, 265
Ayr, 20

B

Bannock, 286
Barberians, 139
Bata Shoe Museum, 133
Battlefield House Museum, 212
Bayfield, 32, 37
Bay Front Quality Inn, 264
Bay of Spirits Gallery, 131
Bay Street Café, 262
Beausoleil Island, 116
Belholme Trading Company, 18
Belleville, 195, 201

Bellevue House, 170
Bell Homestead, 15
Beluga whale, 285
Benjamin's Inn, 59
Benmiller, 40
Best Western Highland Inn, 117
Best Western Inn on the Bay, 106
Bethany, 191
Bethune Memorial House, 245
Bicycling, 77, 127, 228
Big Creek Boat Farm, 213
Big Nickel, 272
Big Nickel Mine, 271, 272
Billy Bishop Heritage, 109
Bingeman Park, 60
Black Creek Pioneer Village, 144
Blacksmith's Shop (Moose
    Factory), 286
Blind River, 263
Bloomfield Inn, 200
Blue Church, 160
Blue Mountain Pottery, 105
Blue Mountain Resort, 105
Boat tours (Ottawa), 179
Boot and Blade, 107
Bootleggers, 80
Bracebridge, 240, 249
Brant County Museum, 17
Brantford, 13
Brantford and Area Sports Hall of
    Recognition, 21
Briars, The, 123
Bridal Veil Falls (Manitoulin
    Island), 255
Bridal Veil Falls (Niagara), 226
Bridgeview Restaurant, 161
Brighton, 202
Brock's Monument, 228, 234
Brockville, 156, 165
Brockville Arts Centre, 158
Brockville Municipal Harbor and
    Marina, 158

Brockville Museum, 159
Brockville Opera House Company, 158
Bruce Brand Tomatoes, 91
Bruce Coast Marine Gallery, 89
Bruce County Museum and
    Archives, 89
Bruce Mines Museum, 263
Bruce Nuclear Power Development, 91
Bruno's Ristorante, 36
Buckhorn, 191
Buckhorn School of Fine Arts, 191
Bunker Military Museum, 281
Burford, 20
Bus tours, 65, 129, 179, 265, 271,
    272, 285
Butterfly Conservatory, 227
Bytown Museum, 184

C

Café Bellevue, 153
Café Les Arcades, 141
Cambridge, 20
Campbellford, 202
Campbell House, 133
Canada's Largest Outdoor Swimming
    Pool, 100
Canadian Automotive Museum, 150
Canadian Football Hall of Fame and
    Museum, 211
Canadian Grenadier Guards, 164, 182
Canadian Military Heritage
    Museum, 21
Canadian Museum of Civilization, 184
Canadian Museum of Nature, 183
Canadian Opera Company, 134
Canadian Tulip Festival, 184
Canadian Vintage Motorcycle
    Museum, 21
Canadian War Museum, 182
Canadian Warplane Heritage
    Museum, 210